The Ältester

The Ältester

HERMAN D. W. FRIESEN,
A Mennonite Leader in Changing Times

Bruce L. Guenther

University of Regina Press

Printed and bound in Canada at Marquis. The text of this book is printed on 100%
post-consumer recycled paper with earth-friendly vegetable-based inks.

Cover design: Duncan Campbell, University of Regina Press
Text design: John van der Woude, JVDW Designs
Copy editor: Kirsten Craven
Proofreader: Nadine Coderre
Indexer: Sergey Lobachev, Brookfield Indexing Services
Cover art: "Herman D. W. Friesen, inspecting crops." Courtesy Herman and Margaretha
    Friesen estate.

Library and Archives Canada Cataloguing in Publication

Guenther, Bruce L. (Bruce Lloyd), 1959-, author
    The ältester : Herman D.W. Friesen, a mennonite leader in changing times / Bruce
L. Guenther.

Includes bibliographical references and index. Issued in print and electronic formats.
ISBN 978-0-88977-572-5 (softcover).—ISBN 978-0-88977-573-2 (PDF).—ISBN 978-
0-88977-574-9 (HTML)

1. Friesen, Herman D. W. 2. Mennonites—Saskatchewan—Biography. 3. Biographies.
I. Title. II. Title: Herman D.W. Friesen, a mennonite leader in changing times.

BX8143.F745G84 2018   289.7092   C2018-903213-8   C2018-903214-6

10 9 8 7 6 5 4 3 2 1

University of Regina Press, University of Regina
Regina, Saskatchewan, Canada, s4s 0A2
tel: (306) 585-4758 fax: (306) 585-4699
web: www.uofrpress.ca

U OF R PRESS

We acknowledge the support of the Canada Council for the Arts for our publishing
program. We acknowledge the financial support of the Government of Canada. / Nous
reconnaissons l'appui financier du gouvernement du Canada. This publication was made
possible with support from Creative Saskatchewan's Creative Industries Production
Grant Program. This publication has also received generous funding from the D. F. Plett
Historical Research Foundation.

In memory of Grampa and Gramma,
Herman D. W. Friesen (1908–69)
and
Margaretha (née Banman) Friesen (1908–97)

I will teach you lessons from the past…
we will not hide them from our descendants;
we will tell the next generation
the praiseworthy deeds of the Lord,
his power, and the wonders he has done.
—Psalm 78:1–4

Contents

Herman and Margaretha Friesen, Osler, Saskatchewan, early 1960s. Courtesy Herman and Margaretha Friesen estate.

Foreword

BIOGRAPHY IS ALWAYS MORE THAN THE STORY OF A SINGLE PERSON.
Certainly, the account of Herman D. W. Friesen is a fascinating one by today's
standards: his life was lived out close to nature, within a small community,
surrounded by kith and kin. Born in a farm village in Saskatchewan in 1908
to an Old Colony Mennonite family, he spent his boyhood in a farm household, attended the local, church-run school, and courted and then married
his neighbour, Margaretha Banman, shortly after being baptized into the Old
Colony Mennonite Church. He and his young bride at first settled with her
family and then created their own farm household, rearing a family of twelve
children. As a community leader, Herman served on the local school board
and roads committee, and then, in his fifties, he was chosen as a minister and
then as the bishop, the *Ältester*, of his church. His life was cut short by a hor-
rific tractor accident at age sixty-one. But by that age he had made his mark as
a person of commitment, generosity of spirit, and intelligence. Herman was a
son, husband, father, neighbour, grandfather, and community leader.

And yet, as Bruce Guenther argues, biography is much more than the
simple account of a single person. It is the story of a man navigating tradition and change, and Herman Friesen was a farmer/preacher from a
particular "moment" of history, a time of tumultuous change, set in a particular place on the Saskatchewan prairie. His story is one of intersection and
even contradiction: as a man committed to a simple lifestyle, he purchases
a brand new Plymouth and brings an organ into his home; as a member of
the exclusive Old Colony Mennonite Church, he nevertheless serves with
non-Mennonites on the local school board and sees his wife spend time in
a public mental hospital; as a father with a strong desire to see his children
follow traditional teaching, he nevertheless opens his house to his daughter
as a single mother and sees most of his children leave for more progressive
churches. There is nothing simple about this story.

The story unfolds in central Saskatchewan, on Treaty 6 lands, based on an 1876 agreement by Cree, Assiniboine, and other First Nations groups to share the land with settlers from Europe. These lands attracted large numbers of settlers, especially after the squelching of an armed resistance to Euro-Canadian encroachment in 1885 and the completion of the transcontinental Canadian Pacific Railway in the same year. This land would become part of the dynamic new Canadian province of Saskatchewan founded in 1905, and, in the decades thereafter, the third most populated province in Canada, one bent on assimilating its settlers into an Anglo-Canadian home. Among a myriad number of settlers were well-received Scandinavian and German immigrants, less easily assimilated Ukrainian and Doukhobor farmers, and even distinctive African American and Jewish communities. Within this cultural matrix, Low German–speaking Mennonites from Russia, by way of Manitoba and Kansas, found their own communities. Historians have commented on the unusual characteristics of a pacifist, Low German–speaking group living in farm villages on this prairie. But the Mennonites in their communities, such as the Hague-Osler Reserve, were part of the diversity of settler communities that comprised rural Saskatchewan.

But this story also recounts the resistance to assimilation and one from a traditionalist group of Mennonites, the Old Colony Mennonite Church. It would stand up to the province's 1917 dictate that children must be educated by the nation-state, and, in 1924, the Old Colonists from Hague-Osler joined a mass migration to Mexico, choosing the State of Durango as their home. For those who remained in Canada, old traditions in particular were tested. The Old Colony Mennonite Church had been one of the largest Mennonite denominations to form in Canada, established in 1875 on the banks of the Red River, announcing itself as comprising an idealistic people committed to the simplicity of Christ. It would mean they would resist state-run schools, members who ran for municipal office, and those who wished to leave the farm villages or purchase the latest technologies, most specifically the car.

But, as the title of this book suggests, this story is about navigating change. A traditionalist church remnant held course in Canada, and lengthy sermons (seven of which are reproduced in this book's Appendix B) laid out the principles by which parishioners were encouraged to stand apart from a complacent and individualistic modern society. The Old Colonists would not fare well in Canada. They would flee the policies of Saskatchewan's education department into far-flung places in northern British Columbia and Alberta, leaving families such as the Friesens a distinct minority within central Saskatchewan. The Friesen children would mostly reject their father's ideas. Some embraced a more open and evangelical faith, one that saw ethics in terms of personal morality rather than communitarian commitment. This is also a story, then, of how evangelical Protestantism arose within a particular community and served to guide a family into the heart of a wider society.

This story is also one of agricultural change. It recounts the move from horse and organic farming to one reliant on fossil fuels and electricity, and the tools and tractors that followed. The steel wheel, that sign of inviolable progress, carrying both the trains that brought the settlers from Manitoba, as well as the massive steam engines that broke the prairie sod, also carried the small gasoline-driven tractors that brought mechanical power and fossil fuels to every farmstead. Along the way, it also introduced full mechanization of the farmstead, bringing unprecedented efficiency to the farm economy. And, given that agriculture is ultimately circumscribed by the availability of land, it was a key factor behind the migration of large numbers of Saskatchewan Mennonites to nearby towns and cities, plying new trades and professions. Agriculture after the Second World War increasingly became the economic activity of the few.

Finally, this is the story of a patriarchal family and household economy, the marriage of a man to his neighbour, and the creation of a family within a close-knit community. Herman Friesen is first and foremost a communitarian man, rejecting the individualistic and personally meritorious masculinity of Anglo-Canada. He is a man because he works hard for his family and identifies with his neighbour, and because he answers the call to lead his community. His identity is linked not to achievement but to belonging, and his household, for one, does not welcome the radio and TV. He is a strict disciplinarian and holds the view that childhood is molded in the early years, but he seems dubious about the idea that adolescence can better a child through higher education and skill development; teenaged years for him are a time of apprenticeship on the farm, when age-old wisdom is passed down through the generations. But it is also a time when parents step back and allow the seeding of "wild oats," in the hope that youth will eventually come home to roost. And, yet, because his is a time of change, some of his children never do return to Old Colony ways, electing instead the path of assimilation.

Bruce Guenther is eminently qualified to tell this story. He is one of Herman's fifty-four grandchildren and a gifted writer. But he is much more. He has been a farmer in Saskatchewan, earned a PhD in history from McGill University, served as a leader within a seminary and a largely urban Mennonite denomination, and is himself a father and husband, and, like Herman, a friend to many. I first got to know Bruce a long time ago and at once enjoyed his affable and intelligent approach to life, a person who ponders the meanings of life in a changing social context, caring deeply for a society trying to find its way, but he is also an optimist, a person of deep faith, who sees within the foibles of humans a hope for a better future. He has published broadly on evangelical Protestantism in Canada, more specifically on the Bible School movement that took Saskatchewan by storm earlier on in the twentieth century, a pathway through which he himself learned to negotiate the wider society.

Most importantly, Bruce is tied emotionally to this story of his grandfather and, indeed, to the extended Friesen family. He is also a thinker, and throughout the book he wonders about the meaning and the context of the information he reaps. He interrogates the historical texts at his disposal, both oral interviews and written texts. He especially contemplates Herman's sermons and has overseen their translation. Mostly it seems Bruce wants to tell us the story of his grandfather, and he does it with the skill of the consummate communicator. He knows when to laugh and cry, when to pull back and contemplate, when to speak broadly or focus narrowly. This is the book that is in your hands; enjoy it as you might Bruce's company.

—Royden Loewen, Chair of Mennonite Studies,
University of Winnipeg

Introduction

Our stories are all stories of searching. We search for a good self to be and for a good work to do. We search to love and be loved. And in a world where it is often hard to believe in much of anything, we search to believe in something holy and meaningful and life transcending.

—Frederick Buechner, cited in Connie (Letkeman) Braun,
Stories in Sepia: A Memoir of Grace

Born on February 4, 1908, in the small village of Blumenheim near Osler, Saskatchewan, shortly after the formation of the province, the life of Rev. Herman D. W. Friesen (1908–69) and his wife Margaretha (nee Banman) coincided with the first six decades of the province's history. Their lives reflected many of the patterns that characterized the experience of homesteading pioneers in rural Saskatchewan during the first half of the twentieth century. During this period, the newly formed province of Saskatchewan, one of Canada's last frontier regions, underwent massive change as government leaders aggressively sought pioneers to populate and farm its wide open grasslands. By 1911, its rapidly burgeoning population made the young province the third largest in Canada, a position it held until the early 1950s. Although the size of its population remained static after 1940, the people of Saskatchewan built a complex societal infrastructure that included an extensive transportation network, a public education system, several large urban centres, and an increasingly diversified economy. Herman and Margaretha experienced changes they never imagined possible as young children, as their lives embodied many of the transitions that took place within Saskatchewan: from the rugged and solitary independence on isolated homesteads, to interconnected communities made possible by networks of railways, roads, and communication technologies; from

dependence on horses for pulling farm implements and providing trans-
port, to the use of motorized farm equipment, personal automobiles, and
even commercial aviation; from intensive pioneering subsistence farming
on homesteads, to specialized automated dairy farm operations producing
goods to serve larger urban markets. Their story exemplifies the adapta-
tions made by many different ethnic immigrant groups in Saskatchewan as
they participated in the transformation of rural Saskatchewan during the
first half of the twentieth century.

In addition to being pioneers, Herman and Margaretha were a part of an
Old Colony Mennonite Church community in Saskatchewan throughout
their lives, as their parents had been before them. The Old Colony Mennonites
are one particular expression of a much larger group of Christians known
as Mennonites, whose origins date back to a radical, sixteenth-century
movement known as Anabaptism. The Anabaptists were a diverse movement; those led by Menno Simons (from which the Mennonites derive their
name) were committed to restoring (not merely reforming) the church to
once again being a community of those adult believers who had voluntarily
accepted baptism upon their own confession of faith. With remarkable
seriousness and devotion, these Anabaptists sought to "follow after Christ,"
believing that true faith will be verified by one's behaviour, which included
loving enemies and a refusal to use violence as a way of seeking revenge.
Despite suffering severe persecution, which scattered the movement across
and beyond Europe, the movement planted the seeds for ideas that eventually became an integral part of contemporary Western culture (for example,
separation of church and state, religious freedom, and religious pluralism).

Both Herman's and Margaretha's families were part of a migration of
approximately eighteen thousand Low German–speaking Mennonites
from southern Russia (present-day Ukraine) to North America during
the 1870s. This first group of Mennonites from Russia to arrive in Canada
became known as *Kanadier* Mennonites to differentiate them from the
Russlaender Mennonites who emigrated from Russia during the 1920s.[1]
These Mennonites were part of a stream whose origins are rooted in the
Dutch and Flemish Anabaptism of the sixteenth century prior to settling
in Danzig and West Prussia. In 1789, many relocated to South Russia to

found the Chortitza Colony. After almost a century, the lack of available land for expanding the Mennonite colonies, and the impending threat of military conscription and the assimilation of Russian culture within Mennonite colonies, prompted some to explore new locations for maintaining their separate way of life according to their religious convictions.[2] After sending a delegation to North America, approximately 7,500 responded to an invitation on the part of the Government of Canada to settle in southern Manitoba on two large land reserves (more than five hundred thousand acres) located along the Red River, which became one of the most prosperous and productive farming areas in western Canada. Eager to attract new immigrants, the government promised the Mennonites exemption from military service, and the freedom to educate their children in their own private schools. Here the new immigrants tried to replicate the subsistence, open-field village way of life with which they were familiar. About 3,200 of the Kanadier immigrants came from the Chortitza and Fuerstenland colonies in Russia to a land reserve west of the Red River in Manitoba. The group's first congregation in the West Reserve was organized in the village of Reinland, hence the group officially registered in 1875 as the Reinlaender Mennoniten Gemeinde. Nevertheless, members of the group were commonly called "Old Colony Mennonites" because of their connection to the Chortitza Colony, the oldest Mennonite colony in Russia.[3] They became known for their tenacious commitment to a distinct Anabaptist-Mennonite religious vision that emphasized simplicity and separation from the larger society, and that is best lived out in isolated, agrarian communities.

Shortly after 1890, some Old Colony Mennonites in Manitoba began investigating the possibility of moving westward with the hope of finding additional tracts of homestead land in isolated locations. This search led many to resettle on the Hague-Osler Reserve, a four-township area located north of Saskatoon that was designated for their use in 1895.[4] Several subsequent extensions expanded the reserve area. After 1904, other Old Colony Mennonites settled on reserves south of Swift Current and east of Prince Albert.[5] By 1910, services were held in numerous villages within these new reserves, and church membership numbered over 1,500 adults. An equal number were present in Manitoba, making the Old Colony

Mennonite Church the largest Mennonite denomination in Canada at the time. Despite an intense desire to safeguard their agrarian village way of life, to preserve intact their private, church-supervised schools, and to minimize contact with outside influences, they witnessed and experienced many of the changes taking place in the province. Church leaders tried to help their parishioners interpret and navigate responses to these changes.

Dedicated to the well-being of his community, Herman Friesen emerged as a leader among the Old Colony Mennonites in the Hague-Osler region during the mid-1930s by serving as a *Vorsaenger* (congregational song leader) in the church, as well as a public school board trustee and municipal councillor in the community. Beginning in the 1920s, leaders of the Old Colony Mennonite Church in Saskatchewan promoted and then organized a successive series of migrations to other locations in both Central America and other parts of Canada in which most members of Herman Friesen's family did not participate. Then, during the watershed decade of the 1960s, and for what turned out to be the final seven years of his life, Herman was elected first as a minister and, a year later, as the *Ältester* (bishop) of the Old Colony Mennonite Church. As such, he became the leader of a group of Old Colony Mennonites in Saskatchewan that had repeatedly refused, or were simply unable, to migrate elsewhere. Despite growing up in an environment filled with intense governmental conflict, and considerable suspicion toward those outside of the Old Colony Mennonite Church, when Herman became Ältester he did not, unlike his predecessors, attempt to organize another migration out of Saskatchewan. He adopted a stance toward culture that was less separationist, and tried to navigate a gradual process of accommodation to the changes taking place in the province. His own family of twelve adult children represents a kind of spectrum of the different cultural tensions experienced and life choices made by those in the Old Colony Mennonite community as the group gradually (and somewhat reluctantly) began moving away from being an intentionally isolated network of small agrarian villages toward adopting a way of life that permitted involvement in a wide variety of trades and industries. A greater degree of cultural integration took place as more and more members began living outside of the original villages and even within the city of Saskatoon.

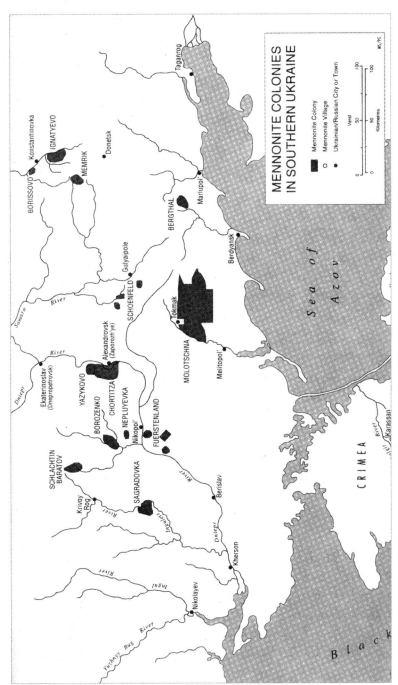

Mennonite colonies in southern Ukraine, 1800s. Courtesy William Schroeder.

Reasons for Writing

My interests in writing a biography of Herman D. W. Friesen arise from both my personal relationship to Herman as well as my academic interests in Mennonite history. I am one of fifty-four grandchildren of Herman and Margaretha, most of whom never had the opportunity to get to know him well, and some never had the opportunity to meet their grandfather at all. This biography created an opportunity to get to know my grandfather in a way that was not possible when I was a young boy. Etched with vivid clarity into my memory as a young child growing up on a mixed farm in rural Saskatchewan north of Saskatoon are several events during the 1960s that many have recognized as monumental moments in the twentieth century: the first occurred on November 22, 1963, as everyday activities were interrupted by shocked radio announcers reporting the shooting death of John F. Kennedy in Dallas, Texas. The second was watching the television coverage, at a neighbour's home because there was no television in our home, of Neil Armstrong taking his first step onto the lunar surface on July 21, 1969, with his famous description of the event as "one small step for man, one giant leap for mankind." Both of these events occurred a long way from the world of the Old Colony Mennonites living in rural Saskatchewan, but, intuitively, I knew that the world would now be different because of these events, even if I did not understand exactly how.

The third memory was not nearly as consequential as far as global events were concerned but profoundly impacted my immediate world. On the afternoon of September 26, 1969, our family received a telephone call informing us of Herman Friesen's fatal tractor accident. As a ten-year-old boy at the time of his death, my personal experience of Ältester Friesen was entirely as "Grampa," that is, my mother's father. My childhood memories of him are limited to recollections of family gatherings at Grampa and Gramma's dairy farm, with uncles crowded into the living room, talking, laughing, with the passing of time marked by the gradual transformation of the floor into a growing carpet of shelled sunflower seeds, and aunts sitting, chatting, holding and feeding babies, preparing *Faspa* (a light, late afternoon meal) in the expansive kitchen and dining room. In the winter, the older grandchildren enjoyed tobogganing down the ravine behind the dairy barn; in the summer, cousins enjoyed exploring (and tasting) the wonders of Gramma's garden. Life seemed peaceful and ordered. Only much later did I discover that the domestic water was not always as calm as it had appeared to my young eyes.

My understanding of Grampa's role as Ältester was limited to an image of austere formality, a man dressed in a dark, tieless, button-up shirt and a long black coat, leading a procession of ministers to their places before the congregation, standing behind the pulpit solemnly dismissing the congregation with the pronouncement, *"und so geht in frieden des Herrn"* (and so depart with Christ's peace), words that, at the time, signalled release from church services that seemed interminably long to young children.

The memory of his austere church presence is balanced by a softer, more pastoral, relational encounter: at one family gathering, several of us grandchildren were playing ball in the yard, when I threw a ball that accidently shattered a glass window in a garage. For this misdemeanour, I was unceremoniously marched into the living room to appear before

Aerial view of Herman and Margaretha Friesen dairy farm and ravine, circa 1960. Courtesy Herman and Margaretha Friesen estate.

Grampa the judge, and what seemed like the grand jury of uncles. Here I was prompted to confess my sin: Grampa listened quietly, and then kindly assured me that accidents happen, that I was forgiven, and that everything was all right. Mortification and dread gave way to relief, and, despite a few bruises of embarrassment, the afternoon gave way once again to light-hearted, joyous play.

My final memories of Grampa have to do with the day, as noted above, during harvest in September 1969, when my parents received the terrible news of his tractor accident and his unexpected death. I remember the devastatingly painful grief experienced by my mother (and others) as she received the news, visiting the site of the accident and seeing the blood-stained, bowl-shaped indentation in the ground left by my grandfather's head as he was pinned underneath the tractor, and being assaulted by a surreal sense of disbelief at his funeral service that was displaced only by the stark presence of the casket holding his now lifeless body. Grampa's death changed the peaceful and ordered world I had experienced. Life was, of course, much more dramatically altered for Gramma, who moved from the family dairy farm near Kronsthal, Saskatchewan, on which she had been born, and on which she had raised her children, to a house in nearby Warman. Family gatherings still took place with regularity, but they never felt the same.

Even as a young boy, I intuitively recognized that Grampa was a person of influence. Through both interviews and research for this book I have learned much about his intense determination to shepherd faithfully the Old Colony Mennonite Church during a time of significant change. Over time, I have also come to appreciate something of the weight that comes with the responsibilities and expectations of public leadership. In addition to getting to know a grandfather I hardly knew while he was alive, writing this book also alerted me to several parallels in our adult lives that intrigued me. Both of us worked as farmers in Saskatchewan (for six years I operated a grain farm operation north of Saskatoon), both of us have been involved in community leadership (I served as a public school board trustee, and have volunteered with numerous advocacy groups and community associations), and both of us have been involved in local church and denominational leadership (for almost two decades I have been a professor with the Mennonite Brethren Biblical Seminary and am active in numerous denominational boards and committees). Although Herman was active in the life of the Old Colony Mennonite Church throughout his life, it was during his fifties and early sixties that he served as minister and Ältester. I am currently in my fifties, a season of life when many people begin to think in terms of how much time they may have left rather than how much has passed. It is a decade more than any other that prompts a major reappraisal of the direction one's life has taken, of priorities, and, most particularly, how best to use the years that remain. While there are many important differences in our lives, these parallels often provided questions and intuitive insights, particularly regarding the challenges of constantly balancing family, farm and public expectations and responsibilities, and the weight and dynamics of leadership. These parallels helped me not only to recognize tendencies within myself but also to empathize with Herman as a human being who experienced longings, concerns, joys, and disappointments.

For almost twenty years I've had a desire to explore my grandfather's story and to understand his influence and legacy within the Old Colony Mennonite Church more fully. The idea emerged when I first became aware of the existence of my grandfather's sermon collection following the death of my grandmother, and the subsequent dispersal of the Herman and Margaretha Friesen estate. At that time, the sermon collection, made up of more than sixty sermons, along with some other personal effects (photos, legal documents, books), was made accessible to members of the family. As a historian with significant interest in Mennonite history, I very much wanted to examine the sermon collection, and discovered that some date back to as early as 1833, and that no other comparable collection of Old Colony Mennonite sermons exists in any Mennonite archive. From that point onward, I knew I wanted to use them as the basis for a writing project featuring the Old Colony Mennonites in Saskatchewan. The immediate challenge was finding capable translators who could read handwritten German Gothic script, and who were also familiar with biblical and theological terminology.

Historiography and Biography

As a professional historian with long-standing specializa-
tions in both Mennonite history and religion in Canada, I have long been
troubled by the unkind and unfair treatment the Old Colony Mennonites
have received at the hands of the media and some scholars. More than
most Mennonite groups, Old Colony Mennonites emphasized the need for
"separation from the world," and therefore intentionally sought out geographically isolated locations that would enable them to pursue a largely
self-sufficient agrarian way of life. As a result, they are often portrayed as a
people staunchly resistant to change. Despite their preference for remaining inconspicuous by living as *die Stillen im Lande* (the quiet in the land),
they obtained notoriety through some remarkably negative media coverage
during the past century, including in local *Saskatoon Capital* and *Saskatoon
Star-Phoenix* newspaper editorials as early as 1909, which portrayed them
as unpatriotic bigots opposed to modern ideals.[6] More recently, they have
been the focus of a national television documentary in 1992, which featured
Old Colony Mennonites involved in smuggling vast quantities of marijuana
into Canada. A similar, more sinister story appeared in *Saturday Night*
magazine in 2004. These incidents served as the foundation for a bizarre
fictional crime drama aired by CBC as a TV miniseries, *Pure*, in early 2017.[7]

Treatment at the hands of scholars has sometimes not been better.
Overtly prejudicial, for example, is C. Henry Smith's assessment of Old
Colony Mennonite resistance to cultural assimilation as "deluded and fool-
ish," and Cornelius Krahn's description of them in the widely distributed
Mennonite Encyclopedia as "culturally retarded."[8] In Canada, the magister-
ial trilogy *Mennonites in Canada*, written by Frank Epp and Ted Regehr,
did much to lift Mennonite historiography beyond denominational stories and to identify and analyze larger national patterns in Mennonite life.
Although respectful mention of Kanadier groups such as the Old Colony
Mennonites is included, their experience does not figure large in the overall
narrative of the series, which devotes most of its attention to the so-called
progressive Mennonite groups that assimilated more fully into Canadian
culture.[9] Regehr casts the story of the Old Colony Mennonites in Canada

as a community in perpetual search for isolated locations beyond the reach of any educational demands by the government. Largely uneducated, and therefore unable to express their theological beliefs effectively, they were particularly vulnerable to the evangelistic interests of other Mennonite groups.[10]

By the mid-twentieth century, Old Colony Mennonites began attracting the attention of scholars in various social science disciplines. These studies were generally sympathetic and helpful in understanding better the communitarian ethos of Old Colony Mennonites, particularly those located in Mexico and South America.[11] Many of these studies are shaped by theories about modernization, secularization, and assimilation. The Old Colony Mennonite experience in Canada serves primarily as the point of departure for the more focused regional studies.

In recent decades, a more concerted effort has been made by both lay and professional scholars from a range of academic disciplines (history, geography, anthropology, health care, sociology) to provide a fuller picture and analysis of Old Colony Mennonites in different places in the world as part of a transnational phenomenon.[12] Many recognize the ongoing dynamic connections between Old Colony Mennonites in Canada and their co-religionists in other locations.[13]

No one in Canada devoted more energy toward the cause of telling the Kanadier Mennonite story than the late Delbert F. Plett, a lawyer based in Steinbach, Manitoba, who collected and published an astounding volume of historical material during his lifetime.[14] Plett's industrious efforts to collect and preserve historical sources featuring communitarian Mennonite groups were motivated by the desire to defend them and their way of life, and to rectify the neglect and unfair treatment experienced at the hands of other Mennonites, historians, and the media.[15] Less helpful were his efforts to present the Old Colony Mennonites as the only true expression of Anabaptism,[16] and his efforts at historiographical revisionism, which were marred by the use of categories that lacked validity and by a strident, sometimes extreme, rhetoric against anyone who dared to critique these Mennonite groups. Despite the limitations of Plett's work, he did contribute to a new impetus for research on the part of numerous lay historians, graduate students, and professional historians who have provided more sophisticated social-cultural studies of Old Colony Mennonite communities around the world that document and analyze the impact of numerous migrations. Many of these present the Old Colony Mennonites as a traditionalist religious community marked by its courage, persistence, and resourcefulness in contesting modern assumptions and cultural practices.[17]

To date, very little scholarly attention has been given to the story of those Old Colony Mennonites in Saskatchewan during the middle of the twentieth century who did not endorse a strategy of migration.[18] This biography of Herman Friesen therefore provides an update to a part of the prairie-based history of the Old Colony Mennonites in Canada that has often been curtailed after the migration to Mexico during the 1920s. The experience of those who have stayed, and the experience of those Old Colony Mennonites who have returned to Canada in more recent decades, needs to be incorporated more fully into Mennonite historiography in Canada. Toward that end, this biography adds a small piece to the much larger historiographical narrative of a traditionalist Low German–speaking "village among nations" that has become, in the words of Royden Loewen, "a 'virtual' transnational community consisting of other Low German speakers, kinship networks, and bearers of a common historical narrative of a people of diaspora."[19]

Herman Friesen's experience is a part of this larger story, but it does not fit neatly into the general characterization of this transnational "village" as those who have consistently rejected the "trajectory of modernization" and participation in nation building. Friesen's biography adds texture to the overarching narrative by exemplifying an instance of an Old Colony *Ältester* whose parishioners chose not to migrate, and who tried instead to navigate a gradual process of accommodation to the changes taking place in Saskatchewan during the first half of the twentieth century. While the Old Colony Mennonites who remained in Canada, like their co-religionists who migrated, did not accept the dominant, progressive, liberal nation-building vision of Canada at an ideological level, they nevertheless participated economically, and in some instances contributed, as did Herman Friesen, in local community building. The research on this Low German–speaking transnational community has been dominated by social-cultural methodologies that have provided many valuable insights. In addition to using these methods throughout this biography, I also explore the way specific theological convictions help shape the internal ethos of a community, and motivate and influence decisions. The story of Herman Friesen and the Old Colony Mennonites in Saskatchewan provides a point of comparison to studies of other Old Colony Mennonite communities elsewhere.

Biography has traditionally fit comfortably within the discipline of history as a useful means for recognizing the relevance of specific locations and circumstances.[20] Nevertheless, the relationship between biography and historiography is often complicated in that biography is more than a form of history, as it integrates contributions from disciplines such as psychology, literary criticism, anthropology, theology, sociology, cultural studies, and more.[21] This book applies the insights from scholars from several disciplines to the available sources of the life story of Herman Friesen to deepen an understanding of the history and culture of Old Colony Mennonites in particular, and of rural pioneers in Saskatchewan during the first half of the twentieth century more generally. As Michael Armstrong Crouch notes, life stories that are well told "capture the relation between the individual and society, the local and the national, the past and present and the public and private experience."[22]

Biographies inevitably raise questions about the role of an individual in human history, particularly when exploring the life story of a leader. As one connects the life story of a single individual to broader narratives, one is constantly forced to weigh the interplay between how much responsibility one can attribute to the agency of one person and the extent to which a person's actions are the product of surrounding socio-cultural forces.[23] Put differently, to what extent was Herman Friesen the maker, or the recipient, of history? While philosophers (and theologians) continue to debate this question, I assume Herman Friesen was both a maker and a recipient, but the line differentiating these two options is not always easily discernible.

Sources and Memory

ONE OF THE MORE DIFFICULT CHALLENGES IN WRITING A BIOGRAPHY of Herman Friesen was the limited number of available primary sources. He did not maintain a personal diary or journal (however, he did try his hand at providing an autobiographical sketch for his family and friends), he never participated in any interviews about his life and ministry experience, and his personal effects did not include any correspondence. His sudden, unexpected death made obtaining any kind of first-hand reflective retrospective impossible. The only primary source materials directly from the hands of Herman are the extant sermons in his collection, but even these do not contain anecdotes drawn from his personal life. In order to obtain as many glimpses as possible into the interior lives of Herman and Margaretha, and the domestic life in their household, I made efforts to interview as many of their children as possible. Many of them live in Saskatchewan, some are scattered across western Canada, and almost all have left the Old Colony Mennonite Church of their parents. Their views regarding their father vary dramatically, with some who suggest he should have been charged with abuse and others who remember him with considerable veneration. A span of twenty-three years separates the oldest and youngest siblings, so the way they remembered and experienced their father and viewed his public leadership roles varied considerably.

The responses to my invitation for a conversation about memories of their parents ranged from eager enthusiasm to considerable reluctance and even outright refusal. A number explicitly expressed a concern that they did not want to have a spotlight shone on their experiences in this biography—the primary focus was to remain on Herman. There are moments, however, in the telling of Herman and Margaretha's family stories, when the experiences of the children and their parents intersect in ways that make it impossible to isolate only the experience of the parents. Critical for alleviating any reticence about openly sharing their memories and experiences, particularly about painful and potentially controversial subjects, was the assurance of anonymity. Such assurance increased considerably the candour of conversations. In order to respect and protect these requests for anonymity, the names of family interviewees have been withheld by mutual agreement, which is the primary reason why there are no citations to family interviews in the critical apparatus that accompanies each chapter.

While this biography does not, like Hans Werner's masterful biography of his father,[24] focus specifically on the nature of memory, it is important nevertheless to recognize the importance of handling family memories with care. As many studies by psychologists, neurologists, and even philosophers have shown, recollective memory is always selective and therefore incomplete, always fallible and therefore not entirely dependable, and always, to some extent, constructed and therefore not impartial.[25] Eliciting memories is not like playing a recording, and while some memories do achieve a kind of stability, accuracy cannot be presumed simply because memories are vivid and clear.[26] Family members' memories were generally limited to their own experiences, with little evidence of critical reflexivity, and with only a few having made the attempt to test their recollections for factual veracity. The most beneficial aspect of the memories obtained from conversations with family members was the identification of specific moments in the life of the Friesen family that they considered particularly notable, and for accumulating factual information for constructing a biographical chronology of Herman's life. Information gleaned from such conversations was examined carefully and corroborated by other interviews or by historical research before being utilized in this biography. Interestingly, no family members offered any broader reflective interpretative comments about the significance of their father's leadership within the larger community, or about the meaning and contribution of his life for the Old Colony Mennonite Church. In part, this was due to the fact that some of the older children were adults and no longer part of the Old Colony Mennonite Church at the time when their father was a minister and Ältester, while others were quite young and not aware of, or interested in, interpretative kinds of questions. In part, it was due to Herman's reserved stoicism, which did not permit his children (or others) easy access to his emotions or internal thoughts, and he was generally careful to protect the privacy of his parishioners and did not talk openly to family members about church matters.

Limited primary sources, and the subjectivity and fallibility of memories, leave a great deal about Herman's life unknown. Understanding social and religious context makes surmising about motivation and rationale for decisions more plausible but never definite. Even with the best of sources, the act of writing a biography is a constant reminder that we "see through a glass darkly" (1 Corinthians 13:12).

Outline of the Book

THE BIOGRAPHY FLOWS IN APPROXIMATELY CHRONOLOGICAL ORDER, as it weaves the mundane, everyday details of Herman and Margaretha Friesen's lives into trends and events in their church life and provincial world. Chapter 1 explores the pioneer homesteading origins of Herman's and Margaretha's families, who arrived in the Hague-Osler Reserve during the 1890s. Here, together with some of their relatives and co-religionists, they organized small villages, which became the birthplaces of Herman and Margaretha. Their childhood years were occupied primarily by doing their part to contribute to the viability of their parents' farms, as well as by attending one of the church-run, German-language schools in the region. In addition to the developments taking place more generally in the newly organized province of Saskatchewan, the school-age years of Herman and Margaretha coincided with a rapidly escalating conflict between the Old Colony Mennonites and several provincial governments that were intent on making attendance at English-language public schools mandatory. Driven by a fervent patriotism, many hailed the public school system as an essential means for transforming the polyglot population in western Canada into patriotic Canadians. Largely unaware of the political circumstances surrounding this conflict, as children, Herman and Margaretha had a front-row seat to the events that precipitated a decision in the 1920s by the leaders of the Old Colony Mennonite Church to migrate to Mexico. In the midst of this struggle, the death of Herman's mother in 1921 dramatically altered his early adolescent domestic world, as did the remarriage of his father and life in a large blended family.

Chapter 2 examines the central role played by the church in the life of an Old Colony Mennonite community, and the way the ethos of this church, and particularly its leaders, shaped the experience of Herman Friesen. Particular attention is given to the role of ministers, who were led by the Ältester. During the first fifty years of Herman's life, the Old Colony Mennonite Church in Saskatchewan was led by three Ältesten, each of whom shaped the life of the church in distinct ways. Elected as Ältester in 1900, eight years before Herman's birth, was Jacob Wiens, who led the

Old Colony Mennonites in resisting English-language public schools, a conflict that culminated in a mass migration to Mexico during the 1920s. This migration was a defining moment for the Old Colony Mennonites in Canada. Once the largest Mennonite denomination in Canada, the move decimated its numbers and the strength of its influence.

Replacing Wiens as Ältester in 1930 was Johann Loeppky, a minister who helped promote the migration to Mexico, but then opted to stay with those in Saskatchewan who either could not, or would not, participate in the migration to Mexico. As a result, he played a critical role in the reorganization of the Old Colony Mennonite Church in the province, which resulted in his appointment as Ältester. After Loeppky's death in 1950, Abram J. Loewen was elected Ältester and continued to explore additional migration possibilities to isolated locations in western Canada. Woven into this chapter are reflections on why the Friesen family opted not to participate in the migration, and how the different approaches on the part of church leaders may have impacted Herman's own perceptions of the narrative of migration as a means for preserving intact the faith and religious practices of the Old Colony Mennonites. I also examine the meaning and practice of baptism in the Old Colony Mennonite Church, and the difficult circumstances surrounding Herman's and Margaretha's baptism in August 1928.

Chapter 3 takes a closer look at Herman and Margaretha's life together as a married couple. After their marriage, the young couple settled on the Banman (Margaretha's parents) family farm. Here they encountered the harsh realities of pioneer life, which were soon made worse by the onset of the dirty thirties, and eventually also the economic boom of the 1940s and 1950s experienced across the country. Greater economic prosperity, along with provincial initiatives that greatly increased the network of roads and made electricity more generally available in rural Saskatchewan, made possible the purchase of motorized farm machinery and vehicles, the construction of a new home, acquisition of more farmland, and the development of a modern dairy operation. Herman was not as hesitant as some other Old Colony Mennonites about utilizing new technology when it became available and affordable.

Large families were the norm among Old Colony Mennonites; the couple had thirteen children, twelve of whom survived to adulthood. The couple was not unfamiliar with hardship and loss, including the death of their first child from whooping cough. During the 1950s, Margaretha faced a number of health issues that required medical attention and that made it difficult for her to participate in the household and farm operation as she had in the past. These challenges included dealing with the stigma of mental illness.

The rhythm of farm and family consisted of regular farm chores, weekly church attendance, school homework, and often also music. Herman, who taught himself to play guitar, enjoyed music, along with many of his children. Eventually, he purchased a pump organ for his children to use. Consistent with the Old Colony Mennonite patriarchal understanding of the structure of family life, Herman was the undisputed head of the household, who, as a strict disciplinarian, occasionally used force that would by today's standards be considered excessive. Although Herman was often absent from the home during evenings on account of his community leadership responsibilities, his election as minister in 1962 dramatically impacted family life.

The chapter concludes by observing how the residential, occupational, and even denominational choices made by Herman and Margaretha's children as they entered adulthood during the 1950s and 1960s reflected the spectrum of options being utilized by young adults in the Old Colony Mennonite Church. These new options contributed to the gradual diversification and fragmentation of the Old Colony Mennonite communitarian way of life.

Chapter 4 focuses specifically on Herman's community and church leadership experience. Although Herman was not the only Old Colony Mennonite elected as a public school trustee or rural municipal councillor during the first half of the twentieth century, it was an unusual departure from the attitudes and strategies promoted by Old Colony Mennonite leaders. His twenty years of experience significantly increased his network of relationships within the region, and also inclined him toward accepting a greater degree of modernization and Canadianization.

His musical interests, talent, and commitment to the community made it almost inevitable that he would be selected as a Vorsaenger, which took place when Herman was a young man in his twenties. This role marked the beginning of his leadership activities within the life of the Old Colony Mennonite Church. His election as a minister at the age of fifty-four, and then Ältester a year later, was life-altering in the way it reshaped the last seven years of his life. The new role meant, among other things, learning to write and deliver sermons on a regular basis. Despite the sombre formality that accompanied Old Colony preaching, his sermons display a surprising degree of personal transparency given the rather stoic personality that people often encountered in conversation. Herman's sermon literature provides a unique glimpse into Old Colony Mennonite theological thought as he sought to guide the church in a strategy of gradual cultural accommodation. The chapter ends with a summary of Herman's most notable challenges as Ältester.

The book concludes with the story of Herman's untimely death in 1969 as the result of a tractor accident. The event came as a devastating shock to his family, as well as to the people of the Old Colony Mennonite Church. It also brought an abrupt end to the strategy of gradual change within the church that characterized Herman's life and church leadership.

𝕳omesteading 𝕺rigins and 𝕰arly 𝕮hildhood 𝕰xperiences   1

BORN ONLY EIGHT YEARS AFTER HIS PARENTS AND
several siblings arrived in Saskatchewan at the turn of the twentieth
century, Herman Friesen's many stories relate to life on a rugged
prairie farm homestead. Unlike many other homesteading families at the
time, the isolation of the pioneering experience on a vast terrain was mitigated by the decision of his parents to participate in the formation of a small
village populated by other Old Colony Mennonites, most of whom were
closely related to either Herman's grandfather or grandmother. The hard
work demanded by subsistence farming was distributed among parents and
children, with everyone expected to contribute in ways appropriate to their
ability and strength. Herman participated in farm chores with six older
siblings and four younger siblings. As a young adolescent, Herman's experience of family life was traumatically disrupted by the death of his mother,
and then readjusted again shortly after by the remarriage of his father and
a blended family experience. His formal education as a young boy took
place at a private German-language school organized by the Old Colony
Mennonites. His time as a student coincided exactly with the skirmishes
between the Old Colony Mennonites and provincial governments over
English-language public schools in both Saskatchewan and Manitoba as
public concern about non–English language schools increased. Although
young Herman was unaware of the circumstances and decisions that
brought his family to Canada, and that made it possible to settle in western Canada, his childhood experiences were nevertheless deeply shaped by
these circumstances.

The Friesen family's efforts at establishing a viable farm operation were a part of a much larger phenomenon taking place on the vast
prairie region still known as the North-West Territories. In 1901, the

settlement of Saskatoon contained a little more than one hundred people; the entire region of what would later become known as the province of Saskatchewan in 1905 had only thirteen thousand farms and a population of about ninety thousand. Despite the sense of isolation among the Old Colony Mennonites within the expanded Hague-Osler Reserve, the newly formed province of which they became a part was experiencing rapid change: during the first decade of the twentieth century, the region's population increased by a staggering 500 per cent (492,000), making it the third-largest province in the country, and the number of farms increased to ninety-five thousand. In the short space of a decade, the community of Saskatoon had expanded to twelve thousand people as it became a service and business centre for the surrounding region. It was not long before the lives of the Old Colony Mennonites became increasingly intertwined with the ever-expanding web of communities linked by railroads and roads making up the province of Saskatchewan.

Herman Friesen was the ninth child of David[1] and Anna (Wiebe)[2] Friesen, both of whom arrived in southern Manitoba from Russia during the 1870s as young children with their Kanadier parents. Herman's father David was born in Blumengart, Chortitza, in Russia in 1870, the sixth child in a family of ten children. David's parents, David L. and Elizabeth (Bueckert) Friesen, arrived in Quebec City on July 1, 1875, on the SS *Moravian* No. 25. Along with their co-religionists, the family made their way to southern Manitoba, where they homesteaded on the West Reserve near Blumengart (Lot #3, SW-21-2-3 W1), southeast of Winkler, Manitoba. Anna, Herman's mother, had a very similar childhood and immigrant experience. She too was born in Russia in 1872, the second child in a family of ten children. Her parents, Jacob and Katharina (Rempel) Wiebe, immigrated to Canada, arriving in Quebec City on July 6, 1879, on the SS *Polynesian* No. 30. They lived on the West Reserve in the village of Schoendorf (Lot #27, NW-10-3-5 W1), east of Morden, Manitoba. David and Anna were married on October 27, 1892, in Manitoba, and shortly after the turn of the century decided to homestead in the District of Saskatchewan of the North-West Territories.

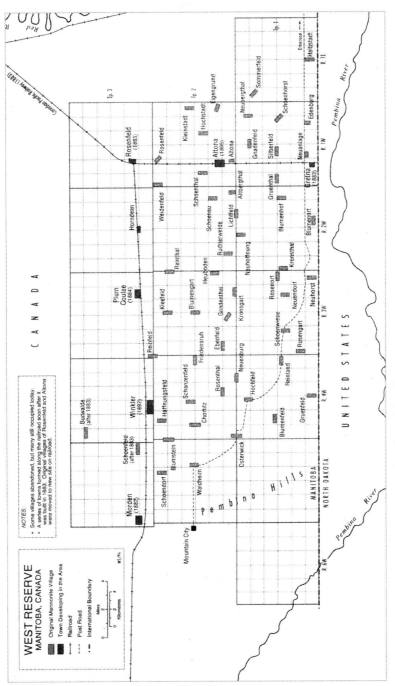

West Reserve, Manitoba, circa 1900. Courtesy William Schroeder.

First Inhabitants

LONG BEFORE THE FRIESEN FAMILY ARRIVED ON THEIR HOMESTEADS in southern Manitoba, and later in Saskatchewan, the region was inhabited by Indigenous peoples who lived on the vast plains of flowing grasses, poplar groves, and winding rivers, where they hunted the herds of buffalo and other wildlife on which they depended for their survival. While the exact origin of these nomadic people remains unclear,[3] over time, descendants of the original inhabitants formed the First Nations groups found across Canada's northwest, making their home on the interior plains with its short, sunny summers and often harsh winter seasons. Their self-sustaining life was characterized by that which comes from hunting-and-gathering cultures: with trade—and sometimes war—with neighbouring tribes, and a deep reverence for the Creator, the land, water, and the animals that sustained them.

This long history of the Indigenous peoples of the Plains changed irrevocably with the arrival of the Hudson's Bay Company in 1670, which took all of the lands draining into Hudson Bay as its trading territory and named it Rupert's Land. Within decades, European fur traders and explorers began to appear across the region. The introduction of iron trade goods dramatically changed the lifestyles, economies, and intertribal relations of the Indigenous people.[4] In time, Christian missionaries arrived, organizing missions and schools.[5] As the buffalo herds were decimated and the fur trade declined, Indigenous peoples found themselves facing starvation in many cases.[6] The immense hardship experienced by Indigenous peoples was used by some to promote the agricultural potential of the region.

In 1867, a new country called Canada was formed. Under the leadership of Sir John A. Macdonald, a vision emerged for extending this nation across the continent as a dominion from the Atlantic Ocean to the Pacific Ocean. Toward that end, the new government acquired the legal right to Rupert's Land in 1870 from the Hudson's Bay Company for $1.5 million, with the condition that treaties be negotiated with First Nations. This purchase drastically altered the relationship that the Indigenous peoples had with the land, and with the Canadian government. As the treaty negotiations were taking place, preparations for settlement began with the passage of the Dominion Lands Act in 1872, which regulated the survey and division of huge areas of the region into square parcels that were offered to prospective settlers willing to homestead. The formation of the North-West Mounted Police in 1873, and the construction of a transcontinental railway, a project that was completed in 1885, helped the government to attract and distribute a diverse group of settlers.

The Mennonites who settled in southern Manitoba were blithely unaware of the political controversies and financial circumstances that preceded their arrival, and the ongoing conflicts that surrounded nineteenth-century efforts to complete treaty negotiations and reserve resettlement with First Nations groups. Even the more violent events of the North-West Resistance of 1885 in the Batoche area, which took place not far from Rosthern, Saskatchewan, after the arrival of Mennonites in southern Manitoba, did not evoke much interest or deter the Mennonites. The subsequent transition of Mennonites from southern Manitoba to Saskatchewan coincided with the start of an aggressive propaganda campaign designed to recruit capable settlers led by Clifford Sifton, minister of the interior (1896–1905), which then resulted in an influx of an additional 1.5 million mostly white European immigrants to the prairies who spoke a multiplicity of languages.[7] Intent on securing a sufficient land base for their economic and religious purposes, the Mennonite settlers did not recognize how the policies that created the prairie homesteading opportunities extended to them were part of a larger project of dispossessing and marginalizing Indigenous people.[8] The cultural diversity created by the infusion of a polyglottal humanity caused considerable concern among those Canadians who had a more culturally, and religiously, homogenous vision of Canada.[9] Despite the federal government's intense desire to see the vast open prairies populated by people of European descent, it would not be long before its assimilationist agenda collided also, rather ironically, with the interests of the German-speaking Mennonites. The stalwart refusal on the part of Old Colony Mennonites to pursue the privileges of political power, and their own subsequent conflicts with governments, complicated their quiet complicity in Canadian strategies for the subjugation of Indigenous peoples.

Nevertheless, individual Mennonites and members of local Indigenous communities occasionally did develop friendly, and sometimes complicated, relationships.[10]

The Homesteading Experience

THE IMPETUS FOR DAVID AND ANNA FRIESEN'S INTEREST IN RELOcating from Manitoba to Saskatchewan likely came from several of David Friesen's older siblings. Frustrated by the lack of available land on the West Reserve in southern Manitoba, David's brother Jacob Friesen (married to Marie Siemens) applied for a homestead in Gleichen, Alberta, approximately eighty kilometres east of Calgary, in early 1891. Jacob was part of a larger group of fifteen families led by a minister, Gerhard Paetkau, from the West Reserve. Some of these settlers, including Jacob, determined quickly that the Gleichen region was not well suited for farming and large-scale Mennonite settlement. Cancelling their homestead, they decided to return to Manitoba. But, prior to leaving Alberta, they received news about the availability of fertile farmland near Rosthern in the District of Saskatchewan. Jacob and Marie, along with twelve other families, including several members of Marie's family, packed their meagre belongings onto a train and arrived in Rosthern in the fall of 1891.[11] The group was excommunicated from the Reinlaender Mennonite Church for not returning to Manitoba.[12] A year later, David's brother Isbrand Friesen (married to Anna Neudorf), and his brother-in-law Johann Siemens (married to David's sister Maria Friesen), both applied for homesteads in the Rosthern area.[13] By 1894, the Rosthern area had acquired a Mennonite population of four hundred people from various sources.[14]

The homesteading experience of these three families prompted the rest of the Friesen family to follow developments in the District of Saskatchewan with keen interest, especially as four townships called the Hague-Osler Reserve were designated for Mennonite settlement in 1895. Three years later, in 1898, when this reserve was expanded to accommodate additional Mennonite settlement, David and Anna, along with four of his siblings and their families, together with David's elderly parents David L. and Elizabeth (Bueckert) Friesen, decided to relocate.

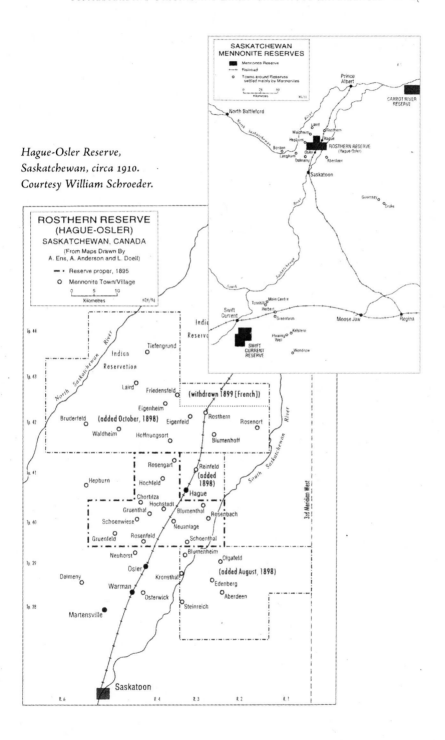

Hague-Osler Reserve,
Saskatchewan, circa 1910.
Courtesy William Schroeder.

The Friesen families were at the centre of forming the village of Blumenheim, not far from the South Saskatchewan River (approximately ten kilometres northeast of Osler). It was not uncommon for family clans to organize villages, but the Old Colony Mennonite immigrants interested in doing so were forced to adapt the more communal village model that was used in Russia to the Canadian system of land ownership, which distributed homesteads on surveyed land to individuals.[15] In 1900, the elderly David L. Friesen was able to purchase a section of land (31-39-3-3W) from the Qu'Appelle Long Lake and Saskatchewan Railroad and Steamship Company, the east half of which was used as the location for the new village of Blumenheim.[16] The name "Blumenheim" (home of flowers) served as a reminder of the Friesen family's past: they had lived in a village named Blumengart in the West Reserve in Manitoba, and, prior to that, moved from the village of Blumengart in the Chortitza Colony in Russia. Although each family applied for, and eventually received, title to their own homestead, they also opted to use the "Hamlet privilege," which waived the usual residency requirement on homestead quarters, and made it possible for groups of families or like-minded individuals to live in closer proximity to one another.[17]

Villages made it possible to continue a way of life that was familiar to the Mennonite immigrants. Close proximity to others greatly helped to mitigate some of the hardships faced by pioneering families in the early twentieth century. Living in villages made it easier for people to socialize, to organize schools and churches, and to share skills and resources. It also brought its share of conflict: little can be hidden from neighbours, and tensions sometimes erupted over insignificant matters.

Despite what seemed like obvious advantages for the homesteading families, and the long-standing preference on the part of Russian Mennonite immigrants for living in villages, the Friesen family's decision to organize a village apparently produced some consternation on the part of Jacob Wiens, the first minister to be ordained as Ältester in the Hague-Osler Reserve. He was concerned that the new village was not located within the boundaries of the original four townships of the reserve. The reason for Ältester Wien's apprehension seems odd given the lack of available homesteads in

BLUMENHEIM VILLAGE

(Established in 1900,
Location: Section 31, Township 39,
Range 4, West of 3rd Meridian)

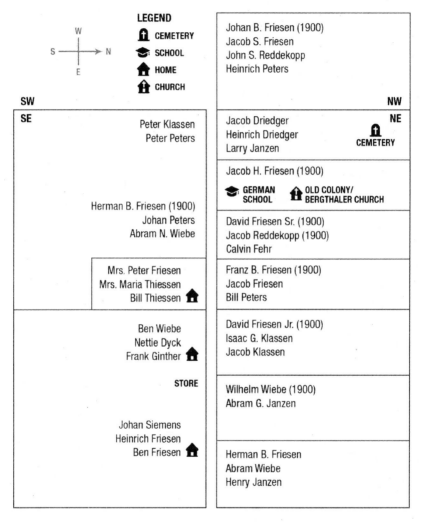

LEGEND

🪦 CEMETERY
🎓 SCHOOL
🏠 HOME
⛪ CHURCH

W — S / E — N

Johan B. Friesen (1900)
Jacob S. Friesen
John S. Reddekopp
Heinrich Peters

SW   NW

SE   NE

Peter Klassen
Peter Peters

Jacob Driedger
Heinrich Driedger
Larry Janzen
🪦 CEMETERY

Jacob H. Friesen (1900)

🎓 GERMAN SCHOOL   ⛪ OLD COLONY/ BERGTHALER CHURCH

Herman B. Friesen (1900)
Johan Peters
Abram N. Wiebe

David Friesen Sr. (1900)
Jacob Reddekopp (1900)
Calvin Fehr

Mrs. Peter Friesen
Mrs. Maria Thiessen
Bill Thiessen 🏠

Franz B. Friesen (1900)
Jacob Friesen
Bill Peters

Ben Wiebe
Nettie Dyck
Frank Ginther 🏠

David Friesen Jr. (1900)
Isaac G. Klassen
Jacob Klassen

STORE

Wilhelm Wiebe (1900)
Abram G. Janzen

Johan Siemens
Heinrich Friesen
Ben Friesen 🏠

Herman B. Friesen
Abram Wiebe
Henry Janzen

Village of Blumenheim, established in 1900. Courtesy Leonard Doell.
The first name on each parcel of land is the original owner of that property. Subsequent names are people who lived on the property but did not necessarily own the land. The original map compiled by Leonard Doell was published in 1995, and any changes in ownership since then are not reflected in this reproduction.

close enough proximity to form a new village within the original boundaries of the Hague-Osler Reserve. Moreover, it was not the only new village to be organized within the extensions to the reserve. The Ältester may have been concerned about the growing challenge of maintaining a close-knit church community as the distances between the first villages and newly formed villages continued to increase. Or it may have been the lingering consequence of a conflict that had resulted in the excommunication of eleven families, including Jacob Friesen (son of David L. Friesen) for his disobedience to Gerhard Paetkau in deciding to move to Rosthern, and the suspicion of a similar independent spirit on the part of the others within the Friesen clan.[18] It is worth noting that each of the three Friesen siblings who settled in Rosthern later decided to move farther south in order to be closer to other members of their family—Jacob and Marie Friesen relocated east of Hague, Isbrand and Anna Friesen moved to the village of Chortitz, and Johann and Maria Siemens joined her parents and siblings at Blumenheim.

With four young children, all five years of age and younger, David and Anna moved to their new homestead in early 1900. David spent the summer building a small (24' x 32') house for his young and growing family at a cost of $400. For David and Anna, more children arrived in rapid succession in their new home. Two boys and a girl were born in Blumenheim prior to Herman's birth on February 4, 1908. By this time, Herman's father had managed to break and crop approximately one hundred acres, and had added a small barn and granary to their yard. The basic structure and routines of Blumenheim village had been put in place. While his two oldest brothers worked with their father in cultivating land, Herman, as a young boy, was kept busy with various farm tasks such as caring for the family's animals, which was the primary source of power for farming and transportation during this pioneering period. Four more siblings arrived after Herman, including a set of twins, which made for a busy and active home.[19]

When Herman was five years old, Canada began participating in a war that was fought in faraway Europe. The terms outlined in a letter written by Secretary of the Department of Agriculture John Lowe to the Mennonite immigrants on July 23, 1873, which were later ratified by the Committee of the Privy Council, promised "entire exemption from military service" for "the denomination of Christians called Mennonites."[20] The ongoing commitment to this agreement on the part of church members and the federal government was crucial for Old Colony Mennonite Church leaders. The move by Russia to impose new conscription laws, and the willingness on the part of some Mennonites to replace their earlier exemption with a proposal advocating alternative service for Mennonite men, was a significant motivation for immigrating to North America. Although several of Herman's brothers were of eligible age, this exemption kept them from being drafted during the First World War.

Despite the lack of any direct involvement in the First World War, Herman's childhood years were punctuated by loss: his paternal grandparents, David L. and Elizabeth, died in 1911 and 1913, respectively. His mother's father, Jacob Wiebe, died three years later in 1916. The deepest loss, and the one that dramatically altered his early adolescent world, was the death of his mother in the summer of 1921, at the relatively young age of forty-eight. As a widower, his father David was left with the daunting task of not only ensuring the ongoing viability of his farm operation but also providing care for eight children still at home, with the youngest being only three years old. It was not uncommon at the time for Mennonite men to remarry quickly after the death of a wife, particularly when there were young children in the home. It is not surprising, then, that less than four months after the death of Anna, Herman's father married Katarina (Wiens) Janzen, a widow whose husband had died the year before in 1920, leaving her with ten children, seven of whom were still in her care. The rigorous demands of an agrarian pioneer setting, and the experience of growing up in a very large blended family with numerous siblings and stepbrothers/sisters shaped Herman's teenage years.[21] One can imagine it would have been difficult for parents to give significant attention to all of the children.

Along with the sad and painful events during Herman's childhood, such as the death of loved ones that would bring family and friends together, there were other more joyful occasions such as seasonal butchering and building bees, and celebratory events such as weddings (including those of four of Herman's older siblings). The social rhythm of village life included

Sundays and religious holidays as designated days of rest that were commonly used not only for attending church but also for visiting neighbours or hosting visitors. These days provided relief from the hard labour demands of a pioneer environment, an opportunity for children to play, for young people to socialize and date, and for adults to renew friendships.

Early School Experience

NINETEENTH-CENTURY MENNONITES FROM RUSSIA BROUGHT WITH them to Canada a long-standing commitment to giving all boys and girls an elemental education. Consistent with their practice in southern Manitoba, and previously in Russia, the Old Colony Mennonites in Saskatchewan were quick to organize their own private German-language schools. Many were located within villages, often near the centre of the village, but some were built on farmyards or conducted in the homes of church members.[22]

The Old Colony Mennonites believed it was the responsibility of the parents and church to provide for the religious education of the children, not the state. It was their understanding that the Canadian government had given Mennonites the right to operate their own schools without any external interference, and that understanding later became a major point of contention. As noted previously, the Mennonites used a letter received from John Lowe as the basis for understanding their agreement with the Canadian government. Lowe's letter stated that "the fullest privileges of exercising their religious principles is by law afforded the Mennonites, without any kind of molestation or restriction whatever; and the same privilege extends to the education of their children in schools."[23] The legal version of this Mennonite *privilegium*, a special charter of privileges, approved by the Privy Council on August 13, 1873, was based upon Lowe's letter and contained a small, but critical, caveat concerning education that read, "the Mennonites will have the fullest privilege of exercising their religious principles, and educating their children in schools, *as provided by law*, without any kind of molestation or restriction whatever."[24] The Mennonites discovered soon enough that education was a provincial matter, not a federal one.

The private, church-supervised schools organized by the Old Colony Mennonites were considered an essential "nursery of Christianity," and were designed to socialize children by reinforcing the values of the home, village, and the church.[25] Historian John Friesen notes that "the school was an extension of a much larger educational process." The curriculum in the classroom was to be coordinated with the work on the farm, and the teaching of the church.[26] It was designed to help all children obtain a basic level of literacy and arithmetic, and to prepare people for baptism and participation in the life of the church and for life in the Mennonite community. Attendance was, therefore, mandatory. Although helping children become literate was a priority, education beyond this elementary level was deemed not only unnecessary but also undesirable. "Children were not expected, nor encouraged to seek ideas or to read sources beyond those which were known and approved; children were to receive information passively, and not to question the sources of authority."[27] Competitiveness in skill and knowledge was discouraged for fear it would manifest pride and disrupt community life. As a result, children were not graded; only laziness was condemned. Leaders of the church were concerned that higher levels of education would encourage independent or critical thinking that might be used to challenge the authority of the church in giving direction to the lives of its members, and it would "alienate people from a simple agrarian way of life."[28]

Unlike the set of grades that was adopted by the public school system to organize students, the Mennonite German schools organized students into four classes: primary reading (using a primer called *Die Fibel*) and arithmetic, catechism, New Testament, and Old Testament. Students remained in a particular class until they mastered the required material before progressing to the next class. While children came to school fluent in Low German (*Plautdietsch*),[29] the language used in the home and community, in school they were introduced to High German, the spoken and written language of the church. Facilities were sparse, textbooks and teaching resources were few, extracurricular activities did not exist, and teachers (always male) seldom had any specialized training for their task.[30] The village school teachers have sometimes been characterized very negatively as people incapable of success in other occupations or as excessively harsh, even at times sadistic, disciplinarians. There were a number of well-trained teachers who immigrated to Canada during the 1890s and settled in the Hague-Osler Reserve, but most of the teachers in the German village schools were local men with limited training.[31] The life of a village school teacher was not easy and required an astounding degree of dedication considering the difficulties under which they worked. Although school teachers were not paid well,[32] and often supplemented their income either by farming or by offering a specialized skill (for example, carpentry, chiropractic services, clockmaking, shoemaking), they were generally well respected and often exercised considerable influence within the community. Most children only attended for half a dozen years or less: girls generally stopped attending at about eleven years of age, and boys at about twelve years of age.

Like most Old Colony Mennonite children in the region at the time, young Herman began attending the small, German-language village school at about six years of age (circa 1914) in Blumenheim. The school was established in the middle of the village around 1901, shortly after the village was started, so young Herman never had far to go to school. The school schedule was arranged to accommodate an annual farming cycle: instruction began, for six hours a day, five days per week, each fall around the middle of October, and continued until seeding time in the spring. Sometimes an additional month of instruction was added during the summer. One of his teachers may have been Heinrich Fehr, who was married to his first cousin Elizabeth Friesen, daughter of Franz B. and Margaretha Friesen. Heinrich taught in many of the private German schools in the Hague-Osler Reserve.[33] Herman probably stopped attending school sometime in the early 1920s, around the time of his mother's death. Despite the fact that the Renfrew School District was organized in 1919, and a school building was built just north of the village of Blumenheim, Herman never attended an English-language public school.

Herman Friesen's years as a young schoolboy coincided both with the First World War and with a rapidly escalating conflict between the Old Colony Mennonites and several provincial governments over the meaning of the Mennonites' agreement with the federal government. These two struggles, despite taking place thousands of kilometres apart, were not unrelated. The massive influx of settlers during the first two decades of the twentieth century meant that public schools could not be built fast enough to meet the growing demand in the new province. This prompted the provincial government to adopt as one of its first pioneering slogans: "A New School Everyday for Twenty Years." As more and more settlers arrived, the number of public school districts in Saskatchewan did indeed grow: from 1906 to 1911, the number grew from 1,190 to 2,546, and, by 1916, the number of districts had increased to 3,873.[34] An intensely patriotic Protestantism, driven by a potent cocktail of nationalism, anti-Catholicism, and xenophobia, hailed the public school system as the primary means for transforming the polyglot population in western Canada into patriotic Canadians. The destruction of non–English language parochial schools became "part of a consistent national policy aimed at the assimilation of ethnics to safeguard national unity and cultural uniformity."[35] As the patriotic fervour surrounding the First World War intensified, so too did the suspicion toward German-speaking immigrants. The conflict created deep divisions among Mennonites in the Hague-Osler region, and prompted many Old Colony Mennonites in Canada to relocate to Mexico during the 1920s. Although he was only a young schoolboy at the time, it is safe to assume that Friesen's observations about this conflict and its consequences influenced his own understanding of cultural accommodation, community involvement, and church leadership.

For the first decade of the twentieth century, it was not mandatory for children in Saskatchewan to attend a public school. If a public school district had not yet been established in a region, people could organize one with a majority vote; the land in the district would then be taxed to pay for the cost of the school. Efforts to organize a public school district in the trading centres in and around the Hague-Osler Reserve were vigorously opposed by many of the Old Colony Mennonites, prompting other residents to utilize unorthodox strategies in order to win referendums (for example, using construction workers in Rosthern to increase the number of votes, or adjusting boundaries for the Osler district to exclude some Old Colony Mennonite villages).[36] Many people expressed frustration and anger to the government about the resistance of the Old Colony Mennonites to the formation of public school districts. For their part, Old Colony Mennonites in the Hague area complained their land had been included in the Hague school district without their approval in order to generate tax revenue for a public school. More than twenty Old Colony members, including several prominent businessmen, who assisted in the formation of public school districts in the Hague-Osler region or decided to send their children to such schools, were excommunicated and shunned by other members of the church, often with severe economic and social consequences.

The struggles of the Old Colony Mennonites in the Hague-Osler Reserve must be seen as part of a larger conflict.[37] The simmering conflict about private versus public schools prompted the provincial government to initiate a formal commission of inquiry to investigate the system of private German schools operated by the Old Colony Mennonites in December 1908, the same year Herman Friesen was born.[38] This commission was conducted in nearby Warman and was widely publicized. As a result, the Old Colony Mennonites who did not enthusiastically support public schools and the government's nationalistic agenda were portrayed as prejudiced and bigoted. Ältester Jacob Wiens, along with Johann Wall, an articulate and uncompromising spokesperson, testified before the commission, describing their private schools and explaining their understanding and practice of excommunication. The commissioners believed that Old Colony leaders had violated the law by advocating a boycott against excommunicated members, and that they were restricting the religious liberty of those members who wished to send their children to public schools. They claimed this was inconsistent with the Ältester's own stated respect for the authority of government and desire for religious freedom.[39] Old Colony leaders were, therefore, warned to stop excommunicating members whose children attended public schools, but this did not lessen their overall resistance to public schools. The commission served to strengthen the resolve of the provincial government to force the Old Colony Mennonites to participate in the public school system.

Various reports, including one written in 1915 by E. H. Oliver, principal of the Presbyterian Theological College, Saskatoon, and vice-president of the Saskatchewan Public Education League, increased public concern (and prejudice) during a particularly sensitive time when people in English-speaking Canada were paying a heavy price for their involvement in the First World War against Germany, from which German-speaking Mennonites were exempt. Oliver took the initiative to conduct his own investigation into the "educational problem" facing the province. He summarized well the prevailing sentiment regarding the purpose of a public education system by stating, "Every effort should be made to furnish the child with such ideas and trend of action as will assist in making him an intelligent and patriotic citizen." As part of his research, he interviewed Ältester Wiens, and visited at least thirteen of the thirty-two private German-language schools operated by Mennonites in Saskatchewan. It is likely he visited the village school in Blumenheim at which Herman Friesen was a student. According to his estimate, more than five hundred children were enrolled in the seventeen German-language private schools in the Hague-Osler area, "about which the Government knows nothing officially and in which from one year's end to another, not one single word of English is ever taught. Not a single teacher knows English well enough to teach if he would." His critical description of conditions within the Mennonite private schools continues:

> In the forenoon they sing and say their prayers, then study Bible History and practice reading. This consumes the morning hours from 8:30 to 11:30. For 3 hours in the afternoon they work at arithmetic and writing. It is simple fare, but is all the teacher himself has ever received. Frequently he does not know even *Hoch Deutsch* [sic] well enough for conversation. So through seven years they go from October 15th to seeding and again for one month in summer ignorant of the fates of Canadian history, untouched by the loftiness of Canadian ideals and taught that the English language will only make it easier to lapse into the great world of sin outside the Mennonite communities.[40]

In 1916, the election of a new premier in Saskatchewan, William M. Martin, who had made English-language schools a major plank in his election platform, followed by the end of the First World War, solidified the

provincial government's resolve that "it was high time that some improve-
ment should take place." For a time, the government considered depriving
Old Colony leaders of the legal right to solemnize marriages if they did not
release members who wanted their children to attend a public school.[41] In
1917, Martin met with Ältester Wiens to inform him that the Mennonite
schools would need to comply with government standards, including the
use of government-authorized textbooks and teachers with recognized cre-
dentials. That same year, the government passed the School Attendance
Act, which made it compulsory in each school district for all children
between the ages of seven and fourteen to attend a government-approved
school.[42] More aggressive action on the part of the government followed
in 1918, and again in 1919, when the provincial government created new
districts by using order-in-council decisions, expropriated land, sent in
construction crews, and built public schools in various Mennonite villages
including Renfrew School in Blumenheim.[43] Trustees were appointed
to oversee these schools, and teachers were hired, even though in some
instances few, if any, children attended. Some Old Colony Mennonite
parents used a variety of tactics to avoid paying fines associated with the
School Attendance Act, including moving to areas that were not part of a
public school district, or sending their children to stay with relatives who
lived in such exempt areas.

With compulsory attendance legislation in place, enforcement actions in
the newly organized public school districts soon followed, which escalated
the conflict and deeply divided the Mennonite community. The actions on
the part of the government would undoubtedly have been a major topic of
conversation in the village of Blumenheim and within the Friesen household during the 1920s when Herman was an adolescent. Despite appeals to
the federal government to intervene, petitions to the provincial government
to relent, and several unsuccessful attempts to negotiate compromises,
prosecutions began in selected areas in 1918 (for example, in Aberdeen)
and continued until the mid-1920s. Between 1918 and 1925, the number
of school attendance prosecutions of Saskatchewan Mennonites probably
exceeded six thousand. During a three-year period (1923–25), there were
1,400 convictions in six school districts in the Hague-Osler area alone

(this included the Renfrew district, with 165 convictions).[44] Penalties were mostly fines, but some Old Colony members were also imprisoned, a practice that was quickly discouraged for fear of creating "martyrs," but it was not entirely discontinued. The fines were not insignificant ($4 per month per child), and they created considerable hardship for pioneering farmers who were cash-poor but still expected to pay school taxes, as well as a church levy to finance their own schools. Some were forced to sell cattle and land in order to make the payments. In 1920–21 alone, $26,000 was collected in eleven Mennonite districts.[45] Those unable to pay had goods seized by the police and sold at public auction. I was unable to verify whether Herman's father David ever paid fines to avoid having to send his children to public school—it seems likely given the number of school-aged children in the blended family household during the early 1920s. Heinrich Banman (Herman's eventual father-in-law), who lived in the nearby village of Kronsthal, not only paid fines but also spent time in prison for not sending his children to public school. Old Colony Mennonite parents were caught on the horns of a difficult dilemma: if they refused to send their children to the new English public schools, they risked destitution.[46] Yet if parents sent their children to school, they risked being reprimanded by, and possibly excommunicated from, the church, which also had severe economic and social implications.

It became increasingly obvious to Old Colony Mennonite leaders that the provincial government had no intention of relenting in its efforts to enforce its policy of compulsory attendance at provincially accredited schools in which English would be the sole language of instruction. The sense of betrayal and hopelessness felt by the Mennonites prompted them to organize meetings where they began considering an alternative course of action. In 1919, delegates were selected and given the mandate of finding a new homeland. This culminated in a mass exodus of Old Colony Mennonite people from Manitoba and Saskatchewan to Mexico during the 1920s.

By the end of the 1920s, most of the Old Colony members who either had chosen not to, or were unable to, migrate to Mexico during the 1920s had conceded to the provincial government's pressure by sending their children to English-language public schools. In 1920, a school inspector named Mr. Coombes visited the Renfrew School and reported that there were forty-three school-aged children in the district, but that only one was attending the public school. By 1930, within only a decade—after Herman was no longer a student—resistance among the Old Colony Mennonites in and around Blumenheim had changed: attendance peaked at seventy-four in the small, one-room Renfrew School.[47] The transition from the private German schools to English-language public schools was smoother in places where trustees hired teachers who could speak German, who belonged to a Mennonite denomination, and who were sensitive to the religious interests of the Old Colony people. Some teachers incorporated a limited amount of German instruction into the curriculum, as well as study of the Old Colony *Catechism* that was used in the private schools. Others organized extracurricular activities that were greatly appreciated by the youth. Particularly helpful were those teachers who organized evening English classes for older youth and young, married adults. These efforts, along with the annual Christmas program and a school closing event, gradually helped the public schools become significant social centres that regularly brought people of the community together.

The petitions submitted by Old Colony leaders to the provincial government made it clear that the English language was not the primary issue, but rather it was about maintaining control over the religious instruction of their children.[48] It is difficult to understand why positions hardened into intransigence, making it impossible to consider the potential in some of the compromise proposals, and making confrontation inevitable. One certainly wonders in what way, if any, Herman's experience as a schoolboy influenced his interest later in life to serve as a trustee of a local public school. Given the intensity of the conflict, and the significant level of distrust between the government and Old Colony Mennonite leaders, it seems odd that such a young member of the church would decide to become involved in community leadership during the mid-1930s, an action that was out of step with church policy. Did this decision have anything to do with perceptions of how this conflict had been managed, both on the part of the government and at times also on the part of the Old Colony

Mennonite leaders? Questions about Herman's involvement in local politics and its impact on his family and relationship to the church are explored more fully in Chapter 4.

ENTRAL IN THE LIFE OF AN OLD COLONY Mennonite community is the church. Not only were church buildings located where they would be easily accessible to the largest number of members but the church defined the way of life for Old Colony Mennonites, with ministers and, particularly, the Ältester assuming prominent positions of leadership. Many of the first Old Colony immigrants who arrived in the Hague-Osler region in 1895 settled in the village of Neuanlage. They were accompanied by Peter Klassen, a minister who conducted services in his home and in a log schoolhouse until a church building was constructed in the village by volunteer labour in 1900.[1]

As more settlers followed, and other villages were developed, church buildings were constructed in Edenburg (near Aberdeen) and Neuhorst. Pioneering conditions made it difficult for some settlers to travel to one of these three church sites, so attendance was often irregular. Depending on the availability of ministers and weather conditions, worship services were sometimes conducted in the German schools, particularly in Blumenthal and Blumenheim. (Services were sometimes also conducted in the homes of members who lived a substantial distance from a church building.) The buildings dedicated for use as public places of worship were plain and unpainted—a visible indicator of simplicity and humility. Men and women used separate entrances and were seated apart on long benches, which, until the 1970s, were without backs. Worship services generally lasted two or more hours and consisted of a combination of singing, a brief "introduction," silent prayers, and a lengthy sermon that was normally read from a manuscript. Behaviour within the building was noticeably hushed and subdued, reflecting the veneration given to the place of worship; even conversation after the service was discouraged.[2]

The Lehrdienst and the Leadership Role of the Ältester

THE HIERARCHICAL LEADERSHIP STRUCTURE WITHIN THE OLD Colony Mennonite Church consisted of three levels. When deemed necessary, ministers and deacons were elected at brotherhood meetings, which were attended by all the baptized men of the church. Any male church member was potentially eligible for nomination as a minister or deacon; if elected, the appointment was expected to be for life. None had any special training for these roles. Ministers were responsible for preaching, officiating at weddings and funerals, and providing pastoral care to members of the congregation. The ministers did not belong to one church location, but together they served all the church locations on a rotation basis that helped distribute the workload. During worship services, ministers wore long black coats as symbols of their authority. Handwritten sermons, often handed down through successive generations, were always read. Eye contact

German school in Blumenthal, Saskatchewan, which was also sometimes used for church services, 1954. Courtesy Leo Driedger.

with the congregation and expressive motions with hands or shoulders were avoided while preaching. Ministers served without payment or compensation, despite the fact that their duties were often onerous, and often placed a considerable burden on their wives and children, and sometimes resulted in the neglect of their farm operations. Although Old Colony Mennonite theology did not ascribe to ministers a mediatorial role between God and humanity, informally they were perceived by many as spokespersons for God, and were given a considerable degree of deference and influence.[3] Deacons were responsible for taking care of various administrative tasks, such as maintaining church records, distributing aid to those in need, ensuring the care of the sick and elderly, preparing the elements at communion services, and organizing building maintenance on behalf of the *Lehrdienst*, a leadership group made up of the Ältester, all ministers, and deacons.

At the head of the church was the Ältester, who was granted considerable authority over the direction and general ethos of church and community life. Elected at a brotherhood meeting, the Ältester was selected from among the ranks of the existing ministers. He led the Lehrdienst, which was responsible for organizing the rotation of ministers, maintaining church records, handling matters of discipline, and making recommendations to the brotherhood regarding major decisions. The Ältester acted as the public spokesperson for the church. He alone administered the rites of communion and baptism. The strength and quality of leadership varied considerably from one Ältester to the next; some had the skills and ability to become strong community leaders in more than just religious affairs, particularly during times of crisis.[4] The organizational structure of the church provided the opportunity for an authoritarian abuse of power, but an Ältester, at his best, understood that his authority could only be exercised fully if it was based upon the ongoing support of the people. Some did not reach old age and died young, exhausted by both carrying the burdens of public leadership and meeting the needs of their own families. Along with the ecclesiastical authority embedded within the role, many Ältesten were highly revered and respected for their sacrificial labour on behalf of the community.

The Friesen family's church experience during their first decades in Saskatchewan was deeply shaped by the individuals selected to lead the church, particularly those who served in the role of Ältester. At first, the visionary Ältester Johann Wiebe (1837–1905), who, in his early thirties, had led the migration of 1,100 people from the Fuerstenland settlement in southern Russia to Canada in 1875, travelled from Manitoba to conduct baptismal and communion services in the Hague-Osler Reserve. Wiebe provided an uncompromising (and controversial) vision for restoring the church to a new level of spiritual purity through a strategy of unified migration and settlement.[5] His regular presence in the Hague-Osler Reserve created a continuity of vision and identity, but the time required for travel, preaching, and pastoral care of Old Colony members living 850 kilometres away did not make this a suitable long-term arrangement. As a result, in 1900, he presided over the election and ordination of Jacob Wiens, a minister with twelve years of experience, as Ältester of the Old Colony Mennonite Church in the Hague-Osler region.[6] Leonard Doell observes that Wiens, who lived in Neuanlage, "led the Saskatchewan group both during its greatest period of material development and through some of its most agonizing years." He describes Wiens as

> a well-respected minister who was knowledgeable about scripture, and whose words were valued as truth by many of his church members. His voice was strong and could be easily heard in the church which had no public address system. He read a lot and was inquisitive about world affairs. In addition to this, he was famous in the area for his chiropractic skills. He also served the community as a veterinarian… (and) was a respected agriculturalist, whose advice was sought by many about how to farm, when to seed, and how to care for the land.[7]

His dedication expressed itself in rather strict, uncompromising, and sometimes autocratic ways: despite considerable pressure from within and without the church, he resolutely refused to allow church members to send their children to public schools. Similarly, he insisted that church members live according to a 1916 vow made by Old Colony church leaders in Manitoba and Saskatchewan to ban the automobile forever. This did not, however, stop a local car dealership from trying to entice Wiens with the offer of a free car, which he flatly refused, knowing that others were closely watching his example. His reputation as a leader was coloured by occasionally allowing petty differences to escalate into public disputes.[8] By 1908, the year of Herman Friesen's birth, the Old Colony Mennonite Church consisted of almost one thousand baptized members in the Hague-Osler region, and was led by Ältester Wiens and six ministers.[9]

Migration to Mexico

AS NOTED ABOVE, ÄLTESTER JACOB WIENS, ALONG WITH JOHANN P. Wall, led the Old Colony Mennonites in the Hague-Osler region in their response to the provincial government on the private school issue. As early as 1913, just before the start of the First World War, Ältester Wiens told of a mystical premonition about an impending relocation. Perhaps evoked by the heightened patriotism experienced during times of war, it took place

> outside the village of Reinland, "while looking out over a field… of swaying wheat with its beautiful ears" [where] Wiens heard "a voice come from above…saying 'You will not be able to stay here [in Canada] forever; the [Mennonite] church will once again have to take up the walking staff.'" When Wiens asked, "but where to?" "in his spirit he received the following answer: 'if the church wishes to maintain itself in the pure gospel, it will once again need to settle among a heathen people.'"[10]

The strategy of migration as a means for preserving intact the faith and religious practices of the Old Colony Mennonites was always kept as an option in the minds of church leaders. The ensuing hardship was consistent with the perception of Christian life as a constant struggle.

The inability to resolve the private school conflict had an irreparable impact not only on Old Colony Mennonite parents with school-aged children in the Hague-Osler region but also on the entire Old Colony church membership in Manitoba and Saskatchewan as leaders tried to mandate a relocation to Mexico during the 1920s. For several years, beginning in 1919, delegations went to South America to explore options in Brazil, Argentina, and Uruguay, to United States in Mississippi and Alabama, and to northern Manitoba and Quebec, before a favourable meeting with President Álvaro Obregón of Mexico led to that country becoming the preferred destination. After some consideration on the part of the president, a *privilegium* was prepared, outlining the conditions the delegates had requested.[11]

Having finalized a destination, church leaders considered the migration to Mexico to be a move of the entire church (*Gemeinde*), which meant that all church members were expected to participate. The mandate to relocate was reinforced by a religious vision that evoked the biblical story of the ancient children of Israel who were called to leave their positions as slaves in Egypt in order to enter a promised land filled with "milk and honey." Church leaders tried to create a parallel with the threat of Russification, which had motivated, in part, an exodus of Mennonites from Russia during the 1870s. Isaak M. Dyck, who eventually became an Ältester in Mexico, depicted Canada as a "heathen" nation shaped by the hegemonic, imperial culture of the "all-British Empire." The English-language school legislation of 1916 was seen as a product of the intense patriotism during the First World War that was intended to produce "an inextinguishable enthusiasm for the art of war," and to lead Mennonite children to embrace the nation-centric mantra of "one king, one country, one fleet, one flag, one all-British empire: love and sacrifice for the Fatherland."[12] In contrast, Mexico was described as the promised land, where Mennonites, as perpetual "pilgrims and strangers" in the world, might find the necessary religious freedom enabling them to procure a heavenly homeland. Canadian historian Royden Loewen notes how the migration of the 1920s was seen as an addition to the "grand narrative of Mennonite diaspora," alongside the story of sixteenth-century Anabaptist martyrs and ancestors who had courageously taken up the "walking staff" from Holland, to Prussia, to Russia, to Canada, and now to Mexico.[13] Encasing the migration with such religious meaning made it much more difficult for church members to resist.[14] Those who refused were suspected of shirking their religious duty because of pride, or the pursuit of wealth, or a preference for assimilation into a culture of modernity. Even more seriously, those who did not obey the directive to relocate were no longer considered to be part of the church. The refusal was interpreted as a serious breach of the vow of fidelity made to the church and to God, an act that would have negative consequences for all of eternity.[15]

Efforts to organize the migration did not always go smoothly: in 1921, leaders from the Old Colony Mennonite Church in Manitoba and Swift Current deliberately excluded those from the Hague-Osler Reserve in a large land purchase in the state of Chihuahua. Some of the leaders from Manitoba and Swift Current did not think the Old Colony Mennonites in the Hague-Osler region had the necessary financial resources. They believed their inclusion would increase the financial burden on others and put the entire relocation project at risk. This action was not well received by the Hague-Osler leaders. As a result of this exclusion, migration plans on the part of those in the Hague-Osler region were delayed. It was not until three years later, in 1924, that they were able to purchase their own land in the state of Durango and proceed with plans to join their compatriots in Mexico. By this time, many of the Old Colony Mennonites from Manitoba had already relocated (approximately four thousand), along with several thousand from the Swift Current region.

Matters were complicated further for the Hague-Osler Mennonites following an unsuccessful and highly controversial attempt in the region to organize a block sale of land with a single land agent that included signing over individual land titles in trust to two men, Benjamin Goertzen and Johann P. Wall, a minister. When the land agent was not able to find a sufficient number of buyers, many wanted to have their land titles returned. This created considerable chaos and misunderstanding. The ensuing conflict surrounding this unfortunate plan disillusioned some.[16] A sudden drop in land prices and the ongoing financial impact of school attendance fines made it impossible for others to consider relocating. The delays experienced by the Hague-Osler group gave them an opportunity to watch and assess the experience of those already in Mexico: negative reports of hardship, banditry, and extreme poverty prompted some to reconsider. In total, historians estimate that approximately eight thousand Old Colony Mennonites left Canada: this included two-thirds (3,340) of the Old

Colony Mennonite members in Manitoba, one-third (1,100) of those members living near Swift Current, and only about one quarter (1,000) of those members living near Hague-Osler. (These membership numbers do not include those who had not been baptized, namely children.)

Although two of David Friesen's brothers (Jacob and Herman) and their families, as well as one daughter (Elizabeth) and her family, decided to move to Mexico, David Friesen (and most of his siblings and children) did not. One can well imagine the agonizing discussions that took place within the Friesen household about whether to go or to stay, as information became available and plans were being made to migrate to Mexico by others. One suspects that the death of David's first wife Anna, his subsequent marriage to Katarina,[17] and the turmoil and demands of adjusting to a large blended family during the early 1920s may well have made the prospect of uprooting yet again, this time at the age of fifty, too daunting to undertake. Regardless of David and Katarina's reasons for not participating in the migration to Mexico, the decision had enormous implications for Herman Friesen. Despite considerable pressure from church leaders, relatives, and friends, the Friesens remained among the approximately 75 per cent of the Old Colony Mennonites in the area who did not migrate to Mexico.[18]

The migration to Mexico was a defining moment for the Old Colony Mennonites in Canada. Once the largest Mennonite denomination in the country, the move decimated its numbers and the strength of its influence. In addition, it created a serious leadership vacuum among those who stayed behind. The Old Colony Mennonite Church essentially ceased to operate in Manitoba for a time. Many of those in the Swift Current region who stayed in Canada, including one minister, joined the Sommerfelder Mennonite Church, a body of Mennonites organized in southern Manitoba during the early 1890s following a series of conflicts regarding cultural accommodation, particularly in the area of higher education.[19] Only in the Hague-Osler region did the Old Colony Mennonite Church manage to remain in operation, largely because two ministers, Johann Loeppky and Abram Wall Jr., opted to remain in Canada despite the fact that they were not able to offer the services of baptism and communion. The two opted to stay, in part, to support and provide pastoral care for those who were not financially able to participate in the migration. As one of the delegates who visited Mexico in 1921, and who initially used his considerable oratorical ability to advocate for relocation, Loeppky, in particular, bore the brunt of severe criticism for this decision from his ministerial colleagues who viewed him as a traitor.[20] Although Ältester Wiens moved to Durango, Mexico, in 1926, he returned in 1927, and again in 1928, to conduct baptisms and serve communion to those who had not relocated to Mexico. These trips demanded considerable time and energy on his part. In 1929, he was unable to travel to Canada because of the death of his wife, and his own failing health.

The Practice of Baptism

A SIGNIFICANT OCCASION IN THE LIFE OF EVERY OLD COLONY Mennonite is baptism. This event marks the moment when individuals are formally accepted as members of the church and considered accountable to the leadership of the church. The ceremony was normally scheduled in spring to coincide with the celebration of Pentecost, and was preceded by several weeks of catechetical instruction (*Jugendunterricht*) led by a minister during which applicants were familiarized with several documents that are vital to understanding the practices and theological thought of the Old Colony Mennonite tradition. The applicants studied the *Katechismus oder Kurze and einsache Unterweisung aus der Heiligen Schrift in Fragen und Antworten durch gesehen unde neu ausgelegt nach dem alten Text zum Gebrauch in Kirchen und Schulen* (hereafter referred to as the *Catechism*), a book that was first published in the late eighteenth century in Elbing, Prussia, and significantly shaped the theological understanding and identity of several Kanadier Mennonite groups, as well as the Amish.[21] It includes the Apostles' Creed and a collection of prayers for specific occasions, and it uses a series of 122 questions and answers as a teaching device to orient readers to basic Christian doctrine. The *Catechism* was accompanied by the *Glaubensbekenntnis der Mennoniten in Manitoba, Nordamerika* (hereafter referred to as the *Confession of Faith*), published in 1881, which contains eighteen doctrinal articles, along with a preface written by Ältester Johann Wiebe after arriving in southern Manitoba.[22] Unlike the *Catechism*, which provides a more comprehensive doctrinal overview, the *Confession of Faith* addresses more particular matters at greater length, including the election of ministers, baptism, communion, foot washing, use of the ban, governmental authority, the swearing of oaths, nonresistance, and more. Together, the *Catechism* and the *Confession of Faith* served as theological handbooks for the Old Colony Mennonite Church as a whole, as reference works in the German private schools, and as devotional tools in family life. Although the exact circumstances around the origin of the *Confession of Faith* remain a mystery, its influence on the theology of Old Colony Mennonites in Canada and beyond has been immense.[23]

The theological concepts surrounding baptism outlined in the *Confession of Faith* are vital for understanding the significance of the practice for Old Colony Mennonites. Believers baptism is without question one of the most central theological emphases within the Anabaptist-Mennonite tradition. It is, therefore, not surprising to see that one of the most extensive articles in the Old Colony Mennonite *Confession of Faith* is devoted to a discussion of "Holy Baptism,"[24] which presents a more sacramental view of baptism than is present within other Anabaptist-Mennonite confessions.[25] It teaches that no one is simply born into the church; every person must make their own decision to be a part of the church. Article 8 declares that "whoever wants to become a follower of Jesus Christ and who wants to confess and accept his Lord, Savior and Redeemer, and who wants to become a partaker of his love, must be baptized." It does not explicitly promote the concept of baptismal regeneration, that is, an individual is saved *by* baptism, but baptism is certainly considered a vital moment in the salvation process ("through baptism we are accepting Christ in faith," and those who "have put on Christ through baptism have become regenerated inwardly"). In response to the question, "Why is baptism necessary?" the *Confession of Faith* states, "Baptism indicates to us the washing away of sins through the merits of the blood of Christ. For as water serves to cleanse the body, so the blood of Christ takes away all the sins of all sinners who faithfully and penitently receive baptism, and it cleanses the conscience of dead deeds, to serve the living God." At least three results ensue from baptism: (1) it "makes us holy"; (2) if penitently received, "the soul will be accepted and received in the church of Christ"; and (3) "through baptism we are accepting Christ in faith and therefore become partakers of his inheritance."

As one of the most sacred and solemn occasions in the life of the Old Colony Mennonite Church, baptism is always officiated by none other than the Ältester. The act of baptism, which is administered by the pouring of a small amount of water on the head of a kneeling candidate, represents an irrevocable vow of faithfulness to God and to the church, and it authorizes the community to excommunicate those who do not remain faithful to their commitment. Old Colony Mennonites understand excommunication from the church as having eternal consequences for an individual. This is consistent with the teaching of early Anabaptists, such as Balthasar Hubmaier, who taught that the decisions made by the true church on earth would be honoured in heaven. Ministers believed it was their duty to use whatever means necessary to help members of their congregation, for their own spiritual well-being, remain true to their baptismal vows.[26] The sacred significance of baptism served as a constant reference point in sermons in which parishioners were reminded of their vows and encouraged to remain faithful. The theological significance ascribed to baptism served as powerful leverage for ensuring obedience and conformity to the expectations of the Old Colony community.

As the event that represented formal reception as a member of the church, baptism was therefore a prerequisite for participating in communion services, which was limited to church members and normally conducted biannually. Many have observed how those who seldom attended worship services would be certain to attend on communion Sundays. Such services were always given special deference because of the theological significance given to the "Lord's Supper." As with baptism, the *Confession of Faith* also takes a more sacramental approach to communion than does the *Rudnerweide Confession* used by many Mennonites in Russia. It states, "What is truly signified by [the] breaking of the bread and the drinking from the cup is this. Just as bread and wine are necessary for the nourishment of the body, in the same way our souls are nourished by the body and blood of Christ. Through and by this eating and drinking our souls are nourished and preserved to eternal life."[27]

Several weeks prior to baptism, the baptismal candidates are expected to recite from memory the *Catechism* answers publicly before the congregation, an exercise often dreaded by those seeking baptism. Young men were generally baptized between the ages of nineteen and twenty-five, while women were often a year or two younger. Theoretically and ideally, individuals joined the church voluntarily as an indication of their spiritual conversion and commitment to a life of discipleship in the church. In actual practice, the motivation for baptism was often more complicated in that it had become a matter of social necessity as it was considered a prerequisite for marriage.[28]

Twenty-year-old Herman, along with his young fiancé, Margaretha Banman, were both baptized on August 26, 1928, during Ältester Wiens's last visit to Canada. The migration to Mexico during the 1920s created considerable uncertainty about whether the Ältester would continue to serve those who had not complied with the church's directive to relocate, and, if so, exactly how. The ambiguity surrounding the future of the Old Colony Mennonite Church in the region was particularly difficult for the young adults with romantic interests who were waiting to be baptized before proceeding with wedding plans. When Ältester Wiens returned to Canada in 1927, he remained in the Hague-Osler area for almost six weeks. During this time, he baptized eighty people, and churches were filled to overflowing for communion services. The following year, Wiens was only able to travel to Canada during the summer months instead of spring. Once again, the number of individuals, including both Herman and Margaretha, who wanted to be baptized was high.

For Herman and Margaretha, the delay in the Ältester's scheduling of baptism in August 1928 had acquired an additional level of urgency: Margaretha discovered she was pregnant with a baby due in November. By the time of their baptism in late summer, her pregnancy was clearly evident. The thoughts and emotions that baptism normally evoked for Old Colony Mennonite young people were overshadowed by the public predicament of this young couple.

The ideal taught by Old Colony Mennonite leaders was that sexual relations belonged exclusively within the bounds of a heterosexual marriage relationship. Premarital, and especially extramarital, sex was a serious religious and social transgression. According to Hans Werner's investigation of Reinlaender Mennonite Church registers of marriages in Manitoba during the late nineteenth and early twentieth centuries, the Old Colony Mennonites were, by comparison, quite successful in "restraining young couples from engaging in sex before their marriage day": the rate of prenuptial conception among these Old Colony Mennonites was considerably less than in most other societies at the time (6.6 per cent versus 15.1 per cent in the United States).[29] He also notes that the "rates of prenuptial conception are of course lower than the incidence of premarital sex." A range of factors contributed toward making such a high degree of social control possible. The close confines of the village and homes, along with a communal sense of responsibility for general watchfulness for illicit behaviour, decreased the level of opportunity. In addition, the low average age of marriage among Old Colony Mennonites at the beginning of the twentieth century (22.5 for men and 19.5 for women), which was much lower than in many other societies, reduced the time between physical sexual maturity and the age when starting a new household was permissible and feasible. Courtship practices that often lacked opportunity for even a private conversation, and that were relatively short in duration before culminating in marriage, further helped regulate the incidence of premarital sex.[30]

While prenuptial conception was not a frequent occurrence, there are some discernible general trends that reflect Herman and Margaretha's experience. By comparing the patterns of conception among married couples and unmarried couples, Werner observes that conception for married couples generally "followed the patterns of the agricultural year" (high during late fall and winter, low during the busy months of spring and fall). "By contrast, the highest periods of premarital sex, as judged by conception dates of prenuptially conceived children,"[31] were during the months of spring, which offered greater opportunity for being out of homes and away from the gaze of family and neighbours. The ability on the part of the community to regulate opportunities for illicit sexual activity was often decreased by the experience of migration, and by the energy required for homesteading and pioneering a community life.

Old Colony Mennonite Church leaders exercised considerable influence on the behaviour of church members. Ministers generally handled minor violations, with more difficult situations brought to the Lehrdienst for discussion and decision. The usual process for church discipline involved the three steps of confession, demonstrated contrition, and attempts at reconciliation. Excommunication (the ban) was reserved as the method of punishment for the most serious offences.[32] Young people such as Herman and Margaretha were not considered members of the church prior to baptism, and therefore were not subject to church discipline. The only recourse for ministers was to encourage parents to be vigilant in monitoring their young people. However, the desire on the part of young people to be baptized created an opportunity to address behaviour that was considered sinful. Herman and Margaretha's circumstance would have necessitated a meeting with the Ältester and possibly other ministers. Baptism would only have been permitted if they acknowledged their sexual activity as sin and offered an adequate expression of repentance that included a clear commitment to getting married in the near future, thereby minimizing the social implications of their prenuptial conception. Their wedding took place less than a month after baptism.

Werner observes that premarital sex was generally considered a "mild form of deviancy" among Old Colony Mennonites if it was followed by marriage and "the formation of a Mennonite household firmly set on a path contributing to village and church life."[33] Nevertheless, a degree of shame was associated with their baptism: Margaretha was expected to wear the same head covering at baptism (and her wedding) that married women were required to wear in church, thereby publicly indicating her loss of virginity. As if obvious pregnancy was not enough, the head covering served as a public reminder of the consequences of sexual deviance. A ceremony that was to be about celebrating a public profession of personal faith and fidelity to the church became simultaneously for Herman and Margaretha a public exhibition of guilt and disgrace. Even though one does not know exactly what the young couple was feeling, one can reasonably surmise that this was a difficult time as the anticipation of, and preparation for, both marriage and parenthood were compressed into a very short period of time.

Church Life during the 1940s and 1950s

GIVEN THE CRUCIAL LEADERSHIP ROLE PLAYED BY ÄLTESTEN IN THE Old Colony Mennonite communities, any change in this position always represented an important transition. The election of Johann Loeppky as the new Ältester in 1930 signalled a new era in the life of the denomination as it began the difficult task of reorganizing and reconsidering its relationship to Canadian society. It also coincided with the advent of a devastating economic depression. His leadership during these challenging decades significantly shaped Herman and Margaretha's church experience during their first twenty years of marriage.

The long absences on the part of Ältester Wiens created confusion and frustration among the Old Colony Mennonites who remained in Canada. Even though it had become increasingly obvious that not all church members would be moving to Mexico, Wiens resolutely refused to organize an election of a new Ältester or additional ministers in Canada. As far as he, and the other ministers who had left Canada, were concerned, the Old Colony Mennonite Church had officially moved to Mexico and no longer existed in Canada.[34] This left those remaining in Canada with both immediate practical problems to solve and some deeper theological questions to consider. With only two ministers, it was no longer possible to conduct worship services on a weekly basis in each of the three church locations in the Hague-Osler area, never mind maintaining all the other aspects of Old Colony Mennonite Church practice.

As a result, in 1930, those members who remained in Canada decided it was time to reorganize and elect their own Ältester. Only the two ministers in Saskatchewan who had opted not to move to Mexico were considered candidates for the role. With majority support from church members in Hague-Osler, Swift Current, and Manitoba, Johann Loeppky was elected as Ältester and ordained with the help of Cornelius Hamm, Ältester of the nearby Saskatchewan Bergthaler Mennonite Church. From this point onward, the group officially became known by its newly registered name, the Old Colony Mennonite Church. The formal reorganization was not received well by Old Colony Mennonite Church leaders in Mexico, who saw the step of selecting a new Ältester in Canada as a further act of defiance and betrayal. In 1936, Ältester Loeppky went further by helping the few Old Colony families remaining in Manitoba to elect new ministers and reorganize as the Old Colony Mennonite Church of Manitoba.[35] Theologically, the decision to reorganize called into question, at least implicitly, the theological assumption that lifelong fidelity to a single Old Colony Mennonite Church was one of the keys to eternal salvation as some Old Colony ministers had suggested. The ongoing insistence on the part of Old Colony Mennonite leaders in Mexico that "we do not consider those left in Canada as our fellow church members" kept tensions alive and made it difficult to facilitate membership releases and transfers for the steady trickle of people who continued to move between Canada and Mexico.

Loeppky's pleasant personality, sense of humour, and oratorical skills helped him to become a popular leader. Services at which he preached were usually well attended. He travelled constantly and was widely revered for his practical approach and wise leadership. Shortly after his ordination as Ältester, he conducted a ministerial election at which two individuals, Isaac Wieler and Johan H. Janzen, were chosen as ministers. Both men had been teachers in the German village schools and were well respected. Five years later, in 1935, three more ministers were elected (Abram J. Loewen, Peter T. Neudorf, and Peter Martens). This once again made it possible to schedule worship services with greater regularity throughout the region.

Old Colony Mennonites had developed a reputation for being suspicious of, if not vigorously resistant to, change. The emphasis on "separation from the world" was in part the by-product of a history of persecution, in part the result of geographical isolation, and in part an attempt to comply with biblical injunctions to avoid worldliness. Combined, these experiences and emphases left the Anabaptist-Mennonite tradition without the theological resources for navigating cultural engagement in places where there was not overt persecution or the possibility of geographical isolation. Because worldliness was often understood as cultural assimilation, the way of life adopted by the entire church community needed to be recognizably distinct from those around it, that is, "the world." Exactly how this "separation from the world" ought to be displayed, and which practices constituted worldliness, was not always clear. The close association between change and worldliness, along with ambiguity over the biblical meaning of worldliness, meant that any adjustments to historical practices and traditions, however minor, had the potential for generating controversy in that they could be interpreted as evidence of worldliness. Deviance from historical practices was understood as a manifestation of worldliness: conformity was enforced by the threat of excommunication and social ostracism. The regular use of the *Catechism* in preparing people for baptism meant that church members all had a similar understanding of basic Old Colony Mennonite doctrine, which helped to ensure a high degree of theological consistency over time. However, the denomination did not have formal governance documents like a constitution, organizational bylaws, or policy manuals, let alone principles or guidelines by which to navigate participation in the broader culture. This left actual church practice more open to interpretation and adaptation by church leaders. Reliance on human memory made it more difficult to detect and to document incremental adjustments over time.

It did not take long for church members to notice that Loeppky was less resistant to change and took a more pragmatic approach to the question of which cultural practices to permit than his predecessor. For example, the assistance from the nearby Bergthaler Mennonite Ältester in his appointment strengthened a fraternal relationship between the two Mennonite groups, and it prompted Loeppky to discontinue the practice of excommunicating Old Colony Mennonite members for marrying a Bergthaler Mennonite member. The new Ältester became more accepting of the use of cars by church members during the 1930s and 1940s than his predecessor, as well as more tolerant toward those who wished to vote in municipal and public school board elections, which had previously been forbidden. Together with other Mennonite church leaders, Loeppky became involved in signing certificates for Mennonite men confirming their status as conscientious objectors during the Second World War. He was pragmatic in his analysis of whether or not to participate in governmental initiatives: the inauguration of a family allowance program by the federal government during the 1940s created fear among some that participating in this program would, in times of war, create a sense of obligation to take part in military service. Loeppky understood more clearly the program's intention of providing financial assistance to needy families in ways that the church was not always capable of doing (or even willing to do). His explanation of the program convinced many eligible Old Colony Mennonites to accept the monthly cheques.[36]

The fact that the majority of Old Colony Mennonites in the Hague-Osler region had not moved to Mexico did not mean they had given up entirely on the strategy of relocating to more isolated frontiers as a way of responding to governmental involvement in education and to other changes taking place within Canadian society. Some were still eager to find a suitable place where they could establish their own German-language private schools. The Great Depression during the 1930s was one of the deepest and longest lasting global economic downturns in the twentieth century. Crop failures due to drought conditions amplified the impact of the Depression for farmers on the prairies. The search for more economically viable agricultural land became an urgent incentive in searching for new migration locations. It was also part of a strategy for ensuring that young people were not forced to find employment in urban centres. In the early 1930s, one of the Old Colony Mennonite ministers from the Hague-Osler region, Isaac Wieler, followed a group that had moved several years earlier to the La Crete and Fort Vermilion region of northern Alberta, which was beyond the boundaries of any public school district.[37] At first the region could only be reached by riverboats in the summer and dogsleds in the winter. For several decades, the group in La Crete lived in almost total isolation and operated its own schools without government interference. It was not until the late 1950s that they too were gradually compelled to accept public schools.[38] During the 1930s, smaller groups went to various locations in Saskatchewan, such as Carrot River, Swan Plain, Mullingar, and Sonningdale. The advent of the Second World War prompted fears that the Canadian government might revoke its promise of exempting Mennonite men from military service, particularly because some young Mennonite men were enlisting. In 1940, Heinrich Bueckert accompanied a group of Old Colony Mennonite members to Burns Lake, British Columbia. Loeppky supported these relocation initiatives and was often instrumental in helping them organize church services and elect their own ministers. A steady stream of Old Colony families flowed between the Hague-Osler region and the various settlements across western Canada.

Following a visit to Mexico in 1946, Loeppky himself became involved in organizing a small migration to Mexico in partnership with a group of Kleine Gemeinde from Manitoba in 1948. He had maintained a keen interest in Mexico ever since serving as one of the delegates who negotiated the original agreement with the Mexican government in 1921. He left with a group in 1948 to establish a new colony in Los Jagueyes. Almost from the outset, the group was plagued by problems and serious internal conflict. Because of his earlier refusal to migrate, the Old Colony Mennonite leaders who had moved to Mexico during the 1920s did not recognize Loeppky as a minister, and refused to help the new colony. Within five years this colony project had disintegrated. He returned to Canada two years later, where he was welcomed back by the other ministers. However, his involvement in this failed migration significantly diminished the confidence the Hague-Osler Old Colony people had in his leadership.

Although Loeppky was a highly personable leader who paid a considerable price for his role in reorganizing the Old Colony Mennonites in Canada, he did not help those remaining in Saskatchewan reconcile their decision not to migrate with the overarching narrative of migration as a necessary strategy for purity and faithfulness that was used to promote the move to Mexico. His amiable support of migrations to other provinces, and his own belated attempt in Mexico, did not offer an alternative vision for how to live as faithful Mennonites in the Hague-Osler region. One is left to wonder about Herman's own perceptions of, and response to, the migration to Mexico, to subsequent efforts to reorganize the Old Colony Mennonite Church in Canada, and to the myriad of questions that surrounded these initiatives. How did these perceptions influence his and Margaretha's decision to remain in the Hague-Osler region, and his eventual approach when he became a leader in the church? Were his reasons for not participating in a migration based only on economic reasons or also on an alternative religious vision?

After Loeppky's death in 1950, Abram J. Loewen was elected Ältester. For a time during the 1950s, Old Colony Mennonites looked at additional migration possibilities near Carrot River, Saskatchewan (1949), Taber, Alberta (1950), and Vanderhoof, British Columbia (1955).[39] The only migration Herman ever seriously considered was to Carrot River in the late 1940s. At first it looked like there might be significant government assistance available for such a relocation, until they discovered that veterans would be given priority. Several family members indicated that any suggestion of relocating to Carrot River was quickly rejected by Margaretha. One can only speculate as to the exact reason, but it may be that, at age forty-one, after twelve pregnancies, with the youngest child only a year old, the prospect of establishing a new farm was overwhelming. In 1953, the church leaders began negotiating the acquisition of a twenty-thousand-acre tract of land near Prespatou, British Columbia, approximately eighty kilometres north of Fort St. John. These migrations included a more direct economic motivation than earlier attempts: the dwindling availability of affordable land made it difficult for young families to establish farms in the Hague-Osler area, thereby forcing the men of these families to find employment in urban centres. The fear that this would fragment the church community's way of life prompted leaders to search for suitable parcels of land.[40] The deal in Prespatou was finalized in 1961, and it prompted almost one hundred Old Colony Mennonite families to relocate, including four ministers, Ältester Loewen, Herman Bueckert, Abram P. Wiebe, and Johan Giesbrecht. It was to be the last migration organized and led by the Old Colony Mennonite Church in Saskatchewan. Despite the ministerial endorsement of the migration to Fort St. John, the Prespatou group did not shun those church members who remained behind in Saskatchewan, as was the case during the Mexico migration. Everyone recognized that it would not be feasible to expect all church members to relocate. As a result, the Old Colony Mennonite communities scattered throughout western Canada generally managed to maintain fraternal relationships, despite some differences of perspective and practice. Ältester Loewen's involvement in this migration set the stage for Herman Friesen's election as minister and then Ältester.

As noted, many of these initiatives were led or accompanied by one or more ministers and therefore repeatedly resulted in a loss of leadership for the Old Colony Mennonite Church in the Hague-Osler region. Ironically, this also increased the level of openness to change and cultural assimilation on the part of those who did not participate in these migrations, as it was often the more conservative factions who insisted on relocation.[41] The decimation of local church leadership resulted in a new kind of "diversification," which took place in all aspects of life, including church affiliation. Some Old Colony members began to pursue occupations in increasingly diverse ways, some explored educational pursuits, some opted to join other denominations.[42] Implicitly, at least, this openness on the part of Old Colony church members represented a disregard for, if not an outright rejection of, a pure church vision that needed to be expressed through migration. Those who remained in the Hague-Osler region were about to face a series of unprecedented changes in the province as telephones and radios became more widely accepted. In 1949, as more technological innovations were introduced in agriculture, the provincial government made plans to create a province-wide electrical grid that would include vast rural areas, as well as a province-wide grid road system to facilitate the growing demand for automobiles and trucks. In 1944, Saskatchewan had only 222 kilometres of hard-surfaced roads, and the vast majority of farms were not accessible by gravel roads.[43] In 1948, only 1,500 farms were connected to the electrical grid, mostly because of their proximity to the lines that linked cities and larger towns. By 1966, less than two decades later, this number had increased to sixty-six thousand. These changes made it virtually impossible to maintain the level of uniformity within the church that had been possible in the past.

Changes gradually continued to take place within the church itself as leaders responded to developments in the region. Shortly after the closure of the last private German-language village schools in the late 1920s, the idea of starting German-language Sunday schools began to be discussed as an alternative strategy for supplementing the religious education of their children. These discussions were precipitated, in part, by the fact that the General Conference Mennonite Church in Neuanlage had started using the private school building in the village to conduct a Sunday school. Old Colony Mennonite leaders quickly curtailed this usage of the school. It was not until 1942 that two Old Colony Mennonite ministers, Peter Neudorf and Abram Wall (a former German school teacher), managed to organize a Sunday school in the Old Colony Mennonite Church in Neuanlage. Several years later, Sunday schools were started in the Steele School (1948), in the German School in Blumenheim (1949), and at the Osler airport. In the early 1950s, the people of Neuhorst raised enough money to construct a Sunday school building. The purpose of the Sunday schools was to prepare a younger generation for active participation in the life of the church by helping them learn both Bible stories and the German language.[44] At first they were scheduled on Saturdays or Sunday afternoons, but eventually the Sunday schools ran concurrently with church worship services. The Ältester at the time, Johann Loeppky, spoke in favour of the Sunday schools but was too heavily involved in organizing a migration to Mexico to participate. Abram Loewen, his successor, was more ambivalent in that he did not seek to prevent, but neither did he encourage, their use. Loeppky's more pragmatic strategy of accommodation prior to his own migration to Mexico modelled an alternative to the strategy used by Wiens, which deeply influenced Herman Friesen's approach to community involvement and eventual leadership in the church.

Farm and Family Life   3

HERMAN FRIESEN AND MARGARETHA BANMAN were married on September 16, 1928, three weeks after their baptism. Because the Banman and Friesen families lived in neighbouring villages, and because both families were part of the Old Colony Mennonite Church, Herman and his wife-to-be Margaretha likely crossed paths numerous times during their childhood and teenage years. A closer relationship between the two families was established in 1923, when, on Christmas day, Herman's older brother Isbrand married Margaretha's older sister Anna. Specific details about Herman and Margaretha's courtship and how it began are unknown, but their fondness for each other, and their interest in marriage, was already evident before they were baptized.

Margaretha (1908–97) was the daughter of Heinrich[1] and Anna (Hildebrand)[2] Banman, who had moved from Manitoba in the early years of the twentieth century (circa 1902). Heinrich and Anna, along with their three young children (all under four years of age), settled approximately five and a half kilometres southwest of Blumenheim, on a quarter section of land purchased from William Bailey, located immediately adjacent to the village of Kronsthal. Here Margaretha was born on April 3, 1908, the sixth child in a family of ten children (the last three died as infants). Although Heinrich had registered for a homestead quarter near Aberdeen, he requested and received permission to reside near Kronsthal in order to be closer to other Old Colony Mennonites while completing the homestead requirements. The two pieces of land were eight kilometres apart but on opposite sides of the South Saskatchewan River.[3] In time, Heinrich built a small, wind-driven flour mill that he used to grist grain for himself and others in the region.[4] Despite being dependent on favourable weather conditions, the mill provided a welcome source of income to supplement the sale of grain.

The two were married at the age of twenty in the village of Kronsthal. Weddings of young people were always joyous highlights in the life of the Old Colony Mennonite community.[5] The actual day of the wedding was generally preceded by a *Felafnis* (engagement celebration), which included a short service and meditation by a minister, as well as a Faspa for all invited neighbours and family. The formal exchange of vows took place a week or two later in a short ceremony at the conclusion of a regular worship service, which was followed by an evening celebration at the home of the bride's family. Despite the festiveness of such occasions, Old Colony Mennonites did not dispense with the custom of wearing plain and modest clothes, which for men meant a black suit without a tie, and, for women, including the bride, a long black (or dark navy) dress full to the neck, with sleeves to the wrist. Honeymoon holidays were not a part of wedding festivities at the time, so following the wedding the bride and groom made an immediate transition to their new home on, and their role as part of, the Banman family farm. It was not possible to learn how Herman's and Margaretha's parents responded to their prenuptial conception, but the fact that the newly married couple was integrated into the Banman farm operation indicates the family's support of the young couple.

Heinrich and Anna Banman farm, 1926. This was the birthplace of Margaretha, and eventual home of Herman and Margaretha. Courtesy Herman and Margaretha Friesen estate.

Starting their married life as part of a more established farm operation instead of a new homestead had the distinct advantage of not having to break and prepare acres of prairie sod for crop production. Nevertheless, farming was back-breaking, labour-intensive activity that relied on the use of horses, which was also, at times, dangerous. Although the soil on the Banman farm was fertile, it was sandy, which made it vulnerable to drought, and it was rocky, which often resulted in damage to farm equipment and

Posing alone, Margaretha in her teens, circa 1924. Courtesy Herman and Margaretha Friesen estate.

was a constant nuisance. For a number of years, four married families lived together on the Banman farm. This included the parents Heinrich and Anna, along with three children and their spouses, Isaac and Sarah (Friesen) Banman, Anna and Isbrand Friesen, and Margaretha and Herman Friesen. Although the close proximity and partnership of four households working together as part of one farm operation would have had some benefit from economy of scale, the farm's capacity to support four families financially serves as an indicator of its economic viability.

Marriage was considered permanent, and clearly defined roles for men and women in the Old Colony Mennonite Church created a structure that eased the adjustment to married life for some. Divorce rarely occurred, and not only because divorce was potentially punishable by excommunication. The strongly patriarchal structure reinforced the maintenance of clearly differentiated and stratified gender roles and established a system of economic and social interdependence. When a young woman married,

Herman (second from left) as a young man, spending Sunday afternoon with cousins and friends, circa 1923. Courtesy Herman and Margaretha Friesen estate.

it was assumed she would take charge of the responsibilities of child care, household tasks, making and cleaning clothes, cooking, gardening, and preserving food. These were time-consuming, tiresome, repetitive chores done without any modern, labour-saving appliances during the first half of the twentieth century.[6] Although women were excluded from partici- pating in brotherhood meetings where major decisions were made, and were expected to conform to the role expectations defined by the church in order to preserve familial stability and the continuity of an Old Colony Mennonite way of life, Kerry Fast astutely observes that Old Colony Mennonite women were often able to find creative ways to exercise agency. She argues that human agency ought not to be understood only as autonomy and self-determination, and that focusing only on the restric- tive practices obscures the often dynamic relationship that Old Colony Mennonite women had with the church.[7] Consistent with the patriarchal structure and practices within the Old Colony Mennonite community, and by the force of his personality, Herman was considered the "head" of the home, that is, the one with the final say in major decisions. Nevertheless, as was the case in many Old Colony Mennonite homes, his wife Margaretha did exercise considerable influence in household decision making. At one point, Herman was intrigued by the economic potential of relocating to the Carrot River area, an idea Margaretha ada- mantly opposed. One does not know exactly how this disagreement was resolved, other than to observe that the family never did move to Carrot River. Herman and Margaretha's marriage was, by all accounts, character- ized by a mutually supportive companionship and loyalty, if not always by open affection.

It was generally assumed among Old Colony Mennonites that married couples would have children. Large families were the norm. Generally, good health and nutrition, and the early average age of marriage, contributed to a relatively high fecundity.[8] Not only were children considered gifts from God but both the survival of their community, which was compelled by the logic of generational succession, and the pragmatic need for many hands on pioneering farm operations to increase their viability reinforced the impor- tance of large families. For many, being a part of a large family brought with it an enhanced social status.[9] Like Canadians generally during the first half of the twentieth century, Old Colony Mennonites rejected the use of artificial methods of birth control.

Herman and Margaretha's first child, a son named Heinrich, was born on November 15, 1928, two months after their wedding. Sadly, the young boy died in April 1931 of whooping cough and pneumonia before he reached the age of three, by which time Margaretha was pregnant with her third child. Margaretha kept a small memento from Heinrich's funeral in a special compartment of a chest she used for storing personal items: it was a small piece of the white shroud used to present the body in the casket and the black ribbon from the sleeve cuff. According to one of her daughters, this tactile reminder of her first-born son, which Margaretha would periodically hold with a kind of pensive sadness, was a helpful way to process her sense of loss and grief. Unexpected death was a commonplace part of the harshness of pioneer life. The boy's death exemplified the high rate of infant mortality prior to the introduction of vaccines and antibiotics during the 1940s and 1950s, which dramatically decreased the death rates from communicable diseases such as whooping cough.

For the young couple, the pain of losing their first child was intermingled with the joy that accompanied the birth of other children. Often there was little time for grief given the unrelenting demands of domestic and farm responsibilities. The couple had a total of thirteen children, with the youngest child born in 1951 when they were both forty-three years of age. Twelve out of the thirteen children, three boys and nine girls, survived to adulthood. All children were expected to participate in domestic or farm chores, and the older siblings had the added responsibility of helping to care for the younger ones.

Long before the term "sandwich generation" was coined to describe the challenges of multigenerational caregiving, a phenomenon that normally falls to middle-aged adults, the young couple learned to balance the responsibilities of simultaneously caring for their own young children as well as for parents who were not in good health. The couple served as caregivers to Margaretha's parents until the death of her father in the summer of 1933, and her mother a year later in 1934.

Funeral of baby Heinrich, April 1931. Courtesy Herman and Margaretha Friesen estate.

Top: *Helping with chores by feeding chickens, circa 1950. Courtesy Herman and Margaretha Friesen estate.* **Bottom:** *Friesen children playing on the farm, circa 1950. Courtesy Herman and Margaretha Friesen estate.*

Children learning to ride a horse, circa 1940. Courtesy Herman and Margaretha Friesen estate.

Surviving the Dirty Thirties

THE DEATH OF MARGARETHA'S PARENTS MADE IT NECESSARY FOR the young couple to assume full responsibility of the farm operation. This took place in the midst of the dirty thirties, as the Depression years were dubbed. It was a cruel calamity following the general optimism on the prairies during the first two decades of the twentieth century. Low grain prices and trade tariffs made it difficult for farmers to make money from the little grain they did manage to produce. Unemployment rates increased to 35 per cent, making it difficult to earn money. One of the worst years was 1937, when drought and grasshoppers destroyed crops in the area. That year, Saskatchewan produced an average of 2.5 bushels of wheat per seeded acre, in comparison to the average seventeen bushels per acre during the 1920s. Export prices for grain plummeted by 50 per cent; cattle prices also declined considerably.[10]

The ability to obtain fresh garden produce, eggs and milk, and various kinds of meat from their farm, along with deeply ingrained habits of frugality, meant that Herman and Margaretha were not dependent solely on a regular cash income for survival. Nevertheless, some cash was necessary to meet the financial needs of their growing family because not everything could be produced on the farm. Watching how his father-in-law's grist mill had provided an additional source to supplement the farm operation probably influenced Herman's approach to financial diversification. Unfortunately, the use of the grist mill was discontinued in the 1930s as flour became more readily available. In order to earn extra money, Herman periodically sought employment with other farmers during the late 1930s and early 1940s, which sometimes meant being absent from his own farm for days at a time. By the late 1930s, two-thirds of the rural population in Saskatchewan was on government relief.[11] It is not clear whether Herman and Margaretha ever accepted relief—attitudes toward it varied considerably as many raised on the virtues of hard work and independence viewed it as humiliation and shame. It is likely they occasionally made use of food shipments (for example, boxes of apples) that were distributed in the region.[12] The first decade of their marriage was characterized by hard work in order to survive and a busy household as Margaretha gave birth to six children during this time. Fortunately, they did not face these challenges alone, given their proximity to the Kronsthal village and other family members.[13]

Greater Prosperity

AS WEATHER PATTERNS CHANGED ON THE PRAIRIES, AND ECONOMIC conditions in Canada improved during the 1940s, Saskatchewan entered a time of prosperity and unprecedented change. Having successfully weathered the difficult conditions of the 1930s, Herman and Margaretha's experience of greater prosperity was consistent with trends taking place more generally in Canada. With well-established habits of thrift and hard work, and multiple children who were now able to contribute their labour to the farm operation, the Friesen family was well positioned to take advantage of these changing conditions. It became possible for the family to experience a higher standard of living as they expanded their land base, acquired motorized farm machinery, purchased vehicles (a car and truck),

Threshing grain on the Friesen farm, circa 1940. Courtesy Herman and Margaretha Friesen estate.

and, in 1950, completed the construction of a new house. Herman was not as hesitant as some other Old Colony Mennonites about utilizing new technology when it became available and affordable.

In the early 1940s, farmers in Saskatchewan began using new methods of surface cultivation to preserve moisture and prevent erosion. The availability and affordability of tractors that could pull cultivators and diskers quickly made the use of horse-drawn implements obsolete. The use of tractors made it possible for Herman and Margaretha to increase the number of acres under cultivation to three quarter sections of land. Two more quarter sections of land south of their farm were purchased in the early 1960s. Herman was among the first farmers in the area to buy a combine in the early 1950s (a tractor-drawn John Deere Clipper). This was a much more efficient, less labour-intensive way of harvesting crops, particularly on land located several kilometres from the farmyard. Not all neighbours were convinced that the technique of leaving swathed grain lying in windrows so it

Aerial view of Herman and Margaretha Friesen farm, early 1950s. Courtesy Herman and Margaretha Friesen estate.

could be picked up and threshed by a combine would enable grain to dry sufficiently for harvest. The previous threshing system required grain to be cut and then bundled into standing stooks. Later, numerous teams of horses transported grain stooks to a stationary threshing machine.

Throughout their married life, Herman and Margaretha kept animals on the farm—chickens provided eggs and meat, hogs were another source of meat as were cattle, and cows provided milk for the family. In order to earn some additional cash during the 1940s, the family began separating the cream from the milk and shipping it in cans to Saskatoon for use in butter production. The cream cans were picked up by truck and, if the roads were impassable, by train from Osler. By 1948, the collection of cows had become a small dairy operation and the Friesens began shipping milk in cans to Saskatoon. Better roads and better trucks for hauling milk cans, and proximity to a processing plant in a growing urban centre, made this move possible and financially attractive. This dairy operation made good use of an existing barn, it utilized available labour, and it provided a more constant stream of revenue than grain production.

Living conditions for the large family improved considerably with the construction of a new home in 1950. Not only did the house provide more space for a family with eleven children ranging in age from two to twenty but it also coincided with the decision to connect the farmyard to the electrical grid. The Friesen family was among the first to benefit from the Rural Electrification Act, which was passed in 1949 to create a province-wide electrical grid. The proximity of the Kronsthal region to the Osler airport, which was established east of Osler in 1940 as part of the British Commonwealth Air Training Plan, helped to bring electricity to the surrounding area sooner than to other rural areas. Access to electricity gradually changed the nature of domestic life, as electrical washing machines, refrigerators, stoves, furnaces, indoor plumbing, water heaters, and other appliances freed many women from daily drudgery.

In 1955, Herman and Margaretha built a much larger hip-roof dairy barn that significantly expanded the farm's capacity for milk production. For a time, the family milked approximately twenty-five cows by hand twice a day. Electricity made it possible to automate aspects of the dairy operation. In the late 1950s, a milking machine system and a bulk tank for milk storage were installed in the barn, as well as an electrical barn cleaner that used a chain-linked system of paddles to move manure from gutters, up a chute, into a waiting manure spreader. These innovations reduced somewhat the level of dependence on the involvement of their children. Six of Herman and Margaretha's children were married during the 1950s, which seriously depleted the family labour pool.

Although the Friesen family had participated for many years in a simple fenceline telephone system that linked several neighbouring farms, during the mid-1950s they had a telephone installed in their home, as did many others who lived in rural parts of the province. Although early efforts on the part of the Department of Telephones to expand its network across the entire province were hampered by the Great Depression and again by the Second World War, in 1947 the department reorganized as a Crown corporation under a new name, Saskatchewan Government Telephones. It immediately embarked on an aggressive program to extend telephone service throughout rural Saskatchewan. During the 1950s, an unprecedented expansion took place as more telephones were installed in the province than in all previous years combined.[14] Despite the strong emphasis within the Old Colony Mennonite community on cultural separation, and even geographical isolation, Herman never expressed any reluctance about the use of electricity and telephones. The question of whether or not to adopt the use of these technologies was not, according to Herman, a question to which the Bible spoke. He saw it instead as an economic opportunity and a convenient means for more efficient communication.[15] The expansion of the electrical grid in the area was used by Herman and Margaretha's son Dave as a vocational opportunity to become a journeyman electrician. Isaac Dyck, who was among the first to start an electrical business in the area, trained him.

Economic prosperity made it possible to purchase not only better farm equipment but also motorized vehicles. It is not clear when Herman and Margaretha purchased their first car, but it was likely during the early to mid-1940s. In addition to a car, the family owned a farm truck, which was sometimes also used to attend church. These vehicles made

Top: Construction of new dairy barn, 1955. Courtesy Herman and Margaretha Friesen estate. Bottom: Herman washing the Plymouth, circa 1953. Courtesy Herman and Margaretha Friesen estate.

attending meetings, making business and shopping trips to nearby Osler and Saskatoon, and going to church considerably more convenient as long as roads were passable. In 1951, Herman purchased a brand new Plymouth sedan for which he was publicly chastised by a minister in a sermon. By this time, many others were using cars, so it is unclear whether such censure was prompted by the perception of extravagance, by petty jealousy, or as a symbolic expression of a more general anxiety about the steady increase in the use of vehicles and acceptance of modern technology. Shortly after, he and Margaretha used it to travel to Mexico to visit Herman's sister Elizabeth in the Durango Colony, as well as other relatives and acquaintances in the Chihuahua Colony who had moved there during the 1920s.[16] Other motor trips followed, including a second trip to Mexico in 1956. After Herman become Ältester, he used the car extensively to visit Old Colony Mennonite communities across western Canada. Motorized travel enhanced Herman's ability to fulfill his community and church leadership responsibilities, and helped him to observe ways of life in other places and to maintain and strengthen relationships with people in distant places. The fact that Herman was elected as a minister a decade later represented at least a tacit endorsement of his pragmatic utilitarian approach to technological innovation.

The Joys and Challenges of Family Life

Most of Herman and Margaretha's children attended Saskatchewan School, a public school located near Kronsthal, until 1947, when East Osler Government Aided School was built near Blumenheim to alleviate crowded conditions. In compliance with the School Attendance Act, the children were required to complete grade eight, and were given a small cash reward by their parents for doing so. After completing grade eight, the children were expected to work on the family farm until adulthood. (Most, but not all, of the Friesen children worked on the family farm until marrying in their late teens or early twenties.) A few of the children would have been happy to stop attending school sooner, while others greatly wished they could have continued their education until at least the end of high school. In part, such variation represented personal preferences, but it also exemplified a growing intergenerational tension within the Old Colony Mennonite Church between an older generation who continued to see elementary education as sufficient for an agrarian communitarian way of life, and a younger generation born in Canada who had begun to adopt the more widely held view in Canada of education as a tool for personal and economic advancement. Many of the children enjoyed participating in the sports days organized by the school teachers, and several had occasion to represent their school in inter-school athletic competitions. Participation

Winter transportation to school, 1940s. Courtesy Herman and Margaretha Friesen estate.

in any inter-school sports was strongly discouraged by Herman and Margaretha, and sometimes even punished: even playing a simple game of catch at home was frowned upon, and in some instances explicitly forbidden, presumably on the grounds that it encouraged a frivolous use of time.

Although involvement in organized sports was not permitted, Herman and Margaretha were not averse to seeing their children develop and use their musical abilities. The enjoyment of music was an important part of life in the Friesen home. Herman was blessed with a good voice and enjoyed singing (unlike Margaretha, who apparently could not carry a tune). As a young man, he taught himself to play the guitar and developed his own unique style of plucking individual strings with his fingers rather than strumming chords. In addition to using a guitar, he purchased a pump organ in the early 1950s for his children to use as their musical interests and abilities emerged.

School teachers were instrumental in helping the Friesen children learn how to read musical notation and to sing harmonies, and they introduced the children (and thus also Herman) to American evangelical Protestant gospel hymnody, through the use of the *Evangeliums-Lieder* (1891) hymn book in particular. This hymn book was a collection of gospel songs from the famous "Moody and Sankey Songbook" that had been translated into German.[17] In addition, the family used German hymnals published by other Mennonite denominations, including a *Choralbuch* that had been introduced to Russian Mennonites by Heinrich Franz. It contained several hundred hymns with four-part music using the *Ziffersystem*, a numerical system of musical notation rather than the more conventional staff system of musical notation.[18] These hymnals were deeply appreciated and their use was encouraged by Herman as a valuable source of spiritual enrichment for the family.

During the early 1950s, Dave Friesen, the fourth child of Herman and Margaretha, who was then a young man in his early twenties employed by a local electrician, purchased a cabinet radio. Use of the radio was carefully monitored in the house, but it did offer more exposure to the evangelical gospel hymns and country gospel music played on various gospel radio broadcasts, including German-language broadcasts prepared by the Conference of Mennonites and the Mennonite Brethren.[19]

Music became a regular activity in the home: some of the siblings organized themselves into musical groups (for example, Tena, Mary, Margaret,
and Dave formed a quartet). The musical talent of the Friesen children was
well known in the church as they were occasionally expected to assist the
less capable Vorsaenger in their task of song leading. The radio also familiarized the family with the country and western music that was popular at
the time, despite the fact that Herman did not approve of using the radio to
listen to popular music. When Dave married in 1954, it meant his siblings
no longer had access to a radio. After much pestering by their children,
Herman and Margaretha purchased a radio of their own. It was used frequently to listen to news broadcasts, and became the means for increasing
a general awareness of developments within the world.

The decade of the 1950s also brought new challenges to the Friesen
household, particularly for Margaretha. Due to failing health, Herman's
widowed stepmother Katarina came to live with the family for a time in
the early 1950s. She was not able to assist with household chores or farm
tasks, and so a greater burden of responsibility for her care came to rest

*Children of Herman and Margaretha Friesen, circa 1951. Courtesy Herman and
Margaretha Friesen estate.*

on Margaretha. Herman's relationship with his stepmother Katarina had never been particularly warm. According to his children, the strained relationship was due in large part to his childhood perception that she treated her own children better than her stepchildren. Her presence in the home occasionally created tension and conflict with Herman. The most notable incident may have been Katarina's insistence that she be included as a passenger on Herman and Margaretha's first car trip to Mexico. Despite considerable entreaties on her part, Herman resolutely refused to include her. In the fall of 1954, Wilhelm Wiebe, a seventy-four-year-old local widower whose wife had died in the spring of that year, came to ask for

Herman and Margaretha Friesen family, 1951. Courtesy Herman and Margaretha Friesen estate.

Katarina's hand in marriage. To reduce the awkwardness that surrounded courting in the presence of numerous children, Wilhelm's visits took place during the day, when most of the children were in school. At age seventy-seven, Katarina decided to marry again, a decision with which Herman's children say he strongly disagreed. The reasons for objecting are unclear, but they might have had to do with concerns about Katarina's health, the relatively short period of time since the death of Wiebe's wife, or concerns about the challenges often experienced by blended families. In any case, the marriage was short-lived, as Katarina died in September 1955, less than a year after her wedding to Wilhelm.

Several years later, as Margaretha began to approach the age of fifty, she faced a number of health issues that required medical attention and that made it difficult for her to participate in the household and farm operation as she had in the past. During the summer of 1958, she was hospitalized with a serious gall bladder inflammation (cholecystitis), a condition that often causes severe upper abdominal pain. Not long after, discomfort and pain experienced from varicose veins intensified. Many of the factors that increase one's risk of developing varicose veins applied to Margaretha, including hormonal changes associated with pregnancy and menopause, obesity, and age. The condition eventually required surgery to alleviate. Each of these maladies, and their treatment, required weeks of recovery time.

Much more traumatic for Margaretha, and for the family, was her admission in 1960 to the North Battleford Hospital, one of two large psychiatric institutions in the province at the time. Here she was diagnosed and treated for clinical depression. This is an event mentioned by many of the family members who were interviewed, and all associated Margaretha's depression with the onset of menopause. Details about her diagnosis are not known, hence one can only speculate about the actual cause(s) of her depression. Scientific research suggests that menopause "may increase the risk of depression for women in middle age," but factors "such as children leaving home, the death and illness of family members, the stresses of daily living, health and the onset of chronic disease" that occur during a woman's menopausal years, rather than hormonal changes, are much more likely to trigger depression.[20] In Margaretha's case, one might consider the cumulative stress created by thirteen pregnancies; the burden of child care resulting from thirteen pregnancies; the relentless responsibility for organizing household and farm labour; life with a strong-minded, patriarchal husband who offered limited support due to his community leadership responsibilities; and the onset of various painful medical conditions. What is known is that she was hospitalized in North Battleford for well over a month, that she received electroconvulsive (shock) therapy, which was first developed as a therapy for depression in 1938, and that the entire experience had been very difficult for her.[21] These times of illness for Margaretha placed an increased level of responsibility and stress on the oldest unmarried children, who were still living in the Friesen home. The relentless demands of a dairy farm, and the distance between Osler and North Battleford, did not make frequent visits on the part of family members possible.

The institution in which Margaretha was hospitalized was at the forefront of innovation in the field of psychiatric medicine at the time. It was one part of a much larger plan that medical historian Stuart Houston argues made Saskatchewan a leader in publicly funded health care during the first half of the twentieth century.[22] Dr. J. W. MacNeill did much to transition the institution from being an "asylum" to being a "hospital" that compassionately treated mentally ill patients as human beings in need of help and treatment, instead of removal from society through isolation and incarceration. He was influential in introducing new treatments and therapies.[23] Nevertheless, admission to the facility often carried a considerable social stigma. The stigmatization of mental illness was not unique to Old Colony Mennonites, as it was common throughout Canadian society.[24] The reluctance to talk openly about the reasons for Margaretha's hospitalization, which meant some of the younger, school-aged children first learned about their mother's admission to North Battleford Hospital from their peers at school, exemplifies not only the feelings of stigmatization and shame that generally surrounded mental health issues, which were often euphemistically identified as "nerve troubles," but also the lack of understanding around mental illness as a form of suffering more generally.[25] The perceived connection between Margaretha's condition and menopause further complicated open discussion, since matters pertaining to human sexuality generally, and the physiology of the female reproductive system in particular, were to be kept strictly private (i.e., not shared with children, particularly boys).[26] Following her release from North Battleford Hospital, other medical issues emerged, including tests for the possibility of diabetes, which turned out not to be the case. Nevertheless, for the remainder of her life, she continued taking medication for various ailments. Chronic illnesses that made it difficult to attend to everyday chores sometimes compounded struggles with self-worth on the part of Old Colony Mennonite women because these were an important measure by which the community determined whether one was a good wife and mother.

The efficiencies gained by the purchase of more modern farm equipment and increased mechanization were offset by expansion of the dairy operation and the purchase of more land. As Herman's community and church leadership responsibilities increased, and the size of his family grew, he was continually faced with the question of how best to balance the demands and complexity of his growing farm operation, his role as a husband and father, and the responsibilities of his public leadership roles. As Herman's involvement in public leadership roles increased, and he was often absent from home in the evenings, Margaretha was compelled to carry the lion's share of the parenting. She was frequently the one to organize and supervise chores and work projects for the children on the farm.

Both parents were known as serious-minded and strict people, which is not surprising given the challenges they faced and the sober (and sometimes sombre) piety of the Old Colony Mennonite faith. Margaretha was softer and more relational in her approach to disciplining the children, but she was more intensely concerned than Herman about usage of the German language and conscientious adherence to the traditions of the Old Colony Mennonite Church and expectations expressed by the ministers. Herman was the more stern, and at times, authoritarian disciplinarian of the two. "What father said, went," observed several of his children. Neither parent felt it necessary to offer extensive explanations for their parenting decisions, given the *Catechism* clearly taught that children are "to obey their parents in all things. Honour thy father and mother, which is the first commandment with a promise." Few, if any, of Herman's children would say they had a close, personal relationship with their father during their childhood and adolescent years. Some wondered whether he truly loved them.

The relational distance experienced by some of the children toward their father was amplified not only by his frequent absences but also by moments when his quick temper got the better of him, which sometimes caused him to lose an appropriate sense of proportion between the seriousness of the offence and a reasonable disciplinary response. Relatively minor misdemeanours were occasionally met with a degree of physical punishment that, by today's standards, would be characterized as violence and abuse. As one of his children put it, "My father wore out more v-belts on me than on his machinery." Like many Canadians at the time, Old Colony Mennonites used corporal punishment but were expected to stay within limits: it was not to be exercised in anger, and the force used was not to be "excessive," which is a rather subjective boundary that provided parents and school teachers latitude in its application.

Old Colony Mennonites believed the responsibility of parents is not only to nurture but also to correct children. The discipline of children, which included the possibility of corporal punishment, was understood as a necessary part of parental responsibility in bringing up "children in the nurture and admonition of the Lord," as mandated in the *Catechism*. Numerous passages from the book of Proverbs in the Old Testament were commonly used to justify, and even argue for the necessity of, physical punishment of children. For example, Proverbs 13:24 counsels, "Those who spare the rod hate their children, but those who love them are careful to discipline them."[27] Alongside (and perhaps because of) this emphasis on parental responsibility, Mennonite leaders had long been aware of the possibility of corporal punishment escalating in intensity to the point where it became a form of violent abuse.[28] To curb such tendencies, leaders emphasized the principle of moderation in how discipline was to be administered in homes and schools. For example, the *Schulverordnung* (*General School Regulations*), written by church leaders during the 1880s and circulated to teachers in the German-language schools in southern Manitoba, states that "the teacher shall discipline the pupils without showing favoritism and shall have the right to punish laziness," but it also warns that "punishment should not be too harsh or applied in anger or vengeance." Teachers are "to act in a manner to deserve love and respect of the pupils."[29] It would, of course, be much easier for church leaders to supervise adherence to such guidelines in schools than it would be to monitor homes. It is odd that the potential for excessive harshness and violent force that sometimes characterized the use of corporal punishment was apparently not perceived by church leaders as inconsistent with the Old Colony Mennonite Church's doctrinal Article 15, "Of Revenge and Non-resistance." The article was primarily understood as a response to "enemies," and as a prohibition against the use of lethal force in times of war, and was not applied, as is common among Mennonite groups now, to the way power or force is sometimes misused in domestic settings, or interactions among church members.

The stress of Herman's various leadership roles and the ongoing invest-ment of energy necessary for parenting over a long period of time may well have increased his irritability and lack of patience when dealing with domestic matters. As a leader in the community and church, he likely felt a heightened degree of pressure as the "head of the household" to maintain the perception that he was "in control" of his household. A lack of aware-ness of alternative disciplinary strategies for motivating children may also have been a factor in resorting almost exclusively to corporal punishment (or the threat thereof) as the means of disciplining his children. Despite the fact that awareness and understanding of domestic violence differs somewhat from era to era, one cannot excuse the physical brutality that some of Herman's children experienced at times. This lack of control was not only inconsistent with the church's cautionary advice of moderation but it damaged his relationship with some of his children.

Several of Herman's younger children observed that "something seemed to change" when he became a minister in 1962—by this time, six of Herman's children were already married and no longer in the home. His new status as a minister increased his sensitivity to what people expected not only him to exemplify but also his family members. The role probably raised Herman's own expectations of himself. He became more austere in his own demea-nour and lifestyle, and stricter about the behaviour he expected from his children: for example, he stopped attending school Christmas programs and community sports days. But there were limits to his acquiescence to pressure from church members. His response after being elected as minister to some who wished him to remove the pump organ from his house was, according to his family, brusquely dismissed with the logic, "If I was good enough to be elected [as minister] with it [the organ] in the house, it will stay in the house after." He recognized, and was possibly anxious about, the way the choices of a leader's children can have an impact on the public perceptions of their parent's leadership. There is no clear indication of an awareness that such pressures are common in most ministerial families, and of the need to balance carefully the concern about the reputational impact of his family with the need to protect his children from inappropriate expectations on the part of church members. Family members agree that he created the perception that the church was of a higher priority than the family, and that they would have wanted Herman to create space where they could be a "normal" family, without carrying the added weight of responsibility for discerning whether their actions might be judged as appropriately exemplary.

Herman's tenure as a minister during the 1960s coincided with some of the more difficult parenting challenges he and Margaretha faced. The younger children were generally bolder than their older siblings had been in pushing the boundaries of acceptable behaviour within the Old Colony Mennonite community. Some began to experiment with a party lifestyle. The most dramatic event may have been the unexpected pregnancy of one of their teenage daughters in 1965, which resulted in the addition of a young baby to the household. Some of the older children thought their parents had simply become too lenient with the younger children. This is doubtful given Herman's position as a minister. It is more likely due, at least in part, to a reaction against Herman's relational aloofness and authoritarian style that did not serve him well in guiding his children in the construction of their own views, hopes, and ambitions. It also represented the initial impact of broader cultural trends on Old Colony Mennonite youth, made possible by a greater degree of mobility and proximity to a growing urban centre. Despite the desire for separation from the "world," the Old Colony Mennonites were not immune from the cultural revolution of permissiveness and pursuit of individual freedom that took place more generally within North America during the 1960s, and that mitigated against the ongoing maintenance of the tight social cohesion that was possible within isolated Old Colony Mennonite village life.

It is not unusual for family members (and others) to note the disparities between the public persona and private life of church leaders. No one lives up to all of the ideals of a faith community perfectly, including leaders. For most people, the most difficult place to live out one's ideals consistently is in the crucible of family life. A leader's weaknesses and inconsistencies within a family setting, along with the complexities of parenting, are among the most powerful sources of self-doubt within a leader. Herman's children experienced varying degrees of dissonance around Herman's public persona as a highly respected community and church leader and the sometimes difficult (and occasionally even abusive) dynamics within the more private world of his immediate family. Although he was often sought out for his wisdom and expertise in mediating local family and business conflicts, his children did not experience him as a confidant or counsellor before they became adults, when some of them developed deeper, more friendship-like relationships with their parents. The varied responses to Herman's sudden death by his children also exemplify this dissonance: on the one hand, his death precipitated a profound sense of loss among those children (and in-laws) who had begun to experience a warmer and respectful relationship with Herman. Their sense of loss was deepened by the fear that, without his leadership, it would not be possible to revitalize a new future for the Old Colony Mennonite Church in the region. Others, on the other hand, were more indifferent to the impact of his death and bewildered by the widespread expressions of reverence and esteem by church members that contrasted sharply with their own intense feelings of resentment toward their father, and perhaps also more generally toward the Old Colony Mennonite Church. The sharp contrast between their stolidity and Herman's popularity as a leader, as evidenced by the one thousand people who attended his funeral, was incomprehensible. Given that his relationships with some of his older adult children had gradually become more like a friendship, had his life not been so suddenly and prematurely curtailed, it is likely that reconciliation would have occurred with some, if not all, of his estranged children.

As noted above, economic conditions improved dramatically for the Friesen family during the 1950s. The decades that followed inaugurated a new stage in Herman and Margaretha's roles as parents as their children became independent adults and began making their own life choices, including marriage—six of their children were married during the 1950s, and another five during the 1960s.[30] (It is curious to note that six chose spouses who were also children of Mennonite ministers.[31]) The Friesen family serves as a kind of microcosm of the transitions taking place within the larger Old Colony Mennonite community in the region. None of their children were old enough to be eligible for military service during the Second World War, so the family did not need to face the difficult and often controversial choices surrounding conscription and alternative service that confronted many other Mennonite families at the time.[32] The Friesen children began entering adulthood in the late 1940s as Canada was experiencing a substantial post-war economic boom. The occupational choices made by Herman's twelve adult children and their spouses spanned a considerable portion of the spectrum of options that were being utilized by many of the young adults within the church at the time. Collectively, they illustrate the diversification that was beginning to take place among the Old Colony Mennonites in Saskatchewan during the 1950s and 1960s as the church community transitioned from being primarily farm-oriented toward more blue-collar trades and labour.

During the 1950s, it became increasingly obvious to the Old Colony Mennonites in the Hague-Osler area that it would not be possible to sustain the same kind of agrarian village way of life in the region that had been in place for more than half a century. The generation entering adulthood were the ones who would feel the impact of this new reality most acutely. There simply was not enough land available in close proximity for the majority of the upcoming generation to farm as a primary way of life, or to expand the area already settled by Old Colony Mennonites north of Saskatoon.[33] Mechanization further reduced the need for workers on the farms in the region. Farming as a viable way of life became an option available only to a minority, thereby calling into serious question the ongoing viability of an exclusively agrarian way of life that had been an integral part of Old Colony Mennonite identity.[34] As noted above, a number of Old Colony Mennonite Church ministers continued to search for geographically isolated areas suitable for agriculture, and tried to encourage migration to these areas. This was an option primarily for those who had capital to purchase land. The vast majority of young adult men, however, opted to pursue readily available employment opportunities in and near Saskatoon, the largest urban centre in the province. At the time, it was generally assumed that Old Colony Mennonite women would be homemakers, even if they were no longer running a farm operation. The few who did seek employment were restricted by their limited education to blue-collar jobs within the agricultural sector, small businesses, and construction trades.

Watching and listening to his adult children and their spouses trying to make decisions regarding their future in a rapidly changing world gave Herman Friesen a close-up and personal view of how church members in general were assessing and navigating the available occupational and residential options. Their experience helped him to see that it was no longer possible (and in some instances not even desirable) for all of his children to pursue a farming way of life within or near the Hague-Osler Reserve area. None of his children showed any interest in joining one of the Old Colony Mennonite migrations. Only half of his children established their own farm operations, with most supplementing their farm income with a range of blue-collar jobs. Those who did not pursue farming obtained a variety of blue-collar jobs. Several men completed the necessary certification to practise construction trades. The majority of Herman's daughters (and daughters-in-law) were homemakers and did not seek full-time employment outside of the home, although a number did supplement household income by working from their home (for example, by providing service as a seamstress or offering child care).

Those young couples seeking off-farm employment were also faced with decisions regarding residential location. Old Colony Mennonite Church leaders actively discouraged members from exposing their families to the evils that might result from living in urban centres, and they refused to organize a congregation in Saskatoon for those interested in residing there and for those members already present. Many sought lots in the villages and towns that were within reasonable commuting distance to Saskatoon. The dilemma prompted the emergence of a new village during the 1950s called Martensville, which literally and figuratively represented a "halfway house" for those who could not join a migration but were seeking to remain loyal to a more rural Old Colony Mennonite way of life, and who therefore needed to remain within commuting distance to Saskatoon.[35] The village, which was located approximately sixteen kilometres north of Saskatoon, became for several decades one of the fastest growing communities in the province. Despite Herman's apprehension, more than half of his children at some point chose to reside in the city of Saskatoon in order to be closer to their place of employment. At least three of his children lived and worked in other provinces.

The gradual diversification and fragmentation of the Old Colony Mennonite communitarian way of life was increased still further by the expanding range of denominational options that were present in the region.[36] Occupational and residential decisions inevitably had implications for church life. Here too the choices made by Herman's children, all of whom grew up participating in the Old Colony Mennonite Church (most were baptized in the Old Colony Mennonite Church), provide a window into the Old Colony Mennonite responses to the growing range of religious options. A number of his children remained with the Old Colony Mennonite Church, some joined other Mennonite denominations, and some chose not to join any at all. While Herman recognized the necessity of occupational diversification, he strongly disapproved of decisions to change church membership. He regularly applied the admonishment to the church in Ephesus in Revelation 2:4 ("You have forsaken your first love") to those who had left the Old Colony Mennonite Church after baptism, and to those who were considering it. This was consistent with the Old Colony understanding of baptismal vows as a permanent commitment.[37] Not all of his children (and in-laws) agreed with Herman's interpretation and use of Revelation 2:4. They argued that reference to "leaving one's first love" is not about changing denominations but rather about the nature of an individual's relationship with Christ, regardless of denomination. Despite Herman's desire to see his children (and other parishioners) remain within the Old Colony Mennonite Church, in some instances there simply was not an Old Colony Mennonite Church to attend in proximity to their place of employment and residence.

Some of the teachers in the English-language public schools were a significant conduit of religious influence upon the upcoming generation of Old Colony Mennonites. As noted above, many of them were Mennonites who belonged either to the General Conference of Mennonites or to the Mennonite Brethren. Like many of the teachers in the earlier German private schools, they too had an interest in nurturing the faith of the children in their schools. They were not directly accountable to any church body, and, depending on the school board to which they were answerable, they often used their freedom to supplement the required curriculum with religious instruction and activities.[38] They often organized evening activities for youth, such as choirs and Vacation Bible School programs, and were often instrumental in promoting organizations that offered Bible memorization programs and mailbox Bible correspondence lessons. Herman generally supported these activities, seeing them as a useful supplement to the preaching within the Old Colony Mennonite Church. Exposure to gospel radio broadcasts was noted above. As the new forms of religious instruction became acceptable, they were sought after by many students, and created a desire among some for different denominational experiences.

Ever present as an alternative denominational option alongside the Old Colony Mennonite Church was the General Conference Mennonite Church, now known as Mennonite Church Canada. It had congregations scattered throughout the Hague-Osler Reserve area, located mostly in the larger village and town centres (for example, Rosthern, Hague, Neuanlage, Osler, and Warman). Their willingness to incorporate new practices, such as Sunday schools, evening services, and *Jugendverein*—a youth program patterned after the Christian Endeavour program that was popular in evangelical Protestant denominations across North America, and their initiative in organizing congregations in Saskatoon attracted a steady trickle of Old Colony Mennonites. The denomination became a kind of melting pot of Old Colony, American, and Russlaender Mennonites during the 1930s through to the 1960s.[39] Several of Herman's siblings, and several of his children, became part of General Conference congregations in Saskatoon.

Another nearby option was the Bergthaler Mennonite Church, a group that was similar in theology and practice to the Old Colony Mennonite Church, and one with which they had close fraternal relations.[40] For a time during the late 1940s, Herman and Margaretha seriously considered joining the Bergthaler Mennonite Church. This helps explain why the Bergthaler church baptized three of their older children.

A more aggressively evangelical-Mennonite option called the Rudnerweider, now known as the Evangelical Mennonite Mission Conference, emerged during the late 1930s. It started as a renewal movement within the Sommerfelder Mennonite Church in Manitoba, akin to the Bergthaler Mennonite Church in Saskatchewan, and then precipitated a split. Inspired by developments in Manitoba, a number of people in the Gruenthal and Chortiz villages began organizing similar services, which eventually led to the formation of a new church group that became part of the Rudnerweider denomination. The new group elected John D. Friesen as their Ältester in Saskatchewan in 1952.[41] He brought a much more explicitly evangelistic, extemporaneous, and emotional style of preaching. The group eventually organized four congregations in the region, including one in Saskatoon: much of the growth experienced by the Rudnerweider was drawn from the Old Colony Mennonites. Despite Herman's objections, several of his children were actively involved with this group.

The Rudnerweider, along with the General Conference of Mennonites, worked together during the 1950s to organize evangelistic tent meetings in the Hague-Osler region that emphasized the necessity of a personal conversion experience. Various English-language evangelists were invited, including the Janz brothers (Leo and Hildor), the American Mennonite Brunk brothers (George and Lawrence), and Ben D. Reimer, a Low German–speaking, Kleine Gemeinde (now known as the Evangelical Mennonite Conference) evangelist from Steinbach, Manitoba.[42] These ministries brought the Hague-Osler Old Colony Mennonites into first-hand contact with some of the techniques used by evangelical Protestant revivalists during the nineteenth and early twentieth centuries. These events provided both religious and social opportunities. On the one hand, some found the evangelical Protestant understanding of soteriology (doctrine of salvation) profoundly attractive. Particularly powerful was the emphasis on "assurance of salvation," which appeared to offer a more joyful and experiential sense of spiritual emancipation. It highlighted a transformation in the subjective character of their religious experience, that is, a move from a spiritual system they considered to be characterized by fear, anxiety, and uncertainty toward one that facilitated emancipation, joy, and confidence through a subjective sense of confirmation of forgiveness and acceptance before a Holy God.[43] Others, on the other hand, were repulsed by what they perceived to be excessive and manipulative emotionalism and overt proselytization driven by a sense of spiritual superiority and dogmatic certainty. In addition, the eschatological schema of dispensational premillennialism that was promoted by many revivalists was completely foreign to an Old Colony Mennonite understanding of eschatology (doctrine of last things, such as death, judgment, and the final destiny of human beings). In addition to different emphases in the theological understanding of salvation, the presence of these revivalists highlighted differences in the area of ecclesiology (understanding of the church): one emphasized the individual, while the other accented the importance of the church as a community; one emphasized the necessity of correct doctrine, while the other accented the importance of holy living. Herman discouraged his children from attending these ministries—participating inevitably generated conflict within the Friesen household, as it also did more generally among the Old Colony Mennonites.

The 1950s and 1960s were watershed decades for Canada in general, and the Old Colony Mennonites in Saskatchewan in particular. Cultural isolation was no longer an option. Although the focus of this book is on the life of Herman Friesen, the dynamics within his family life, including the occupational, residential, and religious choices made by his adult children in response to a rapidly changing world, provide a window into the issues he faced, not only as a parent but as the Ältester of the Old Colony Mennonite Church during the 1960s. One of Herman's challenges as Ältester was helping the Old Colony Mennonite community navigate its transition from an agrarian village way of life to one that required a greater degree of accommodation and engagement with modern Canadian culture than was previously permitted. The possibility of occupational choices amplified the tension between those who wanted to maintain a more uniform communal way of life and those who favoured a greater degree of individual freedom in making life decisions regarding their future.

Community and Church Leadership, 1936–1969

4

HERMAN FRIESEN'S ELECTION AS A MINISTER in 1962 was preceded by more than twenty-five years of experience as a community leader.[1] This experience helped him to develop a broad network of relationships beyond the Old Colony Mennonite community, and provided him with a view and understanding of the political and internal decision-making process within municipal and even provincial governments. These leadership opportunities were an invaluable preparation for his eventual role as Ältester, and enabled him to be more collaborative and more amenable to change than preceding Ältesten.

Public School Board Trustee

HERMAN D. W. FRIESEN'S INVOLVEMENT IN COMMUNITY LEADERship probably began in January 1936, when, at the age of twenty-eight, he was elected as a public school board trustee in the Saskatchewan School District #99.[2] This role began at about the same time as his oldest daughter enrolled as a student at Saskatchewan School. This public school district was unique in that it was the first one to be organized in the region and preceded the creation of the Hague-Osler Reserve. It was formed in 1887 to accommodate English-speaking settlers living near the Clark's Crossing ferry. Classes were initially held in the home of the Caswell family, one of the original pioneers living near the ferry,[3] until a more permanent schoolhouse was built approximately three kilometres southwest of Kronsthal and the Friesen farm in the early 1900s. Because of the strong presence of English-speaking settlers in the immediate vicinity of the school, and the disinterest on the part of the incoming Old Colony Mennonites during the early 1900s, the district avoided the conflicts that characterized the formation of public school districts in and around Hague and Osler, and avoided having an official trustee appointed by the provincial government to oversee the operation of the school. At about the same time as the Mennonite private schools were being closed and more of the Old Colony Mennonites began sending their children to public schools, the original, non-Mennonite, English-speaking settlers in the district began selling their land to local Mennonites who were eager to purchase it because of its adjacency to the Hague-Osler Reserve. By 1930, a good number of the children attending Saskatchewan School were German-speaking Mennonites.

As a young boy, Herman Friesen was well aware of the conflict between the provincial government and the Old Colony Mennonites over the German-language private schools and the ensuing migration to Mexico. He would undoubtedly have observed or heard anecdotes of the ongoing distrust the government had toward any Old Colony Mennonites interested in serving as school board trustees in the region.[4] Although Herman was not the only Old Colony Mennonite to be elected as a public school trustee during the 1930s and 1940s, it was unusual for the way it represented a departure from the policies promoted by many Old Colony Mennonite leaders since their arrival in Canada.[5] It is not possible to determine exactly what motivated Herman to invest considerable time and energy in community leadership roles that included direct participation in the political process, particularly during a time when many Old Colony Mennonites remained opposed to such involvement. Family members noted that he persisted in his involvement in community politics, even though Margaretha apparently did not fully approve of his participation in elections. On election days, he somehow always managed to find convenient reasons for why it was necessary to "go to town." It may be that some of his suspicion of public schools dissipated as a result of the evening English classes he took as a young adult at a local public school, along with some other young Mennonite adults.[6] Was there some regret over educational opportunities he had missed? It may be that he was disappointed with the way the conflicts over private schools and the Mexico migration were handled and he wanted to work toward a different kind of solution for his children that was less divisive. It may be that he saw this role as a way of doing his part in taking responsibility for the education of his children. Serving as a trustee gave him ample opportunity to monitor and influence what was taking place in the classroom. Or it may simply have been that he saw participation as a key to the social and economic well-being of his family and the community at large. His exact motivation(s) will never be known. Also unknown is whether he was ever censured by church leaders for his participation, or whether the Ältesten were quietly grateful to have a member of their church present as an influence.

Like many other country school districts, the Saskatchewan School district was governed by four trustees who met monthly throughout the school year for formal board meetings, and more frequently for informal discussion of issues or the completion of specific tasks. While the provincial government approved curriculum, the district boards managed the operation of a school, including construction and maintenance of the facility, hiring (and occasionally releasing) teachers, setting local education tax rates, and addressing any other matters pertaining to the operation of a particular school. Many of the issues that are referenced in the school minutes are relatively mundane: details about janitorial services, school facility maintenance, purchasing sports equipment, scheduling inoculation days, ensuring an adequate supply of heating fuel, and setting teacher salaries. Presence on the board gave Herman opportunity to assert his preferences on a variety of matters: for example, he approved the purchase of sports equipment but initiated a motion in 1938 stating "that the teacher and the school children are not to play ball against another school," which was consistent with his aversion to competitive sports.[7] Despite the promotion of friendly inter-school competition on the part of the municipality, Herman persistently objected for reasons that were not made clear.[8]

Particularly contentious, however, was the ongoing question of how best to deal with Old Colony Mennonite parents who refused to send their children to school regularly. The issue persisted throughout the 1930s and is referenced frequently within the minutes and correspondence.[9] The animus surrounding governmental intervention and the subsequent exodus to Mexico took time to dissipate, as some families continued to contest the ability of local school trustees to enforce the requirements of the School

Attendance Act. But, in other instances, the economic privation experienced by many at the time prompted parents to circumvent attendance requirements by claiming their children did not have appropriate clothes to wear, lacked adequate means of transportation, or that they needed their children for labour on their farms. Correspondence between the superintendent responsible for Saskatchewan School and the Department of Education debate the merits of turning enforcement over to the RCMP.[10]

At a meeting in early January 1938, the four Saskatchewan School trustees were sharply divided on how to respond to a family that was not sending their children to school. Johan Wahl and Herman Friesen argued in favour of delay in order to provide more opportunity to convince the parents of the wisdom of compliance, whereas the two Lisko brothers wanted immediate and decisive action. As the argument unfolded, even Johan and Herman got into such a heated discussion that the meeting was never formally adjourned. The issue was so fractious it prompted E. Lisko to resign as chairperson at the next meeting. In his place, Herman became the new chairperson, and the board passed a motion to "cancel" the discussion of the previous meeting. On another occasion, one of Herman's neighbours decided to attend a school board meeting to dispute one of the board's decisions. A heated exchange turned violent as the neighbour grabbed a hammer and attempted to strike Herman. These incidents offer a glimpse into the gradual transition that continued to take place among the Old Colony Mennonites regarding their acceptance of public schools, and the struggle on the part of local school board trustees in knowing how best to manage such situations, particularly since they often involved neighbours or close relatives.[11]

Many of the public school boards in the Hague-Osler area hired teachers who were able, and willing, to provide German-language religious instruction after regular school hours. It reflected a conciliatory approach that was appreciated by Mennonite families and made the transition toward the public school system more palatable for many. The specific details were worked out by each school board: in some instances, providing an additional half-hour of German-language instruction was a condition of employment without any additional remuneration. With the onset of the Second World

War, some Department of Education officials questioned the wisdom of continuing this practice, particularly in view of the media criticism directed toward the German-speaking Mennonite men who refused to serve in the armed forces by claiming conscientious objector status.[12] No specific directive about the practice was issued by the local superintendent or the Department of Education, but it was clearly a sensitive issue that had the potential to become a more high-charged controversy.

Herman continued in the role of chairperson until January 1942, when he unexpectedly lost an election. A year later, in 1943, he was re-elected for another three-year term. During the first year of this term, he was again chosen as chairperson, and after that as secretary-treasurer. His involvement occasionally made it possible for him to attend provincial school board trustee conventions during the 1940s, which were sometimes held in Regina. This kind of governmental contact was unusual for laypersons within the Old Colony Mennonite community.

In 1947, the two-room East Osler Government Aided School was built approximately five kilometres east of Osler to relieve the overcrowded conditions in several schools, particularly Renfrew School and Saskatchewan School, with a few additional students from LaBassee School and Pembroke School. Although the new school did not have its own district, it did have its own board of trustees, and Herman Friesen was elected as one of the first trustees.[13] Here he met teachers Ben and Susie Harder, who taught for over a decade at East Osler School and had a profound impact on many of his children. The Harders, who were members of the Evangelical Mennonite Brethren church in Waldheim, Saskatchewan,[14] organized a choir, evening youth meetings, and even a drama as extracurricular activities for students, which were endorsed by the local school trustees.

It was not possible to determine exactly when during the 1950s Herman's tenure as a school board trustee ended, or why it ended. Margaretha's health issues at the time, and possibly also his decision to run for re-election as a municipal councillor in 1958, may have been factors in his decision not to run for re-election as a trustee. His departure from this role meant he was not involved in navigating the move toward consolidation of country school districts during the 1960s into larger school units with centralized high schools located in larger towns, or in the discussions about the negotiation of teacher salaries that culminated in the Teachers' Salary Agreements Act in 1968.[15]

Municipal Councillor

THE SCOPE OF HERMAN'S COMMUNITY LEADERSHIP BROADENED considerably when he was elected as a councillor in the Rural Municipality of Warman No. 374 (now part of the Rural Municipality of Corman Park No. 344) for four years during the 1940s (1946–49) and again for two more years a decade later (1958–59).[16] First organized in 1909, the municipality of Warman quickly became one of the most densely populated, and one of the more prosperous, rural municipalities in the province. The primary focus during this time was on the construction of roads and providing agricultural support for farmers, including the distribution of registered seed and information about animal husbandry. As the governmental avenue by which many provincial government service initiatives and policies were administrated, municipal bodies were involved in a broad range of issues including land-use planning, the development of water and sewer systems, facilitating access to health care, providing police services, and even organizing occasional entertainment and social events. It is unclear why Herman opted to become involved in municipal politics in addition to serving as a public school board trustee, and why, after his initial involvement during the late 1940s, he took a ten-year hiatus before running for election again for only a single term during the late 1950s. His initial interest in municipal politics may well have been due to the influence of his good friend Johan Wahl, who served as both a school board trustee and municipal councillor. In the months preceding his election in early 1958, Herman attended at least three special public meetings with government officials regarding a new grid road program, an indication of his ongoing personal interest in this particular issue.[17]

One of the most meaningful personal outcomes of his public involvement was a highly valued friendship with Johan Wahl. The two were almost the same age, and they served together at various times, both as school board trustees and municipal councillors, and worked closely on innumerable projects. Johan was the grandson of Cornelius Wahl, the central figure in the formation of the village of Kronsthal, which was immediately adjacent to the Banman (and later Friesen) family farm. Johan's father (Peter Wahl) was an Old Colony Mennonite, but Johan married Helena Enns, who was the daughter of a local Mennonite Brethren family. Normally, such a union between members of these two Mennonite denominations would have resulted in the excommunication of one or the other. To reduce the tension within the family that was created by this marriage, the couple agreed to become part of the General Conference Mennonite Church.[18] Both Johan and Helena had attended public schools and therefore knew how to read and write in English (she did a considerable amount of correspondence on Johan's behalf). Johan understood the Old Colony Mennonites well; the friendship provided Herman with an advocate and a capable confidant outside of the Old Colony Mennonite Church.

In addition to his school board and municipality involvement, Herman became a member of the Hague-Osler Snow Club, which was formed in 1953. As the network of roads in the area continued to expand, and as individuals in the region became more economically dependent on regular access to the city of Saskatoon, whether as employees needing to be present at a workplace, or as farmers needing supplies or delivering goods to market, the need for better roads during the winter became more acute. Having expanded their dairy operation, the Friesen family was dependent on regular milk pickup. The Hague-Osler Snow Club developed a reputation as one of the most organized and progressive clubs in the province by building one of the largest snowplows in the province. The work of the club significantly increased the number of cars driving daily to Saskatoon during the winter season (approximately forty per day during the mid-1950s). For a time, Herman served as a member of the board.[19]

Through his twenty years of involvement in local politics, Herman Friesen was involved in numerous issues and decisions that impacted the Old Colony Mennonite community. In addition to providing Herman with opportunities for developing skills in the area of public speaking and leadership, this experience also broadened his awareness of governmental process and significantly increased his network of relationships within the region. It made him more comfortable in accepting a degree of modernization and Canadianization. The information he obtained, particularly from his role as a municipal councillor, often helped him in the development of his dairy operation, as it gave him a better understanding of what was being planned for rural regions (for example, governmental plans for the rural electrification and road improvements in the late 1940s and early 1950s, and information about farming innovations). His reputation as a leader in the region prompted requests for help in resolving family and business conflicts. In some instances, he offered assistance to individuals in financial distress.[20]

One can only surmise as to the reasons why Herman did not continue his community leadership roles after his election as a minister. It would be interesting to know whether he did not do so because of the difficulty in managing multiple volunteer roles, which would certainly have been reason enough, or whether he (or others) considered it inappropriate for an Old Colony Mennonite minister to simultaneously be a publicly elected official. Nevertheless, the example of his former involvement in local politics helped reduce the suspicion of government among some Old Colony Mennonites. Many were surprised to hear him encouraging people to vote in local elections, even after he had become a minister.

Church Ministries, 1930s–1969

HERMAN FRIESEN'S COMMITMENT TO THE OLD COLONY MENNONITE Church was evident throughout his adult life. Long before he became a minister he was already active in the church in a number of ways. His musical interests and talent have already been noted. As a result, it was almost inevitable that he was selected as a Vorsaenger, first in the Blumenheim congregation sometime during the 1930s, and later in the early 1950s in the Kronsthal congregation. In addition to leading music on Sunday mornings, he was often asked to assist with song leading at other church functions. This role marked the beginning of his public leadership activities within the life of the church.

The Vorsaenger were seated in a place of honour on one side of the pulpit facing the congregation; these were the men designated to lead congregational singing by choosing songs, as well as providing the tune by singing the first phrase of the song. The congregation then followed. Each congregation generally designated four to five men to serve in this role. They were seated in order of seniority, with the one nearest the pulpit having the longest tenure.

The Old Colony Mennonites used a nineteenth-century edition of the highly revered *Geistreiches Gesangbuch*, a hymnal containing more than seven hundred hymns without musical notation, compiled by their Mennonite ancestors in Prussia and Russia. Approximately half of the *Geistreiches Gesangbuch* is derived from early-eighteenth-century hymnals prepared by Lutheran Pietists, and half from a range of Anabaptist-Mennonite sources.[21] It was the only book carried to church by members. The songs used by a church community are often as or more important in shaping popular theology than sermons. It is in their hymns, Peter Letkemann notes, "that congregations express the strength of their faith and the depth of their religious devotion."[22] The central purpose of the hymnal was not primarily doctrinal but *Erbauung* (spiritual edification or devotion). Many of the hymns reflect the Pietist concern for spiritual vitality; others focus on the suffering and example of Jesus as a source of strength during times of hardship. The hymnal contains a variety of aids, including a section of prayers for specific occasions, an index of melodies, and a lectionary (*Anweisung der Lieder*), which outlines scripture passages and hymnal selections for each Sunday and religious holiday.

Singing was done without instrumental accompaniment and in unison to symbolize congregational unity. They used a slow, drawn-out, melismatic style of heterophonic singing in which the beauty of tone and regularity of rhythm are not qualities that are of primary importance. "Individual performance in worship (vocal or instrumental)," writes Judith Klassen, "was seen as a distraction from collective humility before God." The melodies are difficult to sing alone. Klassen observes, "The learning, maintenance, and performance of *lange Wiez* in some ways parallels the emphases on community and perseverance in conserving Mennonite life."[23] The style has its roots in reformation Europe and, according to Wesley Berg, represents an "elemental form of music making that is common in societies where notation had not stabilized melodic repertoires."[24] The melodies have been transmitted orally from one generation of Vorsaenger to the next.

During the 1940s, questions surfaced about the possibility of making adjustments to the music in public worship services. Many favoured a change from the *lange Wiez* to the use of *Tsoliwiez*, which uses a slightly faster tempo for singing the same songs.[25] This was not the first time the matter of hymn tunes had surfaced among Old Colony Mennonites. It was one of the first issues facing those who arrived on the West Reserve in southern Manitoba in the mid-1870s. Many of the new immigrants had painful memories of the controversies created by the transition to newer tunes in congregations in the Chortitza and Burwalde colonies in Russia. The newer hymn tunes were introduced in Russia through the *Choralbuch* by Heinrich Franz, so many of the newcomers to Manitoba were already familiar with them. Ältester Wiebe and the majority of members felt that a return to the older tunes would be appropriate for a church community

Old Colony Mennonite Church in Neuanlage, 1954. Courtesy Leo Driedger.

committed to a restoration of Anabaptist ideals.[26] After almost seventy years since that decision, the close association between the older tunes and their sense of identity as a "faithful" church had dissipated somewhat, making it possible to revisit the question. The matter prompted Ältester Loeppky to call a brotherhood meeting in 1950. Following a "lively discussion," the majority voted in favour of this change. The revised musical style was first introduced in the Neuanlage church, and the other congregations in the region soon accepted it. According to his children, this was a change Herman Friesen enthusiastically favoured because of his own familiarity with the *Choralbuch*.

Many of his children remember Herman practising for Sunday morning by using the *Choralbuch* with the Ziffersystem. As noted, he also enjoyed singing songs from the *Evangeliums-Lieder* hymnal, which offered a devotional expression with which he deeply resonated. One of his favourite *Evangelium* hymns was "*Nur mit Jesus will ich Pilger wandern*" ("None but Jesus Would I Have to Guide Me"). The use of this hymnal was not permitted within the Old Colony Mennonite Church. Because of the absence of musical instruments in public worship, and the general lack of musical training, as a Vorsaenger, Herman tried to improve the level of musicality by organizing practice sessions with other song leaders, a suggestion that was not welcomed by all of his colleagues. One Sunday morning during the 1950s, when Herman was unable to be present, the Vorsaenger were struggling to remember how to start a particular hymn: they looked pleadingly at a row of Herman's daughters, who were in church that morning but who silently refused to assist the embarrassed Vorsaenger. This incident greatly amused Herman privately and reinforced publicly his point about the need for more practice. His long-standing involvement as a Vorsaenger, together with other visible positions of community leadership, increased the probability of him being nominated as a minister when ministerial elections took place.

Herman's interest in the well-being of the church was evident in other ways as well. As noted above, Sunday schools were gradually introduced into Old Colony Mennonite congregations during the 1940s. Herman actively supported this decision and made it a priority for his children to attend. It signalled both his interest in the spiritual nurturing of a younger generation as well as an openness to innovation within the church. In the early 1950s, he was involved in establishing an Old Colony Mennonite Church southeast of Osler, near the village of Kronsthal and their farm. The addition of this location made it possible for Old Colony Mennonites in the area to gather for worship weekly, since the only other church building in the vicinity was being shared with the Bergthaler Mennonites.

As noted above, the election of new ministers was necessitated after a group of Old Colony Mennonites, led by Ältester Abram Loewen and all but one of the other ministers, along with almost one hundred families, left Saskatchewan in 1961 to settle near Prespatou, British Columbia. The migration was motivated by a desire to find affordable land for young families who were unable financially to establish farms in the Hague-Osler area, and thereby avoid forcing the men of these families to find employment in urban centres.[27] It was to be the last migration organized and led by leaders in the Old Colony Mennonite Church in Saskatchewan.

Herman Friesen was elected as an Old Colony Mennonite minister at the age of fifty-four on April 3, 1962, at a brotherhood meeting held in the Neuanlage church. Two other individuals, Peter M. Peters and Peter Zacharias, were also chosen at the time. It was a Tuesday evening similar to many others in the Friesen home as Herman left to attend the brotherhood meeting after chores and supper were done. Several of his children, who were adolescents at the time, remember distinctly his return later that evening: the look on his face indicated that something serious had occurred, and he immediately asked Margaretha to join him for a private conversation in their bedroom before announcing the news to his children.[28] Life would not be the same again for the Friesen family.

At age fifty-four, Herman was considerably older than almost all other Old Colony ministers in Saskatchewan at the time of their election. The usual practice was to elect men as ministers in their late thirties or forties. While not explicitly stated as a church policy, Hans Werner notes that involvement in premarital sex sometimes disqualified individuals from being considered as potential candidates for ministry. This might explain why Herman, despite obvious leadership ability and experience, was not elected as a minister sooner.[29] If indeed this previous incident in the lives of Herman and Margaretha had been a consideration in the past, by 1962, more than thirty years had passed, and all of the ministers active at the time of their baptism, marriage, and the birth of their first child had either migrated or died. Regardless of whether the public shame of their prenuptial conception was a factor in the timing of Herman's election as a minister, it did have an impact on his pastoral ministry. After he became a minister, more than thirty years after his baptism and the birth of their first child, couples who found themselves in a similar predicament expressed their appreciation for his understanding and even sympathy. Herman's ordination service took place two weeks later, on April 15, 1962, in the Neuhorst church. A little more than a year later, on June 18, 1963, Herman was elected as Ältester, and ordained as such on June 23, 1963.

As a Preacher

IT WAS NOT UNTIL JUNE 17, 1962, IN NEUANLAGE, TWO MONTHS after his ordination, that Herman preached his first sermon. The two-month delay was intentional in order to give Herman adequate time to prepare for the task of preaching, particularly since spring is a busy season for farmers, and sermon preparation was a new experience for him. After his first sermon, he would become a regular part of the ministerial preaching rotation in the area. Public speaking in general, and the preparation of sermons in particular, were daunting challenges for many new ministers. Like other Old Colony Mennonite ministers in Saskatchewan, Herman did not have any formal theological education to prepare him for the challenges of pastoral ministry, or any homiletical instruction to prepare him for the specific task of preaching. However, he was not unfamiliar with public speaking, as he had occasionally presented public devotionals in his role as a school board trustee.[30] One listener vividly remembers a devotional presented by Herman Friesen featuring a verse from Psalm 23, "*Der Herr is* mein *hirte*" ("The Lord is *my* shepherd"), with a clear emphasis on the word "my."

Herman's inaugural sermon provides a rare moment of transparency into the state of his mind at the time of his ministerial election. The sermon is

a candid attempt by an individual who has been summoned to a leadership
task to find a balance between, on the one hand, an attitude of humility and
dependence on God, without resorting to complete self-deprecation and
effacement, and, on the other hand, a clear assertion of his willingness to
respond obediently to the congregation's call and to the expectations that
accompany that call, without sounding overconfident and self-reliant.[31] It
is typical of the distress experienced by Old Colony Mennonite individuals,
who agonized deeply over the decision of whether to accept such a responsibility, knowing that it represented a significant, life-altering commitment
that would impact their family, farm, and relationships with friends and
extended family. Many struggled with feelings of inadequacy and unworthiness, on the one hand, and the desire to respond with obedience to the
call of God on the other.[32]

It is not hard to sense the anxiety and the almost overwhelming feelings
of inadequacy when reading Herman's first sermon,[33] despite the fact he
was an experienced and competent leader. It is specifically written to com-
memorate his induction into ministry, and it follows the standard structure
found in Old Colony Mennonite sermons: a brief introductory meditation
that includes a prayer led by the minister, an invitation to a time of silent
congregational prayer, a homily featuring a specific biblical text, a second
invitation to a time of silent congregational prayer, and a concluding bene-
diction. The sermon begins with a prayer and an open confession of his
own sinful tendencies and personal limitations. He describes himself as
"weak and needy," as "a poor sinner incapable of all good," and as "a miserable sinner, rotten through and through, from the soles of my feet to the
top of my head." The admission of his own struggles serves as the basis for
a more extended reflection on human sinfulness, and the importance of
staying on the "narrow path." Several times he references his own sense of
inadequacy by describing himself as "weak and lacking in understanding of
this difficult task," as being an "incompetent messenger," and by claiming
that "in me there is no strength or capability for this important work." He
appeals to the congregation to pray that God would "make me capable of
this task," and that he would "be an example in faith, in teaching, in conduct and in love." His own prayer is that God "will give me wisdom and

understanding, a holy and God-pleasing life, and that I might be a good example to the church of God." Despite his flaws and inadequacies, biblical passages such as Jeremiah 1:7 ("You must go to everyone I send you to say whatever I command you"), and 1 Corinthians 9:16 ("Woe to me if I do not preach the gospel") convince him that the election by the congregation is indeed a call from God. To resist would be an act of disobedience: with conviction he states, "The Lord has sent me and by God's help I have determined to go in His name." The sermon concludes with a more confident note that God will provide "grace to enter this work, which God, the Lord, and the congregation have put on me."

Overall, Herman's inaugural sermon presents a prayerful, and poignantly personal, expression of Anabaptist *Gelassenheit*, that is, the humble surrender of one's own interests, combined with a joyous obedience to yielding fully to God's will.[34] The Anabaptist-Mennonite tradition of humility, objectively indicated by the avoidance of ostentatious and attention-seeking behaviour, was seen as not only a key Christian virtue but also a central test of faithfulness. Herman's approach reflected his recognition that, in

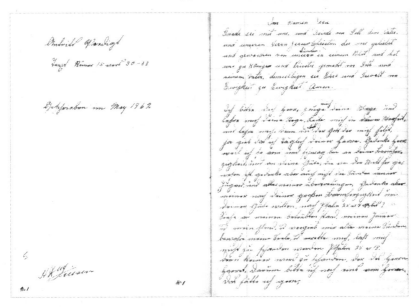

Opening page of Herman's handwritten inaugural sermon, 1962. Courtesy Herman and Margaretha Friesen estate.

order for ministers to be effective, they need the confidence and support of the congregation, and, in turn, ministers need to embody a spirit of humility and model the qualities they wish to see within their parishioners.

As someone learning how to produce written sermons on a regular basis, Herman quickly recognized the value of a consistent routine: his favourite location for sermon preparation was a small writing desk located at the north window of the living room in his home. His sermons were neatly handwritten in small notebooks, using a German Gothic script. Herman was limited in his access to reference works and resources for sermon preparation: there was not an abundance of books in the home, and knowledge about Anabapist-Mennonite history and theology was minimal. In addition to his Bible, the *Catechism*, sermons from other ministers, the *Gesangbuch*, and other hymnals, he sometimes used popular German-language devotional books such as *"Unser Täglich Brot": Biblische Betrachtungen auf alle Tage im Jahre* by Johannes Bachman.[35] He welcomed solitary tasks on the

Herman Friesen sermon collection. Courtesy Mary Guenther.

farm, such as cultivating summer fallow, that did not require much concentration and allowed time for private reflection and mental preparation.

It was not uncommon for Old Colony Mennonite ministers to borrow sermons from the Ältester or from other experienced ministers. Herman had in his possession numerous sermons from other Old Colony Mennonite and Bergthaler Mennonite ministers (for more details, see Appendix B). Despite access to other sermons, his initial trepidation, and the necessary investment of time and energy, Herman prepared his first sermon. There is no indication that any of the sermons Herman preached were written by other ministers, but it is likely he borrowed ideas and expressions from them. Throughout his ministry, he continued to write his own sermons, which reflected both his sense of confidence and ability. Over time, copies of his own sermons were sometimes requested by others—some of his daughters recall the tedious task of hand-copying his sermons so other ministers, particularly those in Mexico, could use them.

Every writer and speaker struggles to find his or her "voice." Aside from the fact that Old Colony Mennonite tradition dictated that sermons were to be read, using a script offered an inexperienced public speaker a level of support and confidence. Nevertheless, Herman occasionally felt free to deviate from his written script to offer short extemporaneous comments. It was often through his sermons that his family, and the larger church community, was able to hear the inner "heart" of Herman's personal faith, which was not as freely expressed in informal conversation. He frequently used poems, or stanzas from hymns, to give more poignant and precise expression to his ideas. It is worth noting that the same level of personal transparency that was present within his first sermon is not as evident in other sermons. Although he does include himself, along with his audience, among those who are in need of admonishment from scripture, he does not incorporate anecdotes from his own life that could serve as instructive examples or that could increase the audience's ability to relate to him as a person. This reflects his awareness that such a convention could have been considered prideful by elevating himself and his own experience as the model for others to emulate. Knowing that his sermons would most likely be used multiple times, and perhaps also by other ministers, might also account for the usage of more general themes and applications, as well as the reluctance to include personal illustrations and anecdotes. Herman frequently posed direct questions to his audience in order to provoke reflection and personal application. The frequent use of expressions such as "dear listener," "dearly beloved," and "dear friends" worked to strengthen an emotional rapport with his audience. This was not merely an artificial convention but rather a genuine indicator of his warm-hearted concern for the spiritual well-being of his parishioners.

Herman's sermons show he quickly adopted the conventional structure used by Old Colony Mennonite preachers for Sunday morning sermons:

- opening invocation/blessing (like a liturgical collect);
- introductory meditation (often taken from a variety of biblical texts);
- invitation to a time of silent congregational prayer;
- reading of the central biblical text (with introductory comments);
- prayer;
- homily (commentary on, and application of, the main biblical text);
- invitation to a time of silent congregational prayer (opportunity for response to sermon);
- benediction/blessing (for example, Numbers 6:24–26);
- dismissal.

Sermons written for specific occasions, such as funerals or engagements, were generally shorter, and did not include all of these components.

Most of his sermons were preached on multiple occasions, some more than a dozen times. This was a practical consideration for lay preachers in an itinerant rotation who did not have the same audience every Sunday. Not only did Herman use his sermons more than once but on numerous occasions sermons were also repeated to the same congregation. One sermon was preached five times to the Neuhorst congregation;[36] other sermons written for specific occasions were also frequently reused. It is not hard to imagine that his hectic combination of farm and ministerial demands might occasionally have created a sense of desperation when considering how he would prepare adequately for all of the more than 430 occasions he was asked or scheduled to speak during his seven-plus years of ministry. Even with the best intentions and planning, unforeseen circumstances arise: it is not possible to schedule sermon preparation for funerals in advance, or plan for emergencies in the lives of his ministerial colleagues (or in his own family).

The inclusion of biblical texts is pervasive within Herman's sermons. It reflects his conviction regarding the Bible's authority in the life of the church. He never considers it necessary to offer an explanation for any appeal to its authority but simply uses the *Catechism's* affirmation of the Bible as the "Word of God" as the self-evident basis from which to call people to repentance and to be followers of Jesus Christ. He avoids questioning biblical texts, and never tries to resolve tensions or difficult statements. When citing a passage of scripture, he tends to read it as if it were written directly to him (and his listeners). This is done without information regarding historical context, genre, exegesis, or any explanation of the interpretation that takes place when an individual reads and uses a text.[37] Textual criticism and hermeneutics are not topics that are addressed within the *Catechism* or *Confession of Faith*, therefore his lack of interest (or awareness) is not surprising. His sermons are not so much about familiarizing people with the Bible itself, or about exploring particular theological ideas, as they are about using specific texts to encourage spiritual self-examination and seek an immediate response from his audience. Seven years of preaching experience is enough time to identify themes and see the emergence of a particular voice and style, but it is too short of a preaching career to detect significant developments in theological perspective and biblical interpretation.

Because of the strong emphasis on admonition and exhortation to ethical living, Anabaptist-Mennonite preaching has been characterized as hortatory.[38] With the exception of the *Catechism* and the *Gesangbuch*, which had been in circulation for a long time, the Old Colony Mennonites did not produce theological or devotional material for distribution to their members that was more responsive to current issues and circumstances. Sermons, therefore, provided one of the few forms of theological discourse in the life of the community. They were clearly the centrepiece of a Sunday morning service, with the greatest proportion of time allocated to preaching. The gravity of the sermon was amplified in the Old Colony Mennonite Church by the authority and deference given to ministers, who collectively were expected to provide an authoritative understanding of the Bible. The role and influence of public oral presentations such as the sermon in shaping the understanding of society is accentuated in religious communities that eschew the use of modern media.

Although Herman was more accommodating toward Canadian society than his predecessors, and was open to some innovation in church practice, his approach to scripture and his theological teaching reflect a high degree of consistency with the theological convictions expressed in the *Catechism* and *Confession of Faith*. The influence of both documents figures prominently in Herman's preaching. Prior to baptism on Pentecost Sunday, several services were allocated to the presentation of baptismal candidates, who were expected to recite publicly the answers to all of the *Catechism* questions. As the presiding minister, Herman used the occasion to insert his own brief commentary on a range of theological issues.[39] Assuming that usage is an indication of priority, it is worth noting that Herman's most frequently used sermon featured the articles of the *Confession of Faith*. He preached on the articles at least once each year, and sometimes as often as four times per year (for example, in 1963 and again in 1967).[40] One of his sermons on the *Confession of Faith* was presented nineteen times. In part, such repetition was due to the role played by the Ältester, particularly as part of the process of baptism. Nevertheless, ensuring a high level of familiarity with the basic theological affirmations of the church was a high priority for Herman.

Although sincerity and strength of conviction are evident in abundance in Herman's life and preaching, absent are indications of familiarity with any works by major theologians, including Anabaptist leaders such as Menno Simons, or awareness of the major theological systems within Christianity. For example, Herman's pervasive emphasis on responding to God's grace and striving to live as faithful Christians to the end of life is consistent with the importance placed on human volition within Anabaptist theology, but nowhere in Herman's sermons is this recognized as an integral feature of Anabaptist-Mennonite theology that differentiates it from some other theological systems such as Calvinism. Occasional lack of nuance in his expression reflects the same lack of theological awareness. For example, in his desire to drive home the reality and depth of human sinfulness to his listeners, his pessimistic description of humanity occasionally sounds vaguely similar to the Calvinist doctrine of total depravity, which was rejected by all early Anabaptist leaders.

Unclear also is the exact role of baptism within the process of salvation. In his introductory meditation addressed to baptismal candidates, Herman asserts that water baptism does not in and of itself bring salvation: "If you don't repent with all your heart and by true faith seek forgiveness in the blood of Christ, external water baptism or joining the congregation simply doesn't suffice."[41] Baptism is considered essential and is more than an outward sign to signal a commitment to a life of Christian discipleship. The lack of precision may reflect some divergence on Herman's part with the more sacramental approach in the *Confession of Faith*, which asserts that baptism is necessary for "the washing away of sins through the merits of the blood of Christ. For as water serves to cleanse the body, so the blood of Jesus Christ takes away all sins of all sinners who faithfully and penitently receive baptism…through baptism we are accepting Christ in faith."[42] Consistent with the Old Colony Mennonite tradition, for Herman, baptism marked a critical moment when, as he tells the newly baptized, "you are not only being accepted into the congregation as members" but "God will write your name in the book of life and graciously accept you into his heavenly kingdom," assuming the appropriate motivation for wanting to be baptized, and an ongoing lifestyle characterized by consistent "holiness and righteousness."[43]

Despite the lack of familiarity with theological systems, Herman's sermons do contain various tensions that are present within the Bible and some theological systems. The extent to which he is aware of these tensions is unclear: he does not draw specific attention to them, or offer explanations or resolutions. The two paradoxical dilemmas that predominate in Herman's preaching are simply accepted without reconciliation. First, when reviewing the entire sermon collection, one frequently encounters the portrayal of God as a fierce and angry judge of human sinfulness, along with occasional juxtaposition with a softer description of God as a gentle father who loves and desires to forgive. As a preacher, Herman tended to place a stronger emphasis on avoiding the terrifying severity of God's judgment of human sinfulness than on responding to the generous grace of God as the means for motivating his parishioners toward a vigilant attentiveness of their spiritual condition.[44] Warning listeners of the need to "put one's house in order," because of the eternal consequences of life choices, was likely perceived as generating a greater degree of urgency in his listeners, which was then amplified further by reference to human mortality and reminders of the inevitability of God's judgment.[45] Second, evident is the simultaneous recognition of personal transformation that accompanies spiritual regeneration and the ongoing persistence of sinful temptations and choices. According to Herman, no one is able to keep God's commandment to love one's neighbour without the strength provided by the Holy Spirit, and, yet, reminiscent of the Apostle Paul's lament in Romans 7:15, he recognizes that no Christian ever loves any neighbour fully or completely.[46] On multiple occasions, he emphasizes the need for consistency between an inner spiritual transformation and the external behaviours exhibited by someone professing to be a Christian. Put differently, the actions of a professing Christian validate the authenticity of any internal spiritual experience, hence the constant need to "test oneself" and the fruits of one's life.[47] For some, such constant introspection generated considerable anxiety and uncertainty about the surety of salvation. Herman's limited range of reading and formal education accounts, at least in part, for the occasional lack of nuance that is present in his discussion of theological concepts.

Without a clear understanding of the Anabaptist-Mennonite theological system upon which the *Catechism* and *Confession of Faith* were based, Herman's preaching centred around a simple narrative.[48] Life is a journey on which one is faced with a choice of two roads—the broad road of sin and the narrow road of salvation—that end with death and the inevitable judgment of God.

Our life is nothing other than a journey—when we are born we begin the journey, and when we die the journey ends and we enter eternity. What counts on our journey here is which path we walked in this life. If we travel on the good path of faith and piety and in the fear of God, with humility, then it will end in the heavenly splendor. If, however, we travel the broad road of unbelief, ill nature, godlessness, or self-created righteousness, it will end in eternal ruin and condemnation. Therefore, let us constantly consider how we lead our lives.[49]

Along with the *Catechism*, Herman affirms that the true way to salvation is by faith in Jesus Christ. Human beings are the ones responsible for their acts of disobedience (sin) and the consequences. They are also, therefore, responsible for neglecting or appropriating God's offer of grace and salvation if one hopes to enter into "the [eternal] house of rest through the grace and mercy of God."[50] And it is not enough to profess faith by words alone. Regeneration invariably produces a godly life, thus actions are a confirmation of real repentance. In the words of the *Catechism*, "Whosoever is born of God, does not commit sin": one must, therefore, continually "prove with words and deeds that we are truly Christ's followers."[51] "No one," emphasizes Herman, "is on the narrow road except the ones who earnestly strive to keep the commandments laid out in the Sermon on the Mount."[52] Adding urgency to his message is the ever-present threat that God could "withdraw His grace from those who have received grace and mercy."[53] Herman encourages his listeners to maintain a constant vigilance against sin, as the temporal world is a dangerous place, filled with distracting temptations that can easily lead an individual astray.

Consistent with the tradition of hortatory, which tends to be a unidirectional and dogmatic form of proclamation, for Herman, the primary goals of preaching were to warn, to admonish, and to encourage his parishioners to persist in their Christian walk. From his inaugural sermon onward, it is impossible to miss the intense seriousness and urgency of his concern for calling people to repentance and holy living. This concern is frequently combined with the sober reminder to prepare for the inevitability of death and the futility of trying to avoid the eventual judgment before God.[54] Herman encourages his listeners to persist in earnestly striving toward selfless holy living, and to test one's spiritual condition regularly for evidence of the fruits of the Spirit: these are the essential components of a faithful

Christian life.[55] According to Herman, the primary calling and duty of Christians is that they, in the words of the Apostle Paul, "work out [their] salvation with fear and trembling" (Philippians 2:12).[56]

Some Mennonites have criticized the Old Colony Mennonite emphasis on "striving" as promoting a "works righteousness" approach to soteriology (doctrine of salvation), but as David Schroeder observes, Old Colony Mennonites tend to emphasize the future tense of salvation (I trust I will be saved), whereas Mennonites that have been more influenced by Protestant theology emphasize the past tense of salvation (I have been saved).[57] The more Protestant understanding of soteriology stands in contrast to the emphasis within Old Colony soteriology, in which the eventual outcome of a person's eternal salvation is not as evident in this life and somewhat dependent upon the individual's trust in God and their persistence in a lifelong faithful obedience to Christ and the church. Old Colony Mennonite soteriology did not emphasize "assurance of salvation" as did evangelical Protestants, not because there was not a high degree of confidence and trust in Christ's salvific work on the cross but to avoid spiritual pride and presumption[58]—it is, after all, only God who knows the ultimate eternal destiny of each person.[59]

In Old Colony soteriology, the lines between justification and sanctification are somewhat intertwined as the individual cooperates with God in living a life of righteousness, which is measured in part by faithful adherence to the ideals demanded by the community of God.[60] Old Colony Mennonite soteriology also has a strong communal dimension. Calvin Redekop notes, "The highest goal is the goal of salvation, which is understood as acceptance by God as faithful people rather than [only] as faithful individuals."[61] An individual's deviance can put the community at risk, at least if deviation is allowed to persist and be copied by other people. Deviance from communal ideals is understood as a manifestation of worldliness: conformity is enforced by the threat of excommunication and social ostracism. This understanding is rooted in the Old Colony Mennonite self-conception as God's chosen (and pure) people, who had covenanted to remain faithful to God and to their church.

Although the call to be separate from the world and to avoid worldliness was unmistakably clear in Herman's preaching, it is surprising to note how seldom he provides any indication in his sermons about what activities he considered to be worldly. The few examples of specific activities Herman renounced as worldly included playing ball, an interest in modern fashions, watching television, visiting beer parlours, and neglecting church attendance.[62] It may be that he offered some additional Low German directives extemporaneously. Nevertheless, the reluctance to name specific activities is surprising because worldliness was a category readily applied by church leaders in more casual conversation to specific activities that leaders did not want people to adopt, and often without clear explanations for how such practices might be sinful (for example, living in urban centres). As Calvin Redekop notes, generally absent in such traditional societies is a philosophy (or theology) of change that sees both the dynamic evolution of culture over time and participation in society as inevitable facts of life.[63]

Unlike some of his predecessors, Herman obviously did not consider complete geographical isolation within Canadian society to be a necessary condition for avoiding worldliness, and therefore did not promote migration. Immersed in a tradition that was not adequately equipped theologically to navigate a strategy of intentional, albeit limited, cultural engagement, on what grounds did Herman assess the legitimacy of the many cultural changes that took place during the course of his life, many of which he adopted? Several scholars who have studied Old Colony Mennonites note how maintaining intact their beliefs and practices (tradition) is often the rationale used to resist cultural changes. The most common explanation among Old Colony Mennonites for the maintenance of specific traditions was simply "So ha' wie daut emma jedohne" (that is how we have always done it). Maintaining both beliefs and practices they assumed were based upon the Bible and their Anabaptist-Mennonite heritage made it unthinkable to countenance change. Obedience to the Ältester's interpretation of acceptable and unacceptable cultural practices served as a test of faith and fidelity to the church. Karen Warkentin argues this phrase is not an accurate description of the Old Colony Mennonite relationship to cultural changes, but rather it is a way of expressing their ongoing commitment to their baptismal vows of obedience and to the needs and identity of the congregation (the Gemeinde).[64] It reflects the desire to retain intact a strong sense of solidarity as a faith-based community over and against the initiatives and interests of an individual. This pursuit emerged out of a theological vision of the church as a living extension of Christ and his disciples. Such a community is defined and reinforced by a communal way of life considered to be consistent with the expectations of faithful Christian discipleship. A certain degree of freedom was necessary in order to live according to their theological convictions (for example, exemption from military service), and consistency was easier to maintain in geographically isolated communities.[65] As Royden Loewen observes, the idea "that Mennonites, unlike other groups, could transplant their societies to North American grasslands [or elsewhere] without much change requires tempering."[66] Herman Friesen's experience suggests the relationship between the Old Colony Mennonites and culture (as with all religious groups) has always been, and will always be, dynamic.

As noted, for some Old Colony Mennonite leaders, an essential aspect of a strategy for avoiding cultural change was a posture of constant preparedness to migrate. The true Christian is a "pilgrim and stranger" in the world, whose life must be characterized by a readiness to sacrifice and suffer. Others emphasized strict adherence to traditional practices within the church while maintaining a degree of control over cultural accommodation outside of the church. Maintaining consistency in matters of faith and church practice was a means for keeping a theological system intact, and perhaps assuring themselves of their faithfulness to unchanging eternal values. Leaders needed some way by which to provide stability and a sense of security in the midst of a rapidly changing world. But, as Herman (at least implicitly) seems to have recognized, it is not possible to define worldliness only by accepting or rejecting specific cultural practices in a consistent way over time. Herman frequently describes worldliness in his preaching as selfishness, a proclivity that does not respect geographical boundaries and cannot always be equated with specific actions.[67] This focus on motivation instead of on a list of specific cultural practices that need to be rejected may have been one principle that Herman used for navigating his own gradual accommodation to Canadian society. As helpful as this approach may have been for himself and others, Herman's written sermons offer little guidance on how to detect such self-interest. A second "biblical" decision-making principle for navigating cultural choices is observable in Herman's response, described in more detail below, to an invitation to assist a group of Old Colony Mennonites who had been excommunicated in Belize (known as British Honduras at the time).

From the first century onward, the life of the church has been structured around the annual cycle of services determined by the main events of the Christian year. In the earliest church, there were two main celebrations: the Lord's Day (Sunday), and the fifty-day period of Pentecost. Like the Ältesten who preceded him, Herman used the lectionary (*Anweisung der Lieder*), with its one-year calendar and pre-assigned cycle of biblical readings that is included in the *Gesangbuch*, as a general guide for church celebrations and preaching throughout the year. The lectionary used by the Russian Mennonites relied heavily on the Lutheran lectionary.[68] It provided a handy schedule for helping ministers reflect regularly on a standardized set of texts that covered a substantial portion of the New Testament. It often made the decision regarding the selection of a biblical text for any given Sunday easier for ministers, as well as for song leaders who could use the index of hymns included in the lectionary. The Old Colony Mennonite Church calendar began with the six-week season of Advent and Christmas, which flowed into New Year's and the six Sundays of Epiphany, followed by the season of Lent, Easter, and Pentecost. Pentecost is followed by Trinity Sunday and twenty-seven weeks of ordinary time. Scattered throughout the year are various high holidays marked by two or even three successive days of services (for example, Christmas, Easter, and Pentecost), and other days of special services (for example, Epiphany, Good Friday, and Ascension). For Old Colony Mennonites, Pentecost Sunday has always been the preferred occasion for baptism (unlike many other Christian traditions that used Easter). Communion was scheduled twice a year, shortly after Pentecost and again after the Canadian Thanksgiving weekend. Communion did not coincide with baptism because, as Donald Stoesz notes, "There had to be at least one sermon on the importance of being reconciled with one's brother and sister before partaking of the Christian symbol of reconciliation."[69]

The use of the lectionary schedule was not rigidly enforced, as it was impossible for the Ältester, who was the only one authorized to conduct baptism and administer communion, to be present in all congregations on the prescribed Sundays. In addition, several Old Colony Mennonite practices were consistently given priority over strict adherence to the lectionary. For example, many of the services during the Easter, Ascension, and Pentecost sections of the lectionary were used to teach the *Confession of Faith* and to give baptismal candidates opportunity to recite their memorized answers to the *Catechism* questions. Flexibility in the use of the lectionary schedule is evident also in the selection of biblical texts that were used in sermons. There is a much closer correlation between the texts used

Painted Old Colony Mennonite Church in Kronsthal, near Herman and Margaretha's farm, 1962. Courtesy Jake Buhler.

in Herman's sermons and lectionary readings for high holidays[70] than for sermons preached on Sundays in ordinary time, that is, the twenty-seven Sundays following Trinity Sunday.[71] Moreover, sermons initially written for a specific Sunday within the church calendar were sometimes used by Herman for other Sundays (for example, a sermon on Matthew 18:23–35, a text for the twenty-second Sunday after Trinity, was used in the months of February, September, and November).[72] For all of its practical advantages, the itinerant system did not always make it possible to maintain a strict adherence to the liturgical calendar within the *Gesangbuch*, so one occasionally notes some unusual sermon selections in Herman's preaching schedule (for example, in 1964, he preached a Palm Sunday sermon in Kronsthal shortly *after* Easter).

Alongside the reading selections within the lectionary, it appears that at least some of the Kanadier Mennonite groups in Canada had developed their own canon of texts for specific occasions. Several of Herman's sermons reflect the same patterns found in a thorough study of Sommerfelder preaching in southern Manitoba, including, for example, the use of Romans 10:9–10 as the key text for sermons featuring the articles in the *Confession of Faith*, and the use of 1 Peter 1:22–23 for sermons on New Year's Day.[73] It is clear Herman was aware of the well-established traditions created by the use of the lectionary, but he also felt a certain liberty to adapt its usage to suit particular situations. It functioned mostly as a convenient aid for planning services and preparing sermons. It may be that a lack of awareness of the internal coherence of the lectionary prevented him from using it more intentionally and fully as a tool for increasing the biblical literacy of the congregation, or as a means for guiding the spiritual formation of a congregation—Herman relied more heavily on the *Catechism* and articles in the *Confession of Faith* as the central documents for this latter task.

It was customary for Old Colony Mennonite ministers to keep a careful record of specific ministerial activities. Herman used a notebook in which he meticulously recorded not only the dates and places where he preached but also home and hospital visitations, number of people baptized, number of people to whom he served communion, notes regarding membership transfer requests, obituary details for funerals, song lists, and other miscellaneous comments regarding ministerial matters. Even though the notebook does not include the innumerable meetings, phone calls, and preparation time, it nevertheless provides a glimpse into the frenetic pace of life of these bi-vocational leaders and the expectations they faced. The information in Herman's notebook, along with his sermons, makes it possible to compile a succinct statistical summary of his ministerial activities (see Table 1 and Appendix A). Herman preached over three hundred times as part of regular church services during his seven-year ministry. This was supplemented by speaking responsibilities at another 115 occasions such as funerals, weddings, major anniversaries, and engagement celebrations. On average, this is almost sixty speaking engagements per year. He presided at nine brotherhood meetings, and served communion to more than 5,500 people, often as part of home or hospital visitations. He conducted two ministerial elections and two ordinations.

But, more than providing a detailed chronological record of Herman's preaching and ministerial activities, a careful reading of the notebook also offers a valuable window into the worship practices and the life of the Old Colony Mennonite Church community. Seeing the details of ministerial activities distributed throughout the year provides a fuller understanding of the pragmatic nature, and the personal impact on ministers, of the bi-vocational, itinerant, pastoral ministry model used by the Old Colony Mennonites, and by many other Christian groups scattered throughout the rural regions of Canada. Participation by ministers in public events that marked major life transitions in the lives of parishioners, such as baptism, engagement and wedding celebrations, and funerals, reflects the importance of the church in shaping community life. Herman's preaching schedule demonstrates not only the important guiding role of the lectionary and liturgical calendar in ordering the experience of corporate worship but also the flexibility given to an Ältester to deviate from lectionary readings when it was deemed necessary. The willingness to customize services so they could be conducted in private homes to accommodate those unable to attend regular services reflects a pragmatic approach to pastoral care.

Table 1: Summary of Ministerial Activities

Year	Regular Preaching	Funeral Services	Wedding Ceremonies	Engagement Talks	Services Conducted in Homes	Communion Services in Homes or Hospitals	Brotherhood Meetings	Individuals Baptized	Communion Served
1962	20	2	1	1	2	0	0	0	0
1963	47	8	3	3	5	13	2	0	408
1964	47	9	3	2	3	14	0	17	858
1965	41	9	4	2	0	13	1	20	775
1966	38	17	4	2	4	14	2	20	825
1967	45	10	1	3	4	14	2	12	822
1968	45	14	3	1	9	19	2	8	1,150
1969	36	7	5	1	1	4	0	6	671
Total	319	76	24	15	28	91	9	83	5,509

As a Leader

IT DID NOT TAKE HERMAN LONG TO MAKE HIS IMPACT FELT AS THE leader of the Old Colony Mennonite Church. As noted, he was the first Ältester in Saskatchewan who did not organize, or even advocate for, another migration. He was certainly aware of discussions among Old Colony Mennonite communities in Canada about locations for new colonies that were being considered at the time (for example, British Honduras and Bolivia): he neither promoted these ventures nor tried to discourage people from participating if they were so inclined.[74] He wisely recognized the potential for division if he were to take a strong position either for or against such migrations. Some members of the church had relatives who had recently migrated elsewhere, or who were themselves sympathetic to the strategy of migration but were unable to do so. This group was generally not interested in seeing changes take place in the life of the church. Other members in the church, particularly younger adults, were not interested in migration or increased isolation, as they were establishing roots in the area not only as farmers but also as labourers and tradesmen in and around urban centres. Many of them were eager to see the church adopt some of the practices already in use in other Mennonite denominations, particularly in the areas of music and language. Herman had a well-established reputation for being an advocate for change, so his immediate challenge as Ältester was to moderate the pace of change—too fast would alienate those interested in conserving intact their church experience, too slow would mean increasing to a stream the steady trickle of individuals opting for other churches in the region.

Herman's ambivalence toward issues that had previously warranted severe censure from church leaders is indicative of a gradual redefinition that was taking place on the part of Old Colony Mennonites living in Canada.[75] Herman neither challenged directly the religious vision that surrounded the numerous migrations nor did he attempt to construct an alternative religious narrative for remaining in Canada. He led less by words and more by his actions in accepting aspects of modern Canadian culture. One mechanism for obtaining feedback from church members was calling a brotherhood meeting. During his brief tenure as Ältester, Herman called nine such meetings. One was used for the election of two new ministers and a deacon in 1964. Several were used to discuss the possibility of building a care home for seniors. Like other Ältesten, Herman often preferred to use the authority of his position to make decisions on more minor matters. Aside from electing leaders, or voting on major initiatives and projects, congregations did not have a great deal of involvement in decision making.

A particularly memorable brotherhood meeting took place in early 1969. Following a schism within one of the Old Colony Mennonite colonies in British Honduras, the Old Colony Mennonite Ältester in Manitoba, Jacob Penner, was asked to assist an excommunicated group in organizing a new Old Colony Mennonite Church. Penner invited Herman to accompany him: the presence of two Ältesten would represent a stronger endorsement of the new group. Perhaps recalling the long-standing rancour that surrounded the reorganization of the Old Colony Mennonite Church in 1930, when Johann Loeppky was chosen as Ältester, Herman called a brotherhood meeting to see whether the church membership would support his involvement. A few expressed reluctance about helping a group that had been excommunicated. Others, including Herman, argued the reasons for excommunication (use of rubber tires on tractors) were not "biblical" and, therefore, the excommunication should not be considered valid. The majority supported his involvement, and he did accompany Penner in February 1969. This incident offers a rare glimpse into the decision-making principle used by Herman to navigate cultural choices. Presumably, if a cultural practice was not prescribed in the Bible, it could potentially be considered permissible. Herman obviously felt sufficiently confident in this approach to risk involvement in the affairs of Old Colony Mennonite Churches elsewhere.

As the leader, Herman was well aware of how multiple migrations had impacted the overall membership of the church in his own region by diminishing the size of the community and depleting its resources. The most recent migration to Prespatou, British Columbia, just prior to his election as minister, had reduced membership by yet another 25 per cent. Herman's inventory of the number of Old Colony Mennonite families that remained in the Hague-Osler area in 1968 reflects the transition from a community comprised primarily of rural farmers to one with a substantial number of urban-based employees. His census (see Table 2) identified 273 Old Colony Mennonite families (approximately one thousand people). By 1968, almost 50 per cent of these families lived in, or within twenty-five kilometres of, Saskatoon. With baptismal numbers barely keeping pace with the number of deaths during the 1960s (see Table 1), the prospects for long-term sustainability lay in retaining the interests of a younger generation. It is not surprising, then, to see that Herman invested energy into such initiatives.

Table 2: Old Colony Mennonite Families in the Hague-Osler Area, 1968 (Arranged in order of distance from Saskatoon.)

Town/City	Number of Families
Hague	20
Hepburn	10
Neuanlage	11
Reinland	4
Blumenheim	32
Gruenfeld	12
Neuhorst	22
Edenburg	9
Osler	10
Kronsthal	10
Warman	58
Martensville	30
Clarks Crossing	4
Saskatoon	41
Total	273

Herman was convinced that Sunday services alone would not suffice as the means for nurturing the spiritual lives of church members. As noted, he was an advocate for those public school teachers who organized evening programs for the young people. He continued to encourage and support the work of the Sunday schools. In addition, he initiated Friday evening *Owentstund* (evening hour) meetings in Neuhorst, which already had a building on site designated for use as a Sunday school. Initially, it began as a combination of hymn singing and catechetical instruction for baptismal candidates. Instruction was in the Low German language, which was more accessible for many than the High German used in Sunday morning services. Herman permitted baptismal candidates to read their responses to catechism questions when presented during Sunday morning services, rather than expecting them to memorize the entire *Catechism*. This adjustment alleviated a great deal of stress for some young people. Over time, the format of Owentstund changed as it became more of an informal service with singing and Bible study.

Still other changes followed. Electricity was installed in the Sunday school building in Neuhorst, extending the hours of usage during evening events. Perhaps most symbolic was the permission to include a short, English-language sermon at funerals to accommodate the inclusion of non-German speaking attendees. With the completion of the Warman Mennoniten Altenheim, a retirement home for Mennonite seniors completed in 1968, he invited families to sing at Altenheim events who were familiar with gospel hymns and four-part harmony. Some speculate that had he remained Ältester for a longer period of time, he might have introduced both language and musical changes in Sunday morning services.

Automobile travel increased substantially during the 1950s and 1960s as roads improved and cars became more affordable. Having been to various places across western Canada, and having driven to Mexico and back twice during the 1950s, he recognized how motorized travel could enhance not only relationships with geographically scattered children and extended family members but also his ability to fulfill his church leadership responsibilities and to maintain relationships with people in distant places. His car was used extensively to make pastoral visits to parishioners scattered beyond the immediate Hague-Osler region: in 1968, he travelled more than 1,500 kilometres for visitation. During his seven-year tenure as Ältester, Herman travelled beyond Saskatchewan regularly on church-related matters that invariably included preaching assignments in local Old Colony Mennonite congregations. This included at least six trips to southern Manitoba, three to both La Crete, Alberta, and Fort St. John, British Columbia, one trip to Fort St. John only, one trip to Aylmer, Ontario, and a trip (by airplane) to British Honduras.[76]

The commitment of time and expense to maintain a network of fraternal relationships among the geographically scattered Old Colony Mennonite communities is an indication of its importance to Herman. At the same time, Herman made it a point to build relationships with some ministerial colleagues in the area from other Mennonite denominations, including, among others, Ältester Abram J. Buhler from the Bergthaler Mennonite Church, John Janzen from the Neuanlage Grace Mennonite Church, Jake Pauls from the Osler Mennonite Church, and individuals from the Nationwide Fellowship Churches. His friendship with these men provided a more distant and detached perspective, and periodically became a valued source of advice.

The hectic combination of farm work, sermon preparation, pastoral care and visitation, funeral and wedding planning, and church leadership and administration meant life was constantly full for Herman. Despite the labour-saving effect of mechanization on the farm, the unrelenting labour demands of operating a dairy farm were increased for Herman and Margaretha as the younger Friesen children became adults and either sought off-farm employment or married. An integral part of Herman's strategy for coping with both the busy pace of his life and the need for competent farm labour was the invitation, in October 1965, to his recently married daughter Helena and her husband John Enns to assist in running the dairy and farm operation. The young couple proved themselves to be very capable and quickly gained Herman's respect and trust. Two years later, Herman's son Jake and daughter-in-law Tina (Dyck) also became partners in the farm operation and moved their family to Herman and Margaretha's farm. The partnership arrangements worked well for all concerned, and enabled Herman to devote his time to church work.

As Ältester, Herman took an interest in the operation of the *Waisenamt*, a trust institution designed to handle the estates of deceased church members. It had a particular mandate to protect the interests of orphans (with boys and girls given an equal inheritance) and widows (to be treated the same as widowers). At times, it also functioned somewhat like a credit union by extending loans to church members from funds being held in trust. As long as borrowers were conscientious and able to repay loans, the system worked well. The Depression years created financial difficulty for some people, which depleted the cash reserves of the Waisenamt; the repayment of debts so estates could be settled took decades to resolve in some instances. The necessity of maintaining this organization decreased by the 1960s due to legislative changes and the emergence of other local institutions such as the Mennonite Trust. By the time Herman Friesen's tenure as Ältester began, efforts were already underway to close down the operation of the Waisenamt. According to Abram G. Janzen, who was the manager of the Waisenamt at the time, Herman's experience in community leadership gave him "a certain understanding of things," which was appreciated.[77] But Herman was also known, even feared by some, as someone who could be very "determined." While he supported the work of the manager by endorsing policies that enabled the Waisenamt to operate more effectively, Herman's occasional efforts to get more directly involved were gently, but firmly, rebuffed. Janzen was very diligent in following advice given to him by his predecessor, Jacob F. Guenter, never to divulge the financial position of the Waisenamt account to members of the ministerial. This protected church leaders from real and/or perceived conflict of interest situations, and from any temptation to utilize their knowledge and power for self-interested actions. By the early 1970s, the work of the Waisenamt had come to an end.

A particularly notable achievement during Herman's tenure as Ältester was the construction of the Warman Mennoniten Altenheim (later renamed the Warman Mennonite Special Care Home), a retirement home where older members of the church who needed special care would be able to reside in a comfortable and familiar atmosphere. The project is one of the best examples of Herman's openness to considering new ideas, his willingness to work collaboratively with other Mennonite groups, and his ability

to navigate relationships with governments in order to accomplish outcomes that would be beneficial for his Old Colony Mennonite community.
A vision for such a project was first presented to the church for discussion at a brotherhood meeting in November 1965. The perceived need for
such an institution reflected the acceptance of contemporary Canadian
trends in the area of elder care that moved away from the expectation that
elderly parents would be cared for by children toward the utilization of
specific-purpose institutions. Early on, Herman realized this undertaking
was too large for the Old Colony Mennonites to carry on their own. As a
result, in 1967, he sought the support and partnership of the irenic Abram
J. Buhler, Ältester of the Bergthaler Mennonite Church.[78] Together the
two leaders guided the joint venture to completion. Despite having an offer
of a government loan, they decided instead to proceed only if they could
raise the funds (over $200,000) that would be necessary for completing the
project. John D. Peters, a member of the Bergthaler Mennonite Church,
generously donated land for the project near the town of Warman. Other
members from the two denominations offered their time and construction skills. Construction began in August 1967, and the home officially
opened on October 30, 1968. The experience gained through Herman's
previous involvement in municipal politics proved to be an invaluable asset
for accomplishing such a project. Over the years, the Altenheim became
home to hundreds of Mennonite seniors in need of affordable housing and
assisted living services. Ministers from the two denominations provided
pastoral care and took turns organizing weekly worship services. Had
Herman remained Ältester, it is possible the Old Colony and Bergthaler
Mennonites would have collaborated on other projects, and some have
speculated that the two groups might have even eventually amalgamated.

Conclusion

On September 21, 1969, Herman preached twice at the Neuhorst church, once in the morning to the congregation, and again at a funeral in the afternoon to the family and friends of an eighty-year-old parishioner. His sermon that day contained a typical, and, in hindsight, prescient exhortation to motivate people to ponder their spiritual state: "It is a sobering truth that many of us may be standing at the edge of eternity. Many die suddenly without an opportunity to reflect on life after death."[79] There was, of course, no sense this might be a foreshadowing of events in his own life in the week to come.

The morning of Friday, September 26, 1969, began like many other days on the Friesen dairy farm, with the early morning task of milking cows. By mid-morning, Herman had decided to use a tractor with a front-end loader to do some tasks on his land located several kilometres south of the farmyard. Margaretha and her daughter Helena were busy harvesting garden produce. Herman left the yard with several steel drums, which were often used to haul water or animal feed, suspended from the front-end loader. When he did not return for lunch, Margaretha and Helena urged John Enns, Herman's son-in-law, to go investigate. To his horror, he discovered Herman almost one kilometre south of the farm by the side of the road, conscious but with his head pinned under an upside-down tractor. As he had made his way along the road, one of the barrels had inadvertently been released from the loader in front of the tractor, causing the tractor to drive over the barrel, overturn, and land on top of Herman. It was not the first time Herman was involved in a tractor rollover mishap. Two years previously, on June 10, 1967, Herman narrowly escaped serious injury in a similar accident in the ravine behind his dairy barn. On that occasion, the tractor pinned only his leg. Fortunately, Herman was discovered shortly after the incident and his leg was released. Only minutes later, the tractor burst into flames.

Working furiously to free Herman as quickly as possible, but unable to do so, John quickly went to get the help of Jake, Herman's son. The family members hurried back to the scene of the incident, and, with Margaretha comforting him, the two men used another tractor to release Herman, and then rushed him by car to hospital in Saskatoon. En route to Saskatoon City Hospital, their speed attracted the attention of a police cruiser. The officer immediately agreed to escort the desperate procession to the hospital, and radioed ahead to prepare emergency room staff. They arrived at the hospital at about 2 p.m., where Herman was immediately rushed into surgery. He died of his injuries later that same afternoon.

News of his accident and sudden death came as a devastating shock not only to his family but also to the people of the Old Colony Mennonite Church, as well as to many friends and neighbours within the community. The funeral was held on October 2, 1969, with a service in the morning at the Warman Altenheim, and in the afternoon in the Old Colony Mennonite Church in Neuanlage. Ältester Jacob Penner, a long-time friend who was the head of the Old Colony Mennonite Church in Manitoba, led the services. The Bergthaler Ältester Abram Buhler, and Peter Zacharias, a local Old Colony Mennonite minister, assisted him. More than one thousand people attended to support the family and pay their last respects. The church community struggled to come to terms with the implications of losing a leader who was regarded by many as, in the words of Jacob Wiebe, one of Herman's ministerial colleagues, "their beloved bishop."

Herman's death brought to an abrupt end the strategy of gradual accommodation among the Old Colony Mennonites in Saskatchewan. A long-standing minister, who had participated in a move to Fort Vermilion, Alberta, during the 1950s, as well as the migration to Prespatou during the early 1960s, Julius Enns, returned from the Fort St. John area to Saskatchewan to become the new Ältester. He was more reserved and conservative as a leader, and emphasized a return to, and the preservation of, historical traditions and practices.

The beginning of Herman's life story coincides with the incorporation of the province of Saskatchewan, and his family is among those immigrant pioneers whose back-breaking labour helped establish the agrarian economic foundation for the region. The changes that he, and his growing family, experienced as part of a farming community serve as a window into the impact of developments in the province of Saskatchewan during the first half of the twentieth century. He was part of a close-knit religious community that came to the province in search of an agrarian refuge that would provide the freedom to practise their faith and pursue their way of life without interference. As part of a bloc settlement, they added to the cultural diversity of the province, and established an agrarian village way of life in which they enjoyed a substantial degree of administrative control and educational autonomy, at least for a time. Rapid population growth quickly reduced their sense of isolation, and their reluctance to integrate into Canadian life put the community on a collision course with the assimilationist interests of the government of Saskatchewan (and Manitoba). The hardships of pioneer life, and the difficulties experienced as a result of an escalating government conflict that precipitated multiple migrations, shaped Herman's childhood and early adulthood. As part of a group of families unable (and perhaps also unwilling) to participate in the migrations out of the province, watching these events unfold deeply shaped Herman's life and subsequent attitudes toward societal and political involvement. His experience as a public school board trustee over several decades, and as a municipal councillor, made him more amenable to change than many of the leaders in his church community.

Herman Friesen's story is part of a growing body of historical research on the Low German–speaking Mennonites found in parts of North America and Latin America. As noted throughout, Herman's experience as an Ältester in the Old Colony Mennonite Church is a unique variation in that he was the first person in that role in Saskatchewan who was less separationist, did not promote a migration, and sought an accommodation with a modernizing Saskatchewan. It represents an example of an Old Colony Mennonite community that adopted a gradual strategy of modernization. Long before he became a minister in the church, Herman was already leading the way by incorporating many of the technological changes taking place that contributed to the prosperity of the province and to his own dairy operation. Later, as Ältester, it became his responsibility to help his church community navigate the complex changes taking place around it.

As he watched the occupational, residential, and religious transitions taking place among the people in his church community, including within his own family, one sees occasional glimpses of concern and bewilderment about the fragmentation taking place as he laments the scattering of "our people" and the growing presence of "factions and opinions."[80] His tragic death in 1969 curtailed his ministry after only seven short years: it would only be speculation to consider how this religious community might have fared if it had maintained the course set during Herman's tenure.

The gradually fading memories of, and stories about, Herman Friesen made the desire to complete this book more urgent. As in all biographical studies, aspects of the story are straightforward and simple, other parts are complex and were made more difficult by the fact that Herman did not reveal much of his interior life. As Ältester, he carried himself with both a stoic reservation as well as a kind of formal, statesman-like authority. Aspects of his story are particular to a specific person, some reflect general patterns among Old Colony Mennonites, while still others (more than one might realize) reflect universal features of the human condition.

While reflecting on the writing of her autobiography, Eva Hoffman, a Jewish editor and writer at *The New York Times* who emigrated from Poland, observed, "To some extent, one has to rewrite the past in order to understand it."[81] My goal in writing this biography was to understand better the life and times of my grandfather by taking the personal experiences and recollections that shape family stories and placing them within a larger context in order to expand an understanding of his choices and impact. Through both the interviews and research for this book, I have learned much about the critical events that shaped his approach to life, and about his sacrificial efforts and intense determination to shepherd faithfully the Old Colony Mennonite Church during a time of significant change. Although his faith was private, introspective, and intensely sober (even melancholy), it deeply shaped his response to life experiences that brought a combination of sorrow and joy, and eventually found more public verbal expression through his preaching.

Writing the past not only helps one understand the past better, it also helps one understand oneself better as one traces the way ethnicity and religion are interwoven for centuries in the lives of ancestors to form our heritage. In addition to getting to know better a grandfather I hardly knew while he was alive, I came to understand much more fully what I had intuitively recognized as a young boy, namely that Grampa Friesen was a person of influence. By exploring his world, I appreciated much more fully the challenges he faced not only as a community and church leader but also as a husband and father. In the midst of it all, he was, like all of us, a person with "feet of clay." The weaknesses and foibles of individuals in public positions of leadership are often more visible, and scrutinized with greater vigour. Over time, I have also come to experience something of the weight that comes with the responsibilities and expectations of public leadership. The various parallels in our lives helped me not only to recognize tendencies within myself but also to empathize with Herman as a human being who experienced longings, concerns, joys, and disappointments. In the midst of the mundane details of everyday life, and the challenges of leadership, I believe Herman recognized, at least implicitly, the inevitability of change. Jill Ker Conway's question, "What can we make of...the network of our kin who constitute our tribal past?" will always have a necessarily personal answer: "If we can know them, they are a set of compass points by which we can chart our own course."[82] This is not to suggest that our choices need to be identical to those of our ancestors, but rather that the decisions of our ancestors should provide wisdom for the choices we will face.

Acknowledgements

AS I HAVE PURSUED THE IDEA DURING THE PAST TWO DECADES OF completing some kind of historical project featuring the life of my grandfather, Herman D. W. Friesen, I have accumulated numerous debts with those who have assisted in making this idea become a reality. The least I can do is to express publicly my gratitude and appreciation for these contributions and support.

This book has been enriched by those individuals who graciously agreed to answer questions and share memories about their relationship with Herman and Margaretha Friesen, and who offered their insights regarding the impact of Herman's leadership in the Old Colony Mennonite Church in Saskatchewan. These often very personal conversations helped to create a kind of vicarious relationship with Grampa and Gramma.

A special thanks to my parents, Cornie and Elizabeth Guenther, who first alerted me to the existence of Grampa's collection of sermons and various family photographs, answered innumerable questions, and offered hospitality on numerous trips to Saskatoon.

It is a gift to have friends who generously provide their time to help make such a project better. A number of people agreed to read an early draft of the manuscript and to offer their responses, namely Leonard Doell, Henry Wiebe, Alan Guenther, Erika McAuley, Donald Stoesz, David Giesbrecht, and Royden Loewen. Your comments improved the book, and your enthusiastic encouragement to persevere with the project was deeply appreciated. Margaret Ewert, David Giesbrecht, and John B. Toews offered their expertise to translate a considerable number of sermons and documents handwritten in German Gothic script. Your work in making this material accessible was invaluable. As well, Erika McAuley's most capable work as a research assistant helped create space in my life for working on this project during an intensely busy season.

Every historical project relies on the availability of source material. The assistance of the staff at the Mennonite Heritage Centre in Winnipeg, and the Saskatchewan Archives in Saskatoon, was deeply appreciated. The generous financial assistance of the D. F. Plett Historical Research Foundation helped facilitate research, sermon translations, and publication of this book. Various individuals graciously granted permission to include certain material in the book: John Enns, on behalf of the Herman and Margaretha Friesen estate, for the use of sermons and family photos; Conrad Stoesz and Leonard Doell for the use of maps; and Leo Driedger, Jake Buhler, and Mary Guenther for the use of their photos.

The deep commitment on the part of University of Regina Press to tell the stories of the people of Saskatchewan made it the perfect publisher for this book. The insightful and helpful suggestions made by the anonymous reviewers commissioned by the press significantly improved the book. The editorial team at the press, particularly Karen Clark, Kirsten Craven, Kelly Laycock, and Nadine Coderre were exemplary in their patient encouragement, wise advice, and professional assistance in preparing the manuscript for publication.

And, finally, I say thank you to my wife, and best friend, Lois. Without your longanimity, support, and deep love, the completion of this book would simply not have been possible. You never fail to remind me of what is most important in life.

APPENDIX A

Herman D. W. Friesen Ministerial Activities

As noted in Chapter 4, it was customary for many Old Colony Mennonite ministers to keep a careful record of specific ministerial activities. Herman used a notebook in which he meticulously recorded not only the dates and places where he preached but also home and hospital visitations, number of people baptized, number of people to whom he served communion, notes regarding membership transfer requests, obituary details for funerals, song lists, and other miscellaneous comments regarding ministerial matters. The notebook does not refer to the innumerable meetings, phone calls, and preparation time that must also have been a part of his life, but it does provide a glimpse, albeit incomplete, into the frenetic pace of life of these bi-vocational leaders and the expectations they faced.

The information in Herman's notebook, along with details included in his sermons, makes it possible to provide a succinct statistical summary of his ministerial activities (see Table 1 in Chapter 4). This appendix provides a more comprehensive list of ministerial events, including information about the numerous home services conducted by Herman Friesen, the dates and locations of preaching events, and even many of the biblical texts used in his sermons. In addition to providing a detailed chronological record of Herman's preaching and ministerial activities, this information offers a valuable window into the worship practices and the life of an Old Colony Mennonite Church community, for example, the shape of pastoral ministry, the significant role of services conducted in the homes of parishioners, the role of the liturgical calendar in ordering the life of the community, and the nature of an itinerant preaching ministry in rural, agrarian settings.

Date	Activity	Sermon Index #	Biblical Text(s)	Location
3 Apr. 1962	Elected as Minister			Neuanlage
15 Apr. 1962	Ordained as Minister			Neuhorst
17 June 1962	Preached—Inaugural Sermon	5	Jeremiah 1:7; Romans 15:30–33	Neuanlage
8 July 1962	Preached—Inaugural Sermon	5	Jeremiah 1:7; Romans 15:30–33	Neuhorst
14 July 1962	Funeral Service			Private Home
15 July 1962	Preached—Inaugural Sermon	5	Jeremiah 1:7; Romans 15:30–33	Kronsthal
22 July 1962	Preached—Inaugural Sermon	5	Jeremiah 1:7; Romans 15:30–33	Edenburg
29 July 1962	Preached	12	Matthew 5–7; 1 Corinthians 9:24–27	Blumenthal
12 Aug. 1962	Preached	12	Matthew 5–7; 1 Corinthians 9:24–27	Neuanlage
19 Aug. 1962	Preached	12	Matthew 5–7; 1 Corinthians 9:24–27	Neuhorst
26 Aug. 1962	Preached	12	Matthew 5–7; 1 Corinthians 9:24–27	Kronsthal
1 Sept. 1962	Engagement Talk	52		Private Home, Martensville
9 Sept. 1962	Preached	12	Matthew 5–7; 1 Corinthians 9:24–27	Edenburg
23 Sept. 1962	Preached	34	Luke 16:1–9	Blumenheim
30 Sept. 1962	Preached—Thanksgiving	33	Acts 14:17	Neuanlage
30 Sept. 1962	Conducted a Home Service			Private Home, Warman

Date	Activity		Scripture	Place
7 Oct. 1962	Preached	34	Luke 16:1–9	Neuhorst
7 Oct. 1962	Wedding Ceremony	60		Reinland
14 Oct. 1962	Preached	34	Luke 16:1–9	Kronsthal
4 Nov. 1962	Preached—After Communion	27	Psalm 100:6	Edenburg
11 Nov. 1962	Conducted a Home Service			Private Home, Blumenthal
14 Nov. 1962	Funeral Service			Neuanlage
25 Nov. 1962	Preached	37	Luke 18:9–14	Neuhorst
2 Dec. 1962	Preached—Advent Sermon			Kronsthal
9 Dec. 1962	Preached—Advent Sermon			Blumenthal
16 Dec. 1962	Preached—Advent Sermon			St. Laurent, MB
26 Dec. 1962	Preached—Christmas	8	Luke 2:15–20	Neuanlage
30 Dec. 1962	Preached—Last Sunday of Year	24	Genesis 32:10	Neuhorst
1 Jan. 1963	Preached—New Year's Sermon	43	1 Peter 1:22–23	Kronsthal
20 Jan. 1963	Preached	37	Luke 18:9–14	Edenburg
27 Jan. 1963	Preached	37	Luke 18:9–14	Blumenheim
10 Feb. 1963	Preached	36	Matthew 18:23–35	Neuhorst
17 Feb. 1963	Preached	36	Matthew 18:23–35	Kronsthal
24 Feb. 1963	Preached	37	Luke 18:9–14	Reinland, near Fort Vermilion, AB

Date	Activity	Sermon Index #	Biblical Text(s)	Location
3 Mar. 1963	Preached	37	Luke 18:9–14	Blumenort, near Fort Vermilion, AB
6 Mar. 1963	Preached			Worsley, AB
6 Mar. 1963	Conducted a Home Service			Private Home, Worsley, AB
10 Mar. 1963	Preached	36	Matthew 18:23–35	Fort St. John, BC
17 Mar. 1963	Preached			Neuhorst
17 Mar. 1963	Conducted a Home Service			Private Home, Warman
24 Mar. 1963	Preached	37	Luke 18:9–14	Neuanlage
31 Mar. 1963	Preached			Neuhorst
7 Apr. 1963	Preached			Kronsthal
15 Apr. 1963	Preached—Easter	20	Mark 16:1–8	Edenburg
16 Apr. 1963	Preached—Articles of Faith	44	Romans 10:10	Blumenthal
21 Apr. 1963	Preached—Articles of Faith	44	Romans 10:10	Neuanlage
21 Apr. 1963	Conducted a Home Service			Private Home, Hochstadt
28 Apr. 1963	Preached—Articles of Faith	44	Romans 10:10	Neuhorst
5 May 1963	Preached—Articles of Faith	44	Romans 10:10	Kronsthal
2 June 1963	Preached—Pentecost			Neuanlage

3 June 1963	Preached—Pentecost			Neuhorst
4 June 1963	Conducted a Home Service			Private Home, Rosthern
18 June 1963	Elected as Ältester			Neuanlage
23 June 1963	Ordained as Ältester			Neuanlage
29 June 1963	Engagement Talk	54		Warman
30 June 1963	Preached—Inaugural Sermon as Ältester	38	Luke 5:1–11	Neuanlage
30 June 1963	Funeral Service			Neuhorst
7 July 1963	Preached—Inaugural Sermon as Ältester	38	Luke 5:1–11	Neuhorst
11 July 1963	Visitation—Communion			Private Home, Duck Lake
11 July 1963	Visitation—Communion			Private Home, Osler
14 July 1963	Preached—Inaugural Sermon as Ältester	38	Luke 5:1–11	Kronsthal
21 July 1963	Preached—Inaugural Sermon as Ältester	38	Luke 5:1–11	Edenburg
28 July 1963	Wedding Ceremony	60		Private Home, Reinland
4 Aug. 1963	Preached	34	Luke 16:1–9	Neuanlage
11 Aug. 1963	Preached	19	Luke 18:9–14	Neuhorst
18 Aug. 1963	Preached	19	Luke 18:9–14	Kronsthal

Date	Activity	Sermon Index #	Biblical Text(s)	Location
18 Aug. 1963	Conducted a Home Service			Private Home, Warman
21 Aug. 1963	Funeral Service	14		
24 Aug. 1963	Engagement Talk	54		Blumenheim
25 Aug. 1963	Preached	19	Luke 18:9–14	Blumenthal
1 Sept. 1963	Preached	49		Neuanlage
7 Sept. 1963	Funeral Service			Neuhorst
8 Sept. 1963	Preached	12	Matthew 5–7; 1 Corinthians 9:24–27	Neuhorst
22 Sept. 1963	Preached	12	Matthew 5–7; 1 Corinthians 9:24–27	Edenburg
28 Sept. 1963	Engagement Talk	54		Martensville
29 Sept. 1963	Preached—Thanksgiving	33	Acts 14:17	Neuanlage
29 Sept. 1963	Funeral Service	14		Private Home
6 Oct. 1963	Preached—Preparation for Communion	35	Revelation 3:20	Neuhorst
6 Oct. 1963	Wedding Ceremony	2	Tobit 8:5–6	Warman
13 Oct. 1963	Communion Service			Neuanlage
13 Oct. 1963	Communion Service			Edenburg
14 Oct. 1963	Visitation—Communion			Private Home, Blumenheim

Date	Activity			Location
14 Oct. 1963	Visitation—Communion			Private Home, Blumenthal
14 Oct. 1963	Visitation—Communion			Private Home, Hochstadt
15 Oct. 1963	Visitation—Communion			Private Home, Duck Lake
15 Oct. 1963	Visitation—Communion			Private Home, Rosthern
15 Oct. 1963	Visitation—Communion			Private Home, Hague
18 Oct. 1963	Visitation—Communion			Private Home, Osler
18 Oct. 1963	Visitation—Communion			Private Home, Warman
20 Oct. 1963	Communion Service			Neuhorst
20 Oct. 1963	Communion Service			Kronsthal
23 Oct. 1963	Funeral Service			Neuhorst
27 Oct. 1963	Preached—After Communion	27	Psalm 100:6	Neuanlage
27 Oct. 1963	Wedding Ceremony	60		Private Home, Blumenthal
1 Nov. 1963	Visitation—Communion			Private Home, Kronsthal
1 Nov. 1963	Visitation—Communion			Private Home, Warman
1 Nov. 1963	Visitation—Communion			Private Home, Saskatoon
2 Nov. 1963	Brotherhood Meeting			Neuanlage
3 Nov. 1963	Preached	34	Luke 16:1–9	Neuhorst
9 Nov. 1963	Brotherhood Meeting—Ministerial Election			Neuanlage

Date	Activity	Sermon Index #	Biblical Text(s)	Location
17 Nov. 1963	Preached			Blumenthal
21 Nov. 1963	Funeral Service	49		Warman
22 Nov. 1963	Funeral Service	47	Romans 6:23	Neuhorst
24 Nov. 1963	Ministerial & Deacon Ordination			Neuanlage
1 Dec. 1963	Preached—Advent Sermon			Neuhorst
8 Dec. 1963	Preached—Advent Sermon			Kronsthal
15 Dec. 1963	Preached—Advent Sermon			Edenburg
15 Dec. 1963	Funeral Service	47	Romans 6:23	Blumenheim
22 Dec. 1963	Preached—Advent Sermon			Neuanlage
25 Dec. 1963	Preached—Christmas	8	Luke 2:15–20	Neuhorst
26 Dec. 1963	Preached—Christmas	8	Luke 2:15–20	Kronsthal
29 Dec. 1963	Preached—Last Sunday of Year	24	Genesis 32:10	Blumenheim
1 Jan. 1964	Preached—New Year's Sermon	43	1 Peter 1:22–23	Neuanlage
5 Jan. 1964	Preached			Neuhorst
6 Jan. 1964	Preached—Epiphany	61	Matthew 2:1–12	Kronsthal
12 Jan. 1964	Preached	25	1 John 1:6	Blumenthal
19 Jan. 1964	Preached	25	1 John 1:6	Chortiz, near Winkler, MB

Date	Activity	Number	Scripture	Location
26 Jan. 1964	Preached	25	1 John 1:6	Neuhorst
2 Feb. 1964	Preached	25	1 John 1:6	Kronsthal
13 Feb. 1964	Funeral Service			Neuhorst
16 Feb. 1964	Preached	36	Matthew 18:23–35	Neuanlage
23 Feb. 1964	Preached	36	Matthew 18:23–35	Neuhorst
1 Mar. 1964	Preached	34	Luke 16:1–9	Kronsthal
1 Mar. 1964	Funeral Service	47	Romans 6:23	Neuhorst
8 Mar. 1964	Preached	19	Luke 18:9–14	Blumenheim
15 Mar. 1964	Preached	25	1 John 1:6	Neuanlage
22 Mar. 1964	Preached—Palm Sunday	30	Matthew 21:1–9	Neuhorst
27 Mar. 1964	Preached—Good Friday	32	John 19:31–42	Neuanlage
29 Mar. 1964	Preached—Easter	20	Mark 16:1–8	Neuhorst
30 Mar. 1964	Preached—Palm Sunday	30	Matthew 21:1–9	Kronsthal
19 Apr. 1964	Preached—Articles of Faith	44	Romans 10:10	Neuanlage
22 Apr. 1964	Funeral Service	50		Blumenthal
3 May 1964	Catechism Examination			Neuanlage
7 May 1964	Catechism Examination			Neuhorst
17 May 1964	Baptism Service			Neuanlage
18 May 1964	Baptism Service			Neuhorst

Date	Activity	Sermon Index #	Biblical Text(s)	Location
24 May 1964	Communion Service			Neuanlage
24 May 1964	Visitation—Communion			Private Home, Neuanlage
26 May 1964	Visitation—Communion			Private Home
26 May 1964	Visitation—Communion			Private Home, Rosthern
26 May 1964	Visitation—Communion			Private Home, Hochstadt
27 May 1964	Visitation—Communion			Private Home, Osler
27 May 1964	Visitation—Communion			Private Home, Warman
30 May 1964	Engagement Talk	54		Neuhorst
31 May 1964	Communion Service			Neuhorst
7 June 1964	Communion Service			Kronsthal
7 June 1964	Communion Service			Edenburg
10 June 1964	Visitation—Communion			Private Home, Rosthern
10 June 1964	Conducted a Home Service			Private Home, Rosthern
13 June 1964	Engagement Talk	54		Blumenthal
14 June 1964	Wedding Ceremony			Neuhorst
28 June 1964	Conducted a Home Service			Private Home, Reinfeld
5 July 1964	Preached			Neuhorst

Date	Activity		Scripture	Location
12 July 1964	Preached			Kronsthal
12 July 1964	Funeral Service	50		Neuanlage
19 July 1964	Wedding Ceremony			Neuhorst
1 Aug. 1964	Wedding Ceremony			Neuhorst
2 Aug. 1964	Preached			Edenburg
9 Aug. 1964	Preached	19	Luke 18:9–14	Neuanlage
16 Aug. 1964	Preached	19	Luke 18:9–14	Neuhorst
23 Aug. 1964	Preached	19	Luke 18:9–14	Kronsthal
30 Aug. 1964	Conducted a Home Service			Private Home, Warman
6 Sept. 1964	Preached			Blumenthal
9 Sept. 1964	Funeral Service	47	Romans 6:23	Neuhorst
20 Sept. 1964	Preached			Neuanlage
20 Sept. 1964	Funeral Service	47	Romans 6:23	Rosthern
27 Sept. 1964	Preached	19	Luke 18:9–14	Gruenfeld, near Fort St. John, BC
27 Sept. 1964	Preached			Reinland, near Fort St. John, BC
4 Oct. 1964	Preached—Thanksgiving	33	Acts 14:17	Kronsthal
4 Oct. 1964	Visitation—Communion			Hospital, Saskatoon
11 Oct. 1964	Preached—Preparation for Communion			Blumenheim

Date	Activity	Sermon Index #	Biblical Text(s)	Location
18 Oct. 1964	Communion Service			Neuanlage
20 Oct. 1964	Visitation—Communion			Private Home, Osler
20 Oct. 1964	Visitation—Communion			Private Home, Warman
20 Oct. 1964	Visitation—Communion			Hospital, Saskatoon
22 Oct. 1964	Visitation—Communion			Private Home, Blumenthal
22 Oct. 1964	Visitation—Communion			Private Home, Rosthern
22 Oct. 1964	Visitation—Communion			Care Home, Rosthern
25 Oct. 1964	Communion Service			Neuhorst
1 Nov. 1964	Communion Service			Kronsthal
1 Nov. 1964	Communion Service			Edenburg
8 Nov. 1964	Preached			Neuhorst
11 Nov. 1964	Funeral Service	49		Neuhorst
15 Nov. 1964	Preached			Kronsthal
26 Nov. 1964	Funeral Service			Kronsthal
6 Dec. 1964	Funeral Service	47	Romans 6:23	Neuanlage
13 Dec. 1964	Preached—Advent Sermon			Neuanlage
20 Dec. 1964	Preached—Advent Sermon			Neuhorst

Date	Activity	Number	Scripture	Location
25 Dec. 1964	Preached—Christmas	8	Luke 2:15–20	Kronsthal
27 Dec. 1964	Preached—Last Sunday of Year	24	Genesis 32:10	Blumenthal
3 Jan. 1965	Preached—New Year's Sermon			Neuanlage
6 Jan. 1965	Preached—Epiphany	61	Matthew 2:1–12	Neuhorst
10 Jan. 1965	Preached			Kronsthal
17 Jan. 1965	Preached	25	1 John 1:6	Blumenheim
4 Feb. 1965	Funeral Service	49		Blumenthal
7 Feb. 1965	Preached	25	1 John 1:6	Neuanlage
14 Feb. 1965	Preached	25	1 John 1:6	Neuhorst
22 Feb. 1965	Funeral Service	49		Warman
14 Mar. 1965	Preached			Edenburg
21 Mar. 1965	Preached			Neuanlage
28 Mar. 1965	Preached			Neuhorst
4 Apr. 1965	Preached			Kronsthal
11 Apr. 1965	Wedding Ceremony			Warman
16 Apr. 1965	Preached—Good Friday	32	John 19:31–42	Blumenthal
19 Apr. 1965	Preached—Easter			Neuanlage
20 Apr. 1965	Preached—Articles of Faith	44	Romans 10:10	Neuhorst

Date	Activity	Sermon Index #	Biblical Text(s)	Location
25 Apr. 1965	Preached—Articles of Faith	44	Romans 10:10	Kronsthal
27 Apr. 1965	Funeral Service	47	Romans 6:23	Warman
20 May 1965	Funeral Service	50		Neuhorst
23 May 1965	Catechism Examination (Part 1)	45		Neuanlage
27 May 1965	Catechism Examination (Part 2)			Neuhorst
1 June 1965	Funeral Service			Blumenthal
6 June 1965	Baptism Service			Neuanlage
7 June 1965	Baptism Service			Neuhorst
13 June 1965	Communion Service			Neuanlage
16 June 1965	Visitation—Communion			Hospital, Saskatoon
20 June 1965	Communion Service			Neuhorst
22 June 1965	Visitation—Communion			Private Home, Rosthern
22 June 1965	Visitation—Communion			Care Home, Rosthern
24 June 1965	Visitation—Communion			Private Home, Osler
24 June 1965	Visitation—Communion			Private Home, Saskatoon
27 June 1965	Communion Service			Kronsthal
27 June 1965	Communion Service			Edenburg

Date	Activity			Location
4 July 1965	Funeral Service	47	Romans 6:23	Neuhorst
11 July 1965	Preached	34	Luke 16:1–9	Blumenheim
24 July 1965	Engagement Talk	54		Blumenthal
1 Aug. 1965	Preached			Neuhorst
7 Aug. 1965	Wedding Ceremony	2	Tobit 8:5–6	Neuanlage
8 Aug. 1965	Preached			Neuanlage
15 Aug. 1965	Preached	34	Luke 16:1–9	Neuhorst
28 Aug. 1965	Preached	34	Luke 16:1–9	Neuanlage
9 Sept. 1965	Funeral Service	50		Warman
12 Sept. 1965	Wedding Ceremony	2	Tobit 8:5–6	Reinfeld
19 Sept. 1965	Wedding Ceremony			Neuanlage
26 Sept. 1965	Preached	28	Jeremiah 51:6	Neuanlage
3 Oct. 1965	Preached—Thanksgiving	33	Acts 14:17	Neuhorst
10 Oct. 1965	Preached	28	Jeremiah 51:6	Kronsthal
17 Oct. 1965	Communion Service			Neuanlage
24 Oct. 1965	Communion Service			Neuhorst
26 Oct. 1965	Visitation—Communion			Private Home, Rosthern
26 Oct. 1965	Visitation—Communion			Care Home, Rosthern
26 Oct. 1965	Visitation—Communion			Private Home, Hague

Date	Activity	Sermon Index #	Biblical Text(s)	Location
28 Oct. 1965	Visitation—Communion			Private Home, Osler
28 Oct. 1965	Visitation—Communion			Private Home, Saskatoon
28 Oct. 1965	Visitation—Communion			Private Home, Saskatoon
29 Oct. 1965	Funeral Service			Martensville
30 Oct. 1965	Visitation—Communion			Hospital, Rosthern
31 Oct. 1965	Communion Service			Kronsthal
31 Oct. 1965	Communion Service			Edenburg
3 Nov. 1965	Visitation—Communion			Private Home, Blumenheim
6 Nov. 1965	Brotherhood Meeting			Neuhorst
14 Nov. 1965	Preached	10	Matthew 24:15-28	Neuanlage
14 Nov. 1965	Funeral Service	49		Neuhorst
20 Nov. 1965	Engagement Talk	54		Edenburg
21 Nov. 1965	Preached	10	Matthew 24:15-28	Neuhorst
28 Nov. 1965	Preached—Advent Sermon			Kronsthal
5 Dec. 1965	Preached—Advent Sermon			Reinland, near Fort St. John, BC
5 Dec. 1965	Preached	28	Jeremiah 51:6	Gruenfeld, near Fort St. John, BC
12 Dec. 1965	Preached—Advent Sermon			Reinland, near Fort Vermilion, AB

Date	Activity		Scripture	Location
26 Dec. 1965	Preached—Christmas	8	Luke 2:15–20	Neuanlage
1 Jan. 1966	Preached—New Year's Sermon	43	1 Peter 1:22–23	Neuhorst
2 Jan. 1966	Preached			Kronsthal
6 Jan. 1966	Preached—Epiphany	61	Matthew 2:1–12	Blumenthal
23 Jan. 1966	Conducted a Home Service			Private Home, Warman
6 Feb. 1966	Preached			Neuhorst
7 Feb. 1966	Funeral Service	49		Neuanlage
12 Feb. 1966	Visitation—Communion			Hospital, Saskatoon
13 Feb. 1966	Preached			Kronsthal
20 Feb. 1966	Preached			Edenburg
23 Feb. 1966	Funeral Service			Neuhorst
5 Mar. 1966	Funeral Service			Neuhorst
10 Mar. 1966	Funeral Service	48		Neuhorst
20 Mar. 1966	Preached			Neuanlage
27 Mar. 1966	Preached			Neuhorst
3 Apr. 1966	Preached—Palm Sunday	30	Matthew 21:1–9	Kronsthal
6 Apr. 1966	Conducted a Home Service			Private Home, Warman
8 Apr. 1966	Preached—Good Friday	32	John 19:31–42	Blumenheim
17 Apr. 1966	Preached—Articles of Faith	44	Romans 10:10	Neuanlage

Date	Activity	Sermon Index #	Biblical Text(s)	Location
21 Apr. 1966	Funeral Service	50		Neuhorst
24 Apr. 1966	Preached—Articles of Faith	44	Romans 10:10	Neuhorst
1 May 1966	Preached—Articles of Faith	44	Romans 10:10	Neuanlage
1 May 1966	Funeral Service	48		Blumenthal
11 May 1966	Conducted a Home Service			Private Home, Warman
15 May 1966	Catechism Examination (Part 1)	45		Neuanlage
15 May 1966	Wedding Ceremony			Rosthern
19 May 1966	Catechism Examination (Part 2)	11		Neuhorst
29 May 1966	Baptism Service			Neuanlage
30 May 1966	Baptism Service			Neuhorst
5 June 1966	Communion Service			Neuanlage
7 June 1966	Visitation—Communion			Hospital, Saskatoon
7 June 1966	Visitation—Communion			Private Home, Saskatoon
12 June 1966	Communion Service			Neuhorst
13 June 1966	Visitation—Communion			Private Home, Osler
13 June 1966	Visitation—Communion			Private Home, Warman
13 June 1966	Visitation—Communion			Private Home, Gruenfeld

Date	Activity		Scripture	Location
16 June 1966	Visitation—Communion			Private Home, Hague
16 June 1966	Visitation—Communion			Private Home, Hague
16 June 1966	Visitation—Communion			Private Home, Rosthern
19 June 1966	Communion Service			Kronsthal
19 June 1966	Communion Service			Edenburg
25 June 1966	Brotherhood Meeting			Neuhorst
5 July 1966	Conducted a Home Service			Private Home, Warman
10 July 1966	Preached	1	Genesis 3:9	Neuanlage
17 July 1966	Preached	1	Genesis 3:9	Neuhorst
24 July 1966	Preached	1	Genesis 3:9	Kronsthal
26 July 1966	Funeral Service	47	Romans 6:23	Neuhorst
28 July 1966	Funeral Service	48		Neuhorst
31 July 1966	Preached	1	Genesis 3:9	Blumenheim
13 Aug. 1966	Engagement Talk	53		Blumenthal
21 Aug. 1966	Wedding Ceremony			Neuanlage
27 Aug. 1966	Funeral Service	50		Neuanlage
28 Aug. 1966	Preached			Neuanlage
30 Aug. 1966	Baptism Service			Neuhorst
4 Sept. 1966	Preached	34	Luke 16:1–9	Neuhorst

Date	Activity	Sermon Index #	Biblical Text(s)	Location
4 Sept. 1966	Funeral Service	50		Neuhorst
11 Sept. 1966	Preached	36	Matthew 18:23–35	Kronsthal
18 Sept. 1966	Preached	25	1 John 1:6	Blumenthal
29 Sept. 1966	Funeral Service	48		Neuanlage
2 Oct. 1966	Wedding Ceremony			Neuhorst
6 Oct. 1966	Funeral Service			Blumenthal
16 Oct. 1966	Communion Service			Neuanlage
23 Oct. 1966	Communion Service			Neuhorst
25 Oct. 1966	Visitation—Communion			Private Home, Osler
25 Oct. 1966	Visitation—Communion			Private Home, Warman
25 Oct. 1966	Visitation—Communion			Private Home, Gruenfeld
27 Oct. 1966	Visitation—Communion			Private Home, Hague
27 Oct. 1966	Visitation—Communion			Private Home, Rosthern
29 Oct. 1966	Engagement Talk	53		Blumenthal
30 Oct. 1966	Communion Service			Kronsthal
3 Nov. 1966	Funeral Service			Neuanlage
4 Nov. 1966	Funeral Service	49		Neuhorst

Date	Activity		Scripture	Location
6 Nov. 1966	Communion Service			Edenburg
6 Nov. 1966	Wedding Ceremony			Neuanlage
12 Nov. 1966	Brotherhood Meeting			Neuhorst
16 Nov. 1966	Funeral Service	47	Romans 6:23	Neuanlage
29 Nov. 1966	Preached—Advent Sermon	63	Matthew 21:1–9	Chortiz, near Winkler, MB
4 Dec. 1966	Preached—Advent Sermon	63	Matthew 21:1–9	Neuanlage
11 Dec. 1966	Preached—Advent Sermon	63	Matthew 21:1–9	Neuhorst
18 Dec. 1966	Preached—Advent Sermon	63	Matthew 21:1–9	Kronsthal
23 Dec. 1966	Funeral Service			Neuhorst
25 Dec. 1966	Preached—Christmas	29	Luke 2:1–14	Blumenheim
30 Dec. 1966	Funeral Service			Neuanlage
8 Jan. 1967	Preached—Sunday after Epiphany	6	Luke 2:41–52	Neuanlage
15 Jan. 1967	Preached	28	Jeremiah 51:6	Neuhorst
22 Jan. 1967	Preached	19	Luke 18:9–14	Kronsthal
29 Jan. 1967	Preached	19	Luke 18:9–14	Blumenthal
1 Feb. 1967	Conducted a Home Service			Private Home, Osler
4 Feb. 1967	Brotherhood Meeting			Neuhorst
5 Feb. 1967	Preached			Kronsthal

Date	Activity	Sermon Index #	Biblical Text(s)	Location
5 Feb. 1967	Funeral Service	50		Neuhorst
12 Feb. 1967	Preached			Neuanlage
19 Feb. 1967	Preached			Neuhorst
25 Feb. 1967	Brotherhood Meeting			Neuhorst
26 Feb. 1967	Preached	34	Luke 16:1–9	Kronsthal
24 Mar. 1967	Preached—Good Friday	32	John 19:31–42	Neuanlage
26 Mar. 1967	Preached—Easter	20	Mark 16:1–8	Neuhorst
27 Mar. 1967	Preached—Easter			Kronsthal
1 Apr. 1967	Engagement Talk	54		Blumenheim
2 Apr. 1967	Preached—Articles of Faith	44	Romans 10:10	Neuhorst
9 Apr. 1967	Preached—Articles of Faith	44	Romans 10:10	Edenburg
9 Apr. 1967	Wedding Ceremony			Neuhorst
16 Apr. 1967	Preached—Articles of Faith	44	Romans 10:10	Neuanlage
23 Apr. 1967	Preached—Articles of Faith	44	Romans 10:10	Neuhorst
4 May 1967	Catechism Examination (Part 2)	11		Neuhorst
14 May 1967	Baptism Service			Neuanlage
15 May 1967	Baptism Service			Neuhorst

Date	Activity			Location
18 May 1967	Funeral Service	48		Neuanlage
21 May 1967	Communion Service			Neuanlage
25 May 1967	Funeral Service	46		Neuhorst
28 May 1967	Communion Service			Neuhorst
28 May 1967	Visitation—Communion			Private Home, Martensville
30 May 1967	Visitation—Communion			Private Home, Osler
30 May 1967	Visitation—Communion			Private Home, Gruenfeld
30 May 1967	Visitation—Communion			Private Home, Hague
31 May 1967	Visitation—Communion			Private Home, Warman
1 June 1967	Visitation—Communion			Private Home, Reinfeld
1 June 1967	Visitation—Communion			Private Home, Rosthern
3 June 1967	Engagement Talk	54		Neuhorst
4 June 1967	Communion Service			Kronsthal
25 June 1967	Preached			Neuanlage
25 June 1967	Funeral Service			Neuhorst
2 July 1967	Preached			Neuhorst
2 July 1967	Preached—60th Anniversary			Kronsthal
6 July 1967	Funeral Service	49		Blumenthal
7 July 1967	Funeral Service	47	Romans 6:23	Neuhorst

Date	Activity	Sermon Index #	Biblical Text(s)	Location
9 July 1967	Preached			Kronsthal
30 July 1967	Preached	10	Matthew 24:15–28	Edenburg
2 Aug. 1967	Funeral Service			Neuhorst
6 Aug. 1967	Preached			Neuanlage
13 Aug. 1967	Preached			Neuhorst
20 Aug. 1967	Preached			Kronsthal
25 Aug. 1967	Groundbreaking Ceremony—Altenheim			Warman
2 Sept. 1967	Engagement Talk	54		Blumenheim
3 Sept. 1967	Preached			Blumenthal
4 Sept. 1967	Funeral Service	48		Neuhorst
17 Sept. 1967	Preached	36	Matthew 18:23–35	Neuanlage
20 Sept. 1967	Conducted a Home Service			Private Home, Osler
24 Sept. 1967	Preached	25	1 John 1:6	Neuhorst
1 Oct. 1967	Preached—Thanksgiving	33	Acts 14:17	Kronsthal
3 Oct. 1967	Conducted a Home Service			Private Home, Gruenfeld
4 Oct. 1967	Conducted a Home Service			Private Home, Warman

Date	Activity		Scripture	Location
8 Oct. 1967	Preached—Preparation for Communion			Blumenheim
15 Oct. 1967	Communion Service			Neuanlage
15 Oct. 1967	Communion Service			Edenburg
22 Oct. 1967	Communion Service			Neuhorst
24 Oct. 1967	Visitation—Communion			Private Home, Osler
24 Oct. 1967	Visitation—Communion			Private Home, Gruenfeld
25 Oct. 1967	Visitation—Communion			Private Home, Warman
26 Oct. 1967	Visitation—Communion			Private Home, Hague
26 Oct. 1967	Visitation—Communion			Private Home, Rosthern
26 Oct. 1967	Visitation—Communion			Private Home, Reinfeld
29 Oct. 1967	Communion Service			Kronsthal
29 Oct. 1967	Visitation—Communion			Private Home, Saskatoon
5 Nov. 1967	Preached	36	Matthew 18:23–35	Neuhorst
12 Nov. 1967	Preached	28	Jeremiah 51:6	Chortiz, near Winkler, MB
2 Dec. 1967	Funeral Service	50		Edenburg
3 Dec. 1967	Preached—Advent Sermon	63	Matthew 21:1–9	Edenburg
10 Dec. 1967	Preached—Advent Sermon	63	Matthew 21:1–9	Neuanlage
17 Dec. 1967	Preached—Advent Sermon	63	Matthew 21:1–9	Neuhorst

Date	Activity	Sermon Index #	Biblical Text(s)	Location
18 Dec. 1967	Funeral Service	47	Romans 6:23	Neuhorst
24 Dec. 1967	Preached—Advent Sermon	63	Matthew 21:1–9	Kronsthal
26 Dec. 1967	Preached—Christmas	29	Luke 2:1–14	Blumenthal
1 Jan. 1968	Preached—New Year's Sermon	43	1 Peter 1:22–23	Neuanlage
6 Jan. 1968	Preached—Epiphany	61	Matthew 2:1–12	Neuhorst
7 Jan. 1968	Preached—Sunday after Epiphany	6	Luke 2:41–52	Neuhorst
14 Jan. 1968	Preached	25	1 John 1:6	Blumenheim
21 Jan. 1968	Funeral Service			Neuanlage
31 Jan. 1968	Conducted a Home Service			Private Home, Gruenfeld
1 Feb. 1968	Conducted a Home Service			Private Home, Hague
4 Feb. 1968	Preached	34	Luke 16:1–9	Neuanlage
7 Feb. 1968	Conducted a Home Service			Private Home, Warman
11 Feb. 1968	Preached	34	Luke 16:1–9	Neuhorst
14 Feb. 1968	Conducted a Home Service			Private Home, Osler
17 Feb. 1968	Brotherhood Meeting			Neuhorst
25 Feb. 1968	Preached	19	Luke 18:9–14	Neuhorst

Date	Activity	Number	Scripture	Location
29 Feb. 1968	Funeral Service	50		Neuhorst
10 Mar. 1968	Preached	34	Luke 16:1–9	Edenburg
17 Mar. 1968	Preached	28	Jeremiah 51:6	Neuanlage
19 Mar. 1968	Conducted a Home Service			Private Home, Aberdeen
20 Mar. 1968	Conducted a Home Service			Private Home, Warman
24 Mar. 1968	Preached	28	Jeremiah 51:6	Neuhorst
12 Apr. 1968	Preached—Good Friday	32	John 19:31–42	Blumenthal
15 Apr. 1968	Preached—Easter			Neuanlage
16 Apr. 1968	Preached—Articles of Faith	44	Romans 10:10	Neuhorst
25 Apr. 1968	Funeral Service	47	Romans 6:23	Edenburg
28 Apr. 1968	Preached—Articles of Faith	44	Romans 10:10	Neuhorst
9 May 1968	Funeral Service	48		Neuhorst
16 May 1968	Funeral Service			Neuanlage
19 May 1968	Catechism Examination (Part 1)	45		Neuanlage
23 May 1968	Catechism Examination (Part 2)	11		Neuhorst
26 May 1968	Wedding Ceremony			Neuhorst
29 May 1968	Conducted a Home Service			Private Home, Osler
2 June 1968	Baptism Service	31	Acts 2:1–18	Neuanlage

Date	Activity	Sermon Index #	Biblical Text(s)	Location
3 June 1968	Baptism Service	31	Acts 2:1–18	Neuhorst
3 June 1968	Visitation—Communion			Hospital, Saskatoon
3 June 1968	Visitation—Communion			Private Home, Saskatoon
3 June 1968	Visitation—Communion			Private Home, Osler
4 June 1968	Visitation—Communion			Private Home, Osler
4 June 1968	Visitation—Communion			Private Home, Gruenfeld
4 June 1968	Visitation—Communion			Private Home, Warman
6 June 1968	Visitation—Communion			Private Home, Hague
6 June 1968	Visitation—Communion			Care Home, Rosthern
6 June 1968	Visitation—Communion			Private Home, Reinfeld
9 June 1968	Communion Service			Neuanlage
12 June 1968	Preached—After Communion	27	Psalm 100:6	Private Home, Warman
16 June 1968	Communion Service			Neuhorst
16 June 1968	Communion Service			Kronsthal
23 June 1968	Preached—Preparation for Communion			Wheatley, ON
23 June 1968	Communion Service			Aylmer, ON

Date	Activity	Number	Scripture	Location
24 June 1968	Communion Service			Wheatley, ON
30 June 1968	Preached	19	Luke 18:9–14	Kronsthal
2 July 1968	Funeral Service	48		Warman
7 July 1968	Preached	1	Genesis 3:9	Rosenhof, near Swift Current, SK
10 July 1968	Funeral Service			Neuhorst
14 July 1968	Preached	1	Genesis 3:9	Blumenthal
27 July 1968	Engagement Talk	53		Neuanlage
28 July 1968	Preached	25	1 John 1:6	Neuanlage
3 Aug. 1968	Wedding Ceremony			Neuanlage
4 Aug. 1968	Wedding Ceremony	2	Tobit 8:5–6	Neuhorst
11 Aug. 1968	Preached	1	Genesis 3:9	Kronsthal
23 Aug. 1968	Funeral Service			Neuanlage
25 Aug. 1968	Preached	1	Genesis 3:9	Blumenheim
28 Aug. 1968	Conducted a Home Service			Private Home, Gruenfeld
8 Sept. 1968	Funeral Service	49		Neuhorst
15 Sept. 1968	Preached			Neuanlage
22 Sept. 1968	Preached			Neuhorst
29 Sept. 1968	Preached			Kronsthal

Date	Activity	Sermon Index #	Biblical Text(s)	Location
20 Oct. 1968	Communion Service			Neuanlage
20 Oct. 1968	Communion Service			Edenburg
20 Oct. 1968	Visitation—Communion			Private Home, Blumenthal
22 Oct. 1968	Visitation—Communion			Private Home, Blumenheim
22 Oct. 1968	Visitation—Communion			Care Home, Rosthern
23 Oct. 1968	Visitation—Communion			Private Home, Warman
23 Oct. 1968	Visitation—Communion			Private Home, Warman
23 Oct. 1968	Visitation—Communion			Private Home, Gruenfeld
23 Oct. 1968	Visitation—Communion			Private Home, Hague
24 Oct. 1968	Visitation—Communion			Private Home, Saskatoon
27 Oct. 1968	Communion Service			Neuhorst
27 Oct. 1968	Communion Service			Kronsthal
28 Oct. 1968	Funeral Service			Reinfeld
3 Nov. 1968	Preached			Neuanlage
10 Nov. 1968	Preached			Neuhorst
10 Nov. 1968	Dedication Service for Altenheim			Warman Altenheim
17 Nov. 1968	Preached			Kronsthal

Date	Activity		Scripture	Location
21 Nov. 1968	Funeral Service			Hague
24 Nov. 1968	Preached			Warman Altenheim
24 Nov. 1968	Visitation—Communion			Private Home, Reinfeld
24 Nov. 1968	Visitation—Communion			Private Home, Warman
28 Nov. 1968	Funeral Service			Neuhorst
7 Dec. 1968	Brotherhood Meeting			Neuhorst
8 Dec. 1968	Preached—Advent Sermon	4	John 1:6–14	Blumenthal
10 Dec. 1968	Funeral Service	48		Neuanlage
11 Dec. 1968	Conducted a Home Service—Advent Sermon	4	John 1:6–14	Private Home, Warman
15 Dec. 1968	Preached—Advent Sermon	63	Matthew 21:1–9	Neuanlage
22 Dec. 1968	Preached—Advent Sermon	4	John 1:6–14	Neuhorst
27 Dec. 1968	Funeral Service	50		Neuhorst
1 Jan. 1969	Preached—New Year's Sermon	43	1 Peter 1:22–23	Reinfeld, near Winkler, MB
5 Jan. 1969	Preached	25	1 John 1:6	Neuanlage
6 Jan. 1969	Preached—Epiphany	61	Matthew 2:1–12	Neuhorst
12 Jan. 1969	Preached—Sunday after Epiphany	6	Luke 2:41–52	Blumenheim
19 Jan. 1969	Preached	34	Luke 16:1–9	Warman Altenheim

Date	Activity	Sermon Index #	Biblical Text(s)	Location
9 Feb. 1969	Preached			British Honduras
13 Feb. 1969	Ministerial Election			British Honduras
16 Feb. 1969	Ministerial & Deacon Ordination			British Honduras
26 Feb. 1969	Funeral Service	49		Neuhorst
9 Mar. 1969	Preached	1	Genesis 3:9	Gruenfeld, near Fort St. John, BC
9 Mar. 1969	Preached	1	Genesis 3:9	Reinland, near Fort St. John, BC
16 Mar. 1969	Preached	34	Luke 16:1–9	Reinland, near La Crete, AB
23 Mar. 1969	Preached	26	Luke 15:1–10; Matthew 9:35–38	Neuanlage
30 Mar. 1969	Preached—Palm Sunday	21	Matthew 21:1–9	Neuhorst
31 Mar. 1969	Funeral Service	48		Neuanlage
6 Apr. 1969	Preached—Easter	20	Mark 16:1–8	Warman
8 Apr. 1969	Preached—Articles of Faith	44	Romans 10:10	Blumenthal
13 Apr. 1969	Preached—Articles of Faith	44	Romans 10:10	Neuanlage
20 Apr. 1969	Preached—Articles of Faith	44	Romans 10:10	Neuhorst
26 Apr. 1969	Wedding Ceremony			Neuhorst
30 Apr. 1969	Funeral Service	46		Neuhorst
11 May 1969	Catechism Examination (Part 1)	45		Neuanlage

Date	Activity			Location
14 May 1969	Conducted a Home Service			Private Home, Blumenheim
18 May 1969	Preached—Articles of Faith	22	Romans 10:9–10	Neuanlage
21 May 1969	Preached			Neuanlage
25 May 1969	Baptism Service			Neuanlage
1 June 1969	Communion Service			Neuanlage
8 June 1969	Communion Service			Neuhorst
10 June 1969	Visitation—Communion			Private Home, Hague
10 June 1969	Visitation—Communion			Care Home, Rosthern
10 June 1969	Visitation—Communion			Private Home, Reinfeld
10 June 1969	Visitation—Communion			Private Home, Neuanlage
15 June 1969	Communion Service			Edenburg
15 June 1969	Funeral Service			Reinfeld
18 June 1969	Funeral Service	49		Neuanlage
21 June 1969	Engagement Talk	54		Mennon
22 June 1969	Communion Service			Warman Altenheim
29 June 1969	Preached			Neuhorst
29 June 1969	Wedding Ceremony			Neuhorst
6 July 1969	Preached			Neuhorst
6 July 1969	Wedding Ceremony			Neuanlage

Date	Activity	Sermon Index #	Biblical Text(s)	Location
20 July 1969	Preached			Warman Altenheim
26 July 1969	Wedding Ceremony			Neuhorst
27 July 1969	Funeral Service			Neuanlage
3 Aug. 1969	Preached	1	Genesis 3:9	Rosenort, MB
10 Aug. 1969	Preached	26	Luke 15:1–10; Matthew 9:35–38	Neuhorst
17 Aug. 1969	Preached	1	Genesis 3:9	Vanderhoof, BC
20 Aug. 1969	Preached			Vanderhoof, BC
24 Aug. 1969	Preached			Blumenheim
24 Aug. 1969	Wedding Ceremony			Neuhorst
7 Sept. 1969	Preached			Blumenthal
14 Sept. 1969	Preached			Neuanlage
21 Sept. 1969	Preached	1	Genesis 3:9	Neuhorst
21 Sept. 1969	Funeral Service			Neuhorst

Appendix B

Selected Sermons

ALTHOUGH SERMONS WRITTEN BY OLD COLONY MENNONITE MINIS-
ters occasionally appear in archives, it is rare to find intact a large, sixty-five
sermon collection like the Herman Friesen collection.[1] In addition to
sermons, the collection also contains copies of correspondence between
Mennonite church leaders in Russia dating back to 1833, items pertaining
to the delegations sent to South America in 1919 in search of a suitable
migration location, and various poems and hymn lyrics. Each sermon is
contained in a single notebook, neatly handwritten in German Gothic
script, which makes accessibility to English-speaking scholars and readers
a challenge. Meticulously recorded at the back of each sermon booklet is
the date and location at which the sermon was presented. Friesen preached
over three hundred times as part of regular church services during his
seven-year ministry. This was supplemented by speaking responsibilities
at another 115 occasions such as funerals, weddings, major anniversaries,
and engagement celebrations. This works out to an average of almost sixty
speaking engagements per year. The number of times he preached may well
have been greater: given the greater degree of informality and variability in
the kind of services conducted in homes, Herman seldom recorded which
sermon, if any, he used on such occasions. At least forty-eight of the sixty-
five sermons in this collection were written by Herman Friesen.[2] This represents more than half of the sermons he wrote and preached during his
seven-year ministry.

With the exception of the *Catechism* and *Gesangbuch*, Old Colony
Mennonites did not produce theological material for distribution to their
members that was designed for devotional use, or that was responsive to
contemporary issues and circumstances. Sermons, therefore, represent
a significant form of theological discourse in the life of the Old Colony

Mennonite community. They were clearly the centrepiece of a Sunday morning service, with the greatest proportion of time allocated to preaching. The gravity of the sermon was amplified in the Old Colony Mennonite Church by the authority and deference given to ministers, who collectively were expected to provide an authoritative understanding of the Bible. The role and influence of public oral presentations, such as a sermon, in shaping the understanding of society is accentuated in religious communities that eschew the use of modern media.

In recent decades, there has been an increase in scholarly interest in Low German Mennonite groups, which has given these groups their place within Mennonite historiography. Social-cultural historians and sociologists have produced much of the scholarly literature featuring the Old Colony Mennonite experience. As valuable as these disciplinary approaches have been, and continue to be, they tend to give only cursory attention to the connection between Old Colony Mennonite theological convictions and the decisions, motivations, views of life, and internal tensions present within this faith community. To date, little effort has been made to examine the connection and consistency between the *Confession of Faith* and the *Catechism*, the teaching of various Old Colony Mennonite leaders, and the broader Anabaptist-Mennonite tradition. Sermon literature provides an important window into the minds of Old Colony Mennonite leaders, and can supplement the historical materials and qualitative interviews from which social-cultural historians and sociologists have gleaned their insights. While the theological analysis of Old Colony Mennonite sermons included in this book is not exhaustive, it does provide a starting point for filling an important gap in understanding the story of Old Colony Mennonites.

Seven representative sermons have been selected to accompany this biography in order to make these important Old Colony Mennonite primary sources available to English-speaking scholars and readers. All of them illustrate well the hortatory approach to preaching. Included are Herman Friesen's first two sermons (#5 and #12), along with his last sermon (#1), because of the way they mark significant moments in his life and ministry, and because of the way they bookend the evolution of his homiletical development. Included also are three special occasion sermons (#54, #50, and #45): one used at engagement celebrations (Felafnis) that preceded weddings, one used at the funerals of adults, and one used at prebaptismal services during which baptismal candidates were expected to recite memorized answers to questions in the *Catechism*. Assuming that frequency of usage is an indicator of Herman's level of satisfaction with the sermon itself, as well as something he thought was of importance for the congregation(s) to hear, one additional sermon (#19) is included that was used at least twelve times.

Sermon #5: Inaugural Sermon
(Jeremiah 1:7; Romans 15:30–33), 1962

This is Herman D. W. Friesen's inaugural sermon following his election as a minister in the Old Colony Mennonite Church. It was first preached on June 17, 1962, in Neuanlage, and then three more times in July 1962 in Neuhorst, Kronsthal, and Edenburg. In it, Herman wrestles with finding a balance between an attitude of humility and dependence on God, and a clear assertion of his willingness to respond to the congregation's call.

Sermon #12: "Run in Such a Way as to Get the Prize"
(Matthew 5–7; 1 Corinthians 9:24–27), 1962

This was the second sermon preached by Herman D. W. Friesen. It was used at least seven times early in Herman's ministry, twice in Edenburg and twice in Neuhorst. Biblical texts from the Sermon on the Mount were generally used on the sixth, eighth, and fifteenth Sundays after Trinity Sunday. The 1 Corinthians 9 text is used on Septuagesima Sunday (the ninth Sunday before Easter). Herman emphasizes the importance of striving to live according to the teachings of Jesus in order to remain on the "narrow road" of salvation.

Sermon #19: Two Praying at the Door of Grace:
The Pharisee and the Tax Collector (Luke 18:9–14), 1963

Written for use on the eleventh Sunday after Trinity Sunday, this sermon was preached twelve times over the span of five years, at least four times in Kronsthal and three times in Neuhorst. It was not always used on the specified date of the liturgical calendar; instead of being used in early fall, Herman used the sermon in winter and early spring on several occasions. The sermon explores how Christian life ought to reflect both an inward and outward transformation.

Sermon #54: For the Occasion of an Engagement Celebration, 1963

This sermon was presented at least eleven times, usually on a Saturday evening several weeks prior to the wedding, in the home of the parents of either the bride or groom. It emphasizes the importance of ensuring that both partners enter a marriage relationship on a common foundation of faith in Jesus Christ, and the importance of practising spiritual disciplines such as prayer and public worship.

Sermon #50: Funeral Sermon for an Adult, 1964

This sermon was used at least eleven times, six times in Neuhorst and twice in Neuanlage. According to Herman Friesen's notes, the ages of those who had died ranged between fifty-eight and eighty-four years. In several instances, the sermon was used at a memorial service for a member of the Old Colony Mennonite Church who had died in Mexico.[3] The sermon is an attempt to motivate those living to consider the importance of putting their own house in order in preparation for their own eventual death.

Sermon #45: For the Preparation of Baptismal Candidates: Part 1, 1965

This sermon was used on the Sundays preceding a baptismal service during which baptismal candidates would publicly recite answers to the questions contained in the *Catechism*. It comprises two short meditations, one preceding the formal recitation, and a second one concluding the occasion. Together, these meditations implore baptismal candidates to continue along the spiritual path on which they have begun, despite the inevitability of struggle and hardship in life.

Sermon #1: "But the Lord God Called Out, 'Adam, Where Are You?'" (Genesis 3:9), 1966

This sermon was preached at least thirteen times between July 10, 1966 (in Neuanlage), and September 21, 1969 (in Neuhorst). These dates fall within the second segment of ordinary time within the liturgical calendar, which is the longest season, beginning with Trinity Sunday and ending with Advent. The biblical text for this sermon is not found in the lectionary, exemplifying the greater degree of flexibility exercised by ministers during this period in the liturgical calendar. Like some of his other sermons, this one was preached multiple times in the same location (Neuhorst, Kronsthal, and Blumenheim), as well as in other locations while travelling outside of the Hague-Osler area (Rosenhof, near Swift Current, Saskatchewan, in 1968, and a year later in Gruenfeld and Reinland, near Fort St. John, British Columbia, and again in Vanderhoof, British Columbia). The sermon is an exhortation to people to ponder their spiritual state: "It is a sobering truth that many of us may be standing at the edge of eternity. Many die suddenly without an opportunity to reflect on life after death." This is the last sermon Herman Friesen preached before his sudden death on September 26, 1969.

Sermon #5

Inaugural Sermon

Texts: Jeremiah 1:7; Romans 15:30–33
Gesangbuch Songs: 318, 478, 511
Written in May 1962 by Herman D. W. Friesen
I.N.J. (In the Name of Jesus)

Invocation/Collect

Grace to you and peace from God the Father and our Lord Jesus Christ, who loved us, washed us from our sins in His blood, and has made us kings and priests before God the Father. To Him be honour and power from eternity to eternity. Amen.

Opening Prayer

Lord, I ask You to show me your ways and teach me your paths, lead me into your truth and teach me, for You are the God who helps me. Grant that I will daily trust in You because I am so weak and needy and dependent on your grace and goodness, which has been since the beginning of the world. Do not remember the sins of my youth and all my transgressions, but think of me in your great mercy because of your goodness according to Psalm 25:4–7. Look on my distress, my misery, my need, and forgive me of all my sins. Protect my soul and save me, let me not be disgraced (Psalm 25:18). For no one will be shamed who trusts in the Lord. Therefore, I ask for one more thing that I would be glad to have, that I may remain in the house of the Lord as a faithful worker as long as I live on earth (Psalm 27:4). But because I am so weak and powerless and my timidity is so great, I need to be taught by others and need to let myself be taught. If You my Lord don't come to help me, I don't know what will happen. You have never abandoned anyone who has come to You in need. Therefore, I call out, "Lord Jesus Christ, have mercy on me in these burdens. Remove them from my heart, for You have atoned for them on the cross with the pain of death so that I need not perish with great pain in misery and despair." O Lord, when I come to realize what I have done in a day, a stone falls on my heart and I am overcome by fright. I sometimes do not know whether I am in or out, but I do know that we are totally lost without your Word. Your healing Word says that all who mourn with tears will be forgiven, and nothing will harm their life. Yes Lord, You predict grace for all who come to You with crushed spirits and who come to You in faith.

I am to teach and admonish others, but when I look at myself, my sins and shortcomings burden my heart so that I need to mourn and confess:

O, I am a child of sin
O, I err far and wide.
There is nothing to be found in me
But only unrighteousness.
All my efforts, all my actions
Are called hatred of God.
My whole life is evil
And continually godless.

Lord, I need to confess
That nothing good lives in me
That what I want to call
I hold before my soul.
Even when trying to force flesh and blood
To perform what is good,
It does not follow as it should.
What I do not want, I still do.

But, O, I fall down
O Father of all grace.
Have mercy on me again
Be patient with your child.
Do not take me to judgment
For I won't endure.
Yes, even for a hundred questions
I won't be able to say a word to You.

Look, Lord, at the deep wounds
That your dearest Son received
When He was fastened to the cross
And hung between earth and heaven.
Look at His death
His pain and His agony
The pain of martyrdom and misery
Which He bore for my good.

Create true repentance, my Saviour,
And a new heart in me.
O, I fall at your feet
Grant that forever and ever
I will withstand all sins,
And walk in your ways.
May all my comings and goings
Be only for your service. Amen.

Introductory Meditation

Beloved brothers and sisters, and yes, you younger listeners, all whom I love in Jesus, I also wish to be loved by all of you. I would earnestly ask all of you to help me, a poor sinner incapable of all good and an incompetent messenger, with your prayers. I hope and trust that you have already sent many prayers to the throne of God that He might stand beside me with His help, so that I may be able to portray His healing words clearly and appropriately.

The words that the Lord spoke to Jeremiah: "You must go to everyone I send you to say whatever I command you. Fear none of them, for I am with you and will keep you safe" (Jeremiah 1:7–8). These words are now my staff to which I cling as I stand at this holy place for the first time today, before the faces of the congregation. Yes, the Lord has sent me and by God's help I have determined to go in His name. He has instructed me to preach to you and so I will, insofar as God gives me grace for it. I will do what He tells me. No doubt there are many hesitations that could develop, as they did for

Jeremiah. Hesitations could arise because of my own incompetence, which I recognize all too well. Or the depraved condition of modern Christianity could make a servant of Christ anxious enough. But the Lord says: "Do not be afraid of them for I am with you, I will save you." So I let this doubtfulness go and with God's help I step before you with full confidence that I will be able to support those of you who need encouragement, for to this God has called me. Oh, that it might happen with great blessing. The Lord will assist me to stand firm, and He will hold me up against all the cunning attacks of Satan. God's side will not be lacking, but how difficult it is for flesh and blood to stay on the narrow path of self-denial, especially for one so weak and lacking in understanding of this difficult task. Only those who have experienced this calling know the problems. Therefore, dear congregation, I ask you to stand beside me with your prayers. Yes, may the Lord bless you and keep you unwearied in the good, so that you can carry on in all highways and byways. May He grant me strength and power in my great poverty and timidity, even if all eyes are on me, so that I will remain steadfast and be able to speak with confidence in God, according to God's holy will and to the benefit of both our souls. What I wish for more than anything is that God would give strength to His weak servant through His grace. Amen.

In the past when progenitor Jacob wanted to give each of his sons a special blessing, he called out in the midst of his situation, "I look for your deliverance, O Lord" (Genesis 49:18). How much more do I, the poor and simple man that I am, find the need to call out "Lord, I wait for your salvation, and for your Spirit's strength and support, so that through the impetus and stimulation of your Holy Spirit I may speak before the congregation according to your holy will!" Yes, faithful head Shepherd, Jesus Christ, strengthen me so that I will be able to steadfastly and tirelessly carry out the difficult task that was placed upon me through your decision and by the congregation. Insofar as You give me strength through your love and grace I will seek to proclaim your will, and place it in the light before You, O Lord.

Lord, make me capable of this task, in spite of my incompetence, because in me there is no strength or capability for this important work. If I take flesh and blood into consideration, I have to say Lord, I am not worthy to teach or preach, as in Jeremiah 1:6. But then when I think of what the Apostle Paul said in 1 Corinthians 9:16: "Yet when I preach the gospel, I cannot boast, for I am compelled to preach. Woe to me if I do not preach the gospel." These words, beloved assembly, have given me much to think about. The "woe to me" became very difficult when I was struggling with flesh and blood, and I pondered how I might be able to avoid it. But it seemed that there was always a voice that said to me, "You are to go where I send you" and thus, "woe to me" if I do not proclaim the gospel. It seemed as though I hardly knew whether to say yes or no, so I almost declined. It was as though I should flee from it, because I did not know how to take on this very important work, as I am so imperfect and sinful. I earnestly prayed to the dear God that He might help me, though I was too evil to serve in this position, yes, too inexperienced with no wisdom in me and lacking everything good. I was useless for this profession. But in all my praying and in my reluctance to accept the position, there still remained the voice, "Woe to you if you do not preach the gospel." If I preach the gospel willingly, God will recompense by grace. If I preach the gospel unwillingly, I am still commanded to do the job. So the position was commanded to me. After all the struggling, praying, wrestling and pleading a thought came to me: Who am I that I should resist God? Didn't His Son, the dear Lord Jesus Christ, do so much for us? He suffered, yes, the horrible death on the cross, and through it His blood saved us. Shouldn't I want to let myself be used for the soul's salvation of many people, if the Lord was able to use me? So finally in the fear of God, I needed to ask myself: What is there to do in all this? Should I excuse myself from the calling and appropriate the calling of Moses, Jonah and other special men of God (Exodus 4:10–14 and Jonah 1–2). I would have to ask with David: "Where shall I go before your Spirit, and where shall I flee before your presence? If I go up to the heavens, You are there, if I make my bed in the depths, You are there. If I take the wings of the morning, and dwell in the uttermost parts of the sea, even there your hand will guide me, and your right hand will hold me fast. For your eyes saw my unformed body" (Psalm 139:16).

If all the days that are still to come are written in your book even before they come about, I felt the need to present myself in the fear of God to give my voluntary response: Lord, here I am, You have called me. Send me and make me willing and fit for this task. Yes, who am I Lord, and what is my house that You have brought me here (2 Samuel 7:8)? Heavenly Father, could You not have elected someone else in my place, someone who would have been more faithful and obedient in following your way, as I have been a miserable sinner? Yes Lord, You who test hearts, You do not demand more of your followers than that they be found faithful according to 1 Corinthians 4:2. But where have I made my faithfulness visible, since all my life I have been in the company of sinful people, have had sinful thoughts, and have often done things that You have forbidden? Yes, if I were to take the time and use it for repentance, take the Holy Scriptures before me and pray for the Spirit and for a holy, God-pleasing life, so that I might have wisdom and understanding, but I have been idle and have sought my pleasure and joy in the world, even though I felt many things and had many fears in my heart because of it. Many times I prayed to God that He might give me a different heart and grant me a different mind, but I remained unchanged and did not attain the new birth. I had many misgivings, especially when the Lord spoke to us so harshly through thunder and lightning during the dark night. How afraid I was then that I might die an unsaved death. But when the storm passed, the thought to earnestly try to be better went away and I lived freely in the world again. Yet, at the age of fifty-four it has pleased the Lord to put on me, through a vote by the congregation, the task of being a minister, even though I am a miserable sinner, rotten through and through, from the soles of my feet to the top of my head. Yes, when I think of how the Lord has so graciously protected and preserved me for so many years on the many roads I have walked and travelled, though I spent so much time following the lusts of the flesh, I am moved to say with the prophet Jeremiah: "O Lord, I am not worthy to be a preacher because I am too young, even if not in years in true seriousness and understanding. But the Lord spoke to me and said: Do not say you are too young, but you are to go where I send you and preach what I tell you to preach" (Jeremiah 1:6–7). If I judge correctly there will be difficulty in preaching, and in the trembling that is involved in finding one's own salvation according to Philippians 2:12, how heaven suffers violence and the mighty seek to grasp it for themselves. How also one must struggle to enter through the narrow gate into eternal life, according to Matthew 7. It is difficult then to help provide for the salvation of members of the congregation. It is difficult enough to be responsible for oneself and even more so for the congregation. Yes, when I weigh the fact that the blood of the one who missed out will be demanded by the Lord from the hands of the watchman, then I would rather say with Moses: "Lord, send whom You will" (Exodus 4:13). I see so many faults in me and there is much lacking in my righteousness in Christ. If my heartfelt wish for you might be fulfilled it would be that along with Timothy I might be an example in faith, in teaching, in conduct and in love (1 Timothy 4:12).

Yes, dear friends all together, as difficult as I find it, I very much want to give myself over to God and gather comfort in the knowledge that the work is the Lord's and the strength to do it comes from God. So hopefully God will be able to bless my work, so that souls may be rescued from eternal damnation and brought into the arms of Jesus. So I will be confident. Yes, insofar as the Lord gives me grace to enter this work, which God, the Lord, and the congregation have put on me. And hopefully you will accept everything in love. I will earnestly plead with God that He and the Holy Spirit will give me wisdom and understanding, a holy and God-pleasing life, and that I might be a good example to the church of God.

> O, my Lord and my God
> Come near to me and make it easy
> That which seems almost impossible to me
> And bring it to a good ending
> What You yourself have begun
> Through the wisdom of your hands.
> Even though the beginning is difficult
> And even if I need to go into the deep ocean
> Of bitter sorrows to bear
> So drive me, Lord, constantly
> To sighing and to prayer.

Invitation to Participate in a Time
of Silent Congregational Prayer

So now, before we go to the discussion of the text and to prayer, I would ask that in this prayer, in great awe and humility, you would plead to God that He might strengthen and fortify me with as many gifts of His Holy Spirit as are necessary for me to carry out my service, so that until my death I may be a faithful worker. Also you may well have reason to pray seriously, and to call on God for anything needed. So at this time turn with me to God, the Lord, in prayer.

The Lord grant a favourable hearing to our prayer and be gracious to us. If we prayed with longing and sincerity for His help, we can be hopeful that the Lord will have heard our prayer.

Reading of the Text

Let us now turn to the words of our text, which we find written in Romans 15:30–33. "I urge you, brothers, by our Lord Jesus Christ and by the love of the Spirit, to join me in my struggle by praying to God for me. Pray that I may be rescued from the unbelievers in Judea, and that my service in Jerusalem may be acceptable to the saints there, so that by God's will I may come to you with joy and together with you be refreshed. The God of peace be with you all." Amen.

Thus far from the words of our text, which we want to look at in order to see how miserable and sinful we have become because of sin. By nature all of us are incapable of anything good, but there is an unexceptionable salvation available to all penitent sinners who find forgiveness for their sins, and through these means become blessed.

Homily

Let us pray, "O faithful Saviour Lord Jesus, be among us now because of your merciful promise. Bless the words that are spoken by this weak and unworthy vessel, in great imperfection, in the present hour. Grant me strength and words to speak according to your holy will. Remove the hardened hearts from our bodies and give us a sincerely reformed heart, which lets itself be ruled by your Holy Spirit. Do so that in this time of grace we may rightly recognize that You save us from the hands of the enemy, so that we may be prompted to heartily repent. Do this because of your infinite love and mercy." Amen.

Our text, dear friends, was sent by the highly enlightened Paul as admonishment to his brethren, and was written as a teaching for us. The text shows how we need to struggle with prayer, and that Paul has come to a conclusion that all people have fallen so deeply by the fall into sin. Of our own selves we are in no position to think anything good, much less do anything good. This is why Paul comes with the admonishment as it is stated in our text: "I urge you, dear brothers, that you help me in the struggle by praying for me to God, so that my service in Jerusalem be acceptable to the saints, so that I may come to you in joy and be refreshed with you." In Romans 7:18–19 Paul says: "I know that nothing good lives in me, that is in my sinful nature. For I have the desire to do what is good, but I cannot carry it out. For what I do is not the good I want to do; no, the evil I do not want to do—this I keep on doing." In verse 23 he says: "I see another law at work in the members of my body, waging war against the law of my mind and making me a prisoner of the law of sin at work within my members." From this we can understand that a person in this world will never be completely able to overcome the evil urge of original sin or to be rid of it. But we are not to let it reach the point where we are ruled by sin and evil works. Much more, in the power of Christ, we are to rule over sin, which gives us a reason for constant prayer. For the law in our body, that is our spoiled nature, constantly struggles against the law or will of our soul, which is the law of God. So, through the strength of God's great grace, which is available to all prayers, and which has conquered sin and death and Satan, we are not to let sin rule over us.

See, dear ones, Paul was an illustrious Apostle of the Lord, yet he kept himself quite low and realized that only through Christ, the crucified One, could he be justified. Paul said that he had the desire to do what was good, but could not carry it out, for the flesh struggles against the spirit, and the spirit against the flesh. However, he did not spend a long time considering flesh and blood, but bravely practised the fight of faith, and at the same time challenges his fellow humans to enter the battle, as he says in the text:

"I urge you, dear brothers, through our Lord Jesus Christ, and through the love of the Spirit, that you will help me strive, by praying to God for me."

So this highly talented Apostle humbled himself as an example for us. How much more will we have to acknowledge that we have been so lax, and have spent our lives in the pursuit of vanity and sensual pleasure? Then I need to confess that I have been far too lax, that I have lived too loosely and have not let myself be taught. And now I am to teach others? O Lord, I pray through the blood of Christ, do well with this poor sinner. O Lord, be gracious to me in your great goodness, and blot out my sins according to your unending mercy. Wash away my sins, for I acknowledge my misdeeds, and my sins are always before me. Create in me a pure heart, and give me a new confident spirit, for the sacrifices that please God are a broken spirit; a broken and contrite heart, O God, You will not despise according to Psalm 51.

I have every reason to be heartily downcast when I think of my great weakness, how slow and indolent I have been against all encouragements, and how quick and easily I have been led into sinfulness. I look at how irreproachable a teacher is to be, how he is to admonish day and night with tears, as Paul did (Acts 20:31). O, when I think of that, I have often been forced to cry out:

I come now to You alone
striding in my distress
And with bended knee
plead with all my heart
Graciously pardon me.
What in my life here
I have committed against You,
O Lord, my God, forgive me
For your name's sake.
And quiet in me the terrible burden of my transgressions
So that my heart will be at peace
And from here on live to your honour
In childlike obedience. Amen.

O Lord, have mercy on this poor sinner. Forgive me of all my sins and grant me strength and wisdom for my calling that has been laid on me, so that in the confidence of your grace I may untiringly and steadfastly carry it out according to your holy will. May I, this poor sinner bought by Christ's blood, be able to say with the Apostle Paul: Who can separate us from the love of Christ?

Whether there be distress, or fear, or persecution, or hunger, or nakedness, or danger, or the sword. May nothing separate us from the love of God, which is in Christ our Lord according to Romans 8:35. But before a person reaches this stability, many a sigh, yes many a prayer, will be sent to heaven, and with the prodigal son making his way to the father saying: "Father, I have sinned against heaven and against you, I am not worthy to be called your son, but make me one of your servants (Luke 15:18–19). Yes, poor person, weep over your situation as Peter did. Come with an eager heart, like Maria. Let your heart be full of love and your eyes full of tears. Call out with the woman from Canaan, Jesus, Son of God, have mercy on me, for my soul is troubled by many sins. Can you not already hear the comforting answer, be comforted, your sins are forgiven. So do not give up, but call even more: Jesus, Son of God, be merciful to me. Look at all my misery and distress, help me in my need. If the time becomes long while you are waiting for your God, you must say with David: "I am worn out calling for help; my throat is parched. My eyes fail, looking for my God." And if your faith grows weak, you sad heart, then call out with the half-discouraged disciple: "Help, Lord, or I will perish." If you, sad sinner, have such remorse over your sins of the past, whether you are old or young, if you seek with all your heart to be rid of them, have a deep longing for the grace of God, and come with a weeping heart looking for grace and forgiveness by God, the Father cannot long refrain from helping. It breaks His heart and He will have mercy on you, as we can see in the story of the prodigal son, who is the example of all penitent sinners. So, people, do not neglect to repent, for who knows how long we still have until we will need to appear before the Judge of the world and give account of our life's journey. So I, unworthy as I am, call to all of you earnestly: "Hurry and save your soul." If you do that with sincere repentance and living faith, you will become a completely different person. Then everyone will be able to see that you have become a new character. If before you have been arrogant, after your conversion you will become quite humble. Along with Abraham you will acknowledge that you are nothing but dust and ashes. Yes, you will learn gentleness and humility according to Matthew 11. If before you have been stingy, have rightly or wrongly amassed temporal goods, taken advantage of the neighbour and have closed your heart against the poor neighbour, you will become quite mild. You will no longer look at your belongings as though they are yours, but as if God has given them into your care in order to help your poor brother in his time of need.

Therefore, my dear listeners, let us begin again to make a greater effort to live in such a way as to be ready for the great judgment day. Yes, when I think back on the past two months I am reminded of the election for ministers and the confirmation where I promised to serve God and the congregation faith-fully, and then the teaching of the young people (*Jugendunterricht*) where we checked ourselves carefully as to how far we had lived up to the confessions we had made before God and the congregation, we all had to confess that we had frequently failed. If we look at the present time, where everything rushes along in the stream of life, and how the Lord warns us through illness and accidents, which occur so that we may draw closer to God.

Let us give ear to His voice, so that we too will become different people. As with Samuel, you too will become a different person. Let us remember the words of Jesus when He says that "it is better to give than to receive" (Acts 20:35). If previously we were angry if someone offended us with words, we will become calm, and even pray for them, as Jesus teaches. We become completely different people in heart and mind. Then what Samuel said to the newly crowned Saul will be fulfilled in us: that you will become a new person (1 Samuel 10:6).

Therefore, my dear ones, let us not neglect to pray and plead to God, the Lord, as we read in Psalm 38:21: "O Lord, do not forsake me; do not be far from me, O my God." And let us pray with a poet thus:

O stay with me Lord, when the dark time breaks in
When night comes, leave me not alone.

When everything flees, when each prop breaks,
Thou, reliable refuge, leave me not.
The short day of life flees like a rapid stream
The delights of earth wither, their luster fades
All around decay stares in my face
Thou unchanging one, leave me not.
Not a glance, a fleeting word of grace
I ask for, no, graciousness, full of patience.
And as your mouth promises to your disciples
Forever, Lord, come, do not forsake me.
Come as the doctor, who heals our illness,
As a mild friend, who shares all our sorrow.
Come, not frightful, as if for the world's judgment
No, as a Saviour come, do not forsake me.
Even at my cradle You stood smiling,
And if I was unfaithful, a prodigal son
You faithfully went after the scoundrel
So to the end, O Lord, do not forsake me.
If your grace does not stand by me from hour to hour
How can I quench Satan's tyranny?
Who is there like You, an anchor and a light?
Be it clear, or cloudy, only do not abandon me.
If only I have You, no enemy frightens me
Sweet are the tears, light the sorrow's pressure
Yes, when the thorn of death afflicts me
The victory is mine, as long as You do not leave me.
And if my eyes grow dim, hold your cross before me
Show me through the darkness the door of heaven
The shadows flee, your eternal light shines.
In death and life Lord, do not forsake me. Amen.

When it was decided on which Sunday I should present my introductory message, I tried to prepare. In the beginning I had a fair amount of time for preparation, but from time to time there were interruptions that kept me from my work. But the day approached when I was to begin my work. The date was set, and in the same way our day of death is also determined and we are always drawing closer. Often something happens and we postpone our preparation for death, so we want to make good use of the time, so death does not find us unprepared. If we look at the world, we soon hear of a gruesome murder, or about a terrible accident. Then it is a sudden death, or a serious illness that causes the ill person's thinking to be compromised. So often we hear of much strife and lack of peace in our day, and Jesus said: "Blessed are the peacemakers."

Therefore, let us be watchful, for our days are also determined.

The grace of our Lord Jesus Christ, the love of God the Father, and the comforting presence of the Holy Spirit be with us all. Amen. In the name of Jesus, Amen.

Invitation to Participate in a Time
of Silent Congregational Prayer

For any other concerns that anyone may have on their hearts for which they feel prayer is necessary, they can call on our Lord, not only here in this place, but also at home, evening and morning, at any time during the day or night. With this, turn again with me to the Lord in prayer.

The Lord hear our prayer and give heed to the voice of our appeal.

Benediction/Dismissal

In connection with this morning's worship service I have nothing more to say to the congregation, except to thank you heartily for your acceptance and your love for the services. In conclusion I say with the man of God, Moses: "The Lord bless you and keep you; the Lord make His face shine upon you and be gracious to you, the Lord turn His face toward you and give you peace" (Numbers 6:24–26). May the Lord protect our comings and goings into eternity. Amen.

Go in the peace of God.

Sermon #12

"Run in Such a Way as to Get the Prize"

Texts: Matthew 5–7; 1 Corinthians 9:24–27
Written in July 1962 by Herman D. W. Friesen
I.N.J. (In the Name of Jesus)

Invocation/Collect

Grace be with you, and peace from God the Father of our Lord Jesus Christ, who gave Himself for us so that He could save us from this wicked world according to the will of God, our Father, to whom be honour and power from eternity to eternity. Amen.

Introductory Meditation

"Enter through the narrow gate. For wide is the gate and broad is the road that leads to destruction, and many enter through it. But small is the gate and narrow the road that leads to life, and only a few find it" (Matthew 7:13–14). Dear friends, those are words of the Lord Jesus that He Himself said to His Apostles when they asked Him if only a few would be saved. He did not tell them how many, but warned them that they must struggle and see to it that they themselves be saved. We hear it here, dear souls, out of the mouth of truth itself that there is only one way to salvation, namely the narrow way, and to this way there is only one gate, the narrow gate. Therefore, dear listeners, let us think about it. Only two roads are before people, a narrow one, which is clearly described in the Word of God, and a broad one, which leads to eternal ruin because those who follow it do not live according to the prescribed limitations of the narrow road. The quoted words, dear friends, are from the conclusion of Jesus's Sermon on the Mount.

Obviously here the dear Lord summarizes what He says in the Sermon on the Mount as He admonishes, "Enter through the narrow gate and travel on the narrow road" (Matthew 7:13). The road that leads to life is none other than the road that is described in the Sermon on the Mount. So no one is on the narrow road except the ones who earnestly strive to keep the commandments laid out in the Sermon on the Mount. So all those who do not act in accordance with the Sermon on the Mount, find themselves on the broad road that leads to destruction. On the broad way that leads to destruction are those who do not strive to follow the teachings of Jesus. The Lord clearly describes in the Sermon on the Mount the rules of His kingdom and the conditions under which we become citizens of His kingdom, and remain in the same.

He who does not keep the laws of the Kingdom cannot be a citizen thereof because he is not under the rule of Christ. So he who is not under the rule of the Saviour is not on the narrow way that leads to life, but rather he is on the way to destruction. On the narrow way, which leads to life, dear souls, are only those who really feel the burden of their sins, and are truly spiritually poor. Only those who carry their regret with a godly sorrow, only the meek, only those who hunger and thirst for righteousness, only the compassionate, only the pure of heart will let themselves be prompted by the spirit of God. Only those who seek peace and love it, who then also for the sake of Christ may be persecuted and suffer scorn and unjust treatment, only those are on the narrow way, the way that leads to life. But those who do not seek a greater righteousness than that of the scribes and Pharisees, who do not love their brother whom they see, who are not obliging to their opponent on the way, who do not seek the truth everywhere, who still lie, still swear, and protest, who then practise retribution against others instead of suffering wrong themselves, who even hate their friends, and do not try to love them or pray for them, all those are on the way to destruction.

For children of God seek to shine outwardly with their works, and they don't have a divided heart between God and Mammon. They put their faith in the living God, they cast their burdens on Him. They are always concerned with taking the beam out of their own eyes, before trying to see if they can move the splinter out of their brother's eye. They are careful in their walk in the world, and they have a spirit of prayer so they can let their concerns be known to the Lord with pleas and entreaties. They seek to love their neighbour as themselves. See, dear listeners, the narrow way that leads to life. For this reason we want to test ourselves and see if we find ourselves on the narrow road, the road that leads to eternal and blessed life.

Our wish, dear listeners, is that we will all be saved, but when we test ourselves according to the Sermon on the Mount, our consciences often accuse us of walking in a direction we should not have gone, and that we have lost ourselves on the broad way. Instead of being poor in spirit we are rich, conceited, proud, and self-righteous. In light of this, are we sorry for our sins? Aren't we too often more concerned about earthly things? Do we hunger and thirst for righteousness? Are we compassionate like our Father in heaven is compassionate? He who carries us one day after another in His great patience, who still lets His sun of grace shine over us. Our Saviour says, "Blessed are the peacemakers," and we have joy in lack of peace, and often strive for that? Or we create lack of peace by our carelessness.

Dear ones, be compassionate, as also the Father is compassionate. Do not judge, so you will not be judged. Do not condemn so that you will not be condemned. Forgive, and you will be forgiven. O, beloved friends, how we can be encouraged by these words to strive ever more with great earnestness toward these great goals. Our heavenly Father, as a faithful shepherd, is so compassionate and long-suffering. He goes after the lost sheep, looks for the lost coin, and is happy when He finally finds it. Yes, I say again, should not our total attention be in this direction? Should this not lead us to repentance? Have we, dear friends, really tested ourselves in our relationship to our God and Saviour? Have you considered, with faith-filled eyes, the love and compassion of your Saviour, experienced them in your heart, and with thankful lips praised Him? Have you called on God and the Saviour for forgiveness of your sins? If you have not done that, then the sermon has been in vain, and you have not let it lift up your heart as it was intended to do. O, dear souls, do we not testify with our actions and with our walk that the Word of God has been made available to us and is still sent to us? We have not reacted to it, or we have even despised it. And how can we practise the godly attributes and qualities we have if we do not want to hear or follow His commandments and precepts? We cannot be Jesus's followers or His disciples if we do not pay attention to the teachings He has left for us. The admonition—be merciful as your Father in heaven is merciful—is given us as a command from the Lord Jesus. Therefore, we want to begin to follow more earnestly, and pay heed to this teaching, and to let go of the lack of mercy toward friends and enemies. Let us practise mercy in the same way our heavenly Father lets mercy come over us, daily and even hourly. For James says: "Because judgment without mercy will be shown to anyone who has not been merciful" (James 2:13). And we see in Matthew 18:34 what kind of judgment follows lack of mercy. Despite the warning, such unmerciful treatments happen among us. Therefore, let us take the words of our dear Saviour, Jesus Christ, which He left us as a prediction in the Sermon on the Mount, when he says "blessed are the merciful, for they shall be shown mercy" (Matthew 5:7).

Now, dear listeners, from these words we understand clearly that we will be treated according to the way we have treated our neighbour, so let us be more careful in our relationships to our neighbours. Let us first look at ourselves and then at our neighbour. Yes, let us show mercy so that we too shall receive mercy. Further, Jesus says: "Do not judge, or you too will be judged" (Matthew 7:1). Oh beloved and dear listeners, in this too we fail so often when we judge the faults of another, and do not see our own. Paul says in Romans 2:1: "You, therefore, have no excuse, you who pass judgment on someone else, for at whatever point you judge others, you are condemning yourself, because you who pass judgment do the same things." Dear friends, even here we are again encouraged to look first at ourselves before we begin to blame or judge another. But what is it that daily experiences teach us? How often do we judge another according to our natural instincts, instead of sympathizing with another and seeking to show them a better way? Too often a strong criticism is expressed and we forget ourselves. How often do we overstep the bounds? Therefore, believing friends, do not judge, that you will not be judged (Matthew 7:1). If we would first look at our own shortcomings, we would not find as many mistakes in others.

Further, Jesus calls to the people: "Blessed are the peacemakers, for they will be called sons of God. Blessed are those who are persecuted because of righteousness, for theirs is the kingdom of heaven" (Matthew 5:9–10). How many are persecuted today for the sake of Jesus and for righteousness? When we hear that in some countries the Word of God is repressed, and even here in our area some are beginning to show indignation to the church and thereby they create disharmony, thinking they are doing a service to

God. In Acts 4:25 we read: "Why do the nations rage and the peoples plot in vain?" So, dear listeners, let us not undertake what is useless so that our work is in vain because God is not a God of disorder, but of peace according to 1 Corinthians 14:33. Jesus says: "Blessed are the peacemakers, for they will be called the sons of God" (Matthew 5:9).

So "let us fix our eyes on Jesus, the author and perfecter of our faith," (Hebrews 12:2) for He says in John 14:6: "I am the way and the truth and the life. No one comes to the Father except through me." So this is the only path open to us, to come to the heavenly Father to attain eternal life. Therefore, dear souls, let us strive in all seriousness not to miss the right road, so that no one is left behind. O that we might all pray along with King David: "Show me Your ways, O Lord, teach me Your paths; guide me in Your truth and teach me" (Psalm 25:4–5). King David was so concerned, he wanted to know the way of the Lord, and to follow in the path of His holy commandments. But because he recognized his own shortcomings, his spiritual blindness and incompetence, he turns to God and pleads for Him to guide and lead him along the path that he might reach true and eternal redemption. That is the reason why he begs: "Lord, show me your ways, and teach me your paths, guide me in your truth and teach me" (Psalm 25:4–5). In this sincere pleading and asking, we want to emulate King David, a man after the heart of God.

It should be a concern for each of us that we do not miss the right path to everlasting bliss, and that no one is left behind. We should pray to the Lord to show us the right way and teach us His paths. Lord, my God, rescue me from the path of unrighteousness, and guide me on the way that leads to life. Yes, lead me in your truth, and teach me, for You alone are the God who helps me. In line with this I call on all of you to heed the Lord's words: "Stand at the crossroads and look; ask for the ancient paths, ask where the good way is, and walk in it, and you will find rest for your souls" (Jeremiah 6:16).

Invitation to Participate in a Time
of Silent Congregational Prayer

We will together consider more of God's Word in this text, but before that let us all kneel on our knees before God, and come to His throne and in childlike fashion plead that He would grant me, this weak instrument, to be equipped ever more and more. Then, bolstered by the assurance that among the dear listeners there are praying hearts beating for us poor servants, we want to kneel down and in prayer and intercession bow down to request the assistance of the Holy Spirit, so that everything be done to His honour, and that it may serve to the well-being of our souls. So with this, join me in turning to God in prayer.

The Lord hear our prayer and be gracious to us.

Reading of the Text

If we have called on God the Lord not only with our lips but also with our hearts, we may comfort ourselves and be happy that He will hear us and bless us in this hour. With this certainty I turn confidently to the words of the text that we find described in 1 Corinthians 9:24–27: "Do you not know that in a race all the runners run, but only one gets the prize? Run in such a way as to get the prize. Everyone who competes in the games goes into strict training. They do it to get a crown that will not last; but we do it to get a crown that will last forever. Therefore, I do not run like a man running aimlessly; I do not fight like a man beating the air. No, I beat my body and make it my slave so that after I have preached to others, I myself will not be disqualified for the prize." Thus far the words of the text.

Homily

Dear Friends, before we go to a discussion of the text, let us pray together. Dear Saviour, Lord Jesus, You are the only treasure, You are the only blessing that will last forever. Grant us the grace that we may constantly have You before our eyes and in our hearts. Protect us, so that we will not consider the joys and goods of this world as more important than the peace of God and eternal salvation that You have promised us. You have given us this world and our life in it as preparation for the other world. Therefore, O Lord, open our eyes that we can see which road we find ourselves, and grant that we be able to do what is necessary in faith to reach the treasure that You have promised us, which holds before us the heavenly calling to eternal life with God through Jesus Christ. Amen.

Dear listeners, I first must remark that when I speak of the race for the heavenly treasure, I do not speak of those who are still dead in their transgressions and sins, and are living without any urge within themselves toward the kingdom of God. We are speaking of such who have awakened from their sin-sleep, and are striving to live a pious life. For those who feel no regret for their miserable sinful condition, spend all their time of grace with various vanities and conceits of the world, are pleased with their own virtues and integrity, still hang onto their lusts of the flesh, conceits, and idleness, and still set their confidence on their outward Christianity without considering the changes that have happened in heart and mind, such are still without life from God. They are still far from the Saviour, and have not yet entered the ranks of the fighters for Christ. They all find their dismissal, brief and decisive, in the words of Jesus: "Wide is the gate and broad is the road that leads to destruction, and many enter through it" (Matthew 7:13). But here the talk is of such who recognize their condition, and are concerned about the one thing that is needful. The talk is of those who have already recognized in their hearts why they are in this world, namely as being designated for eternal blessedness in the kingdom of God and His righteousness, and for which they strive. I wish with all my heart that we might all be like this.

Therefore, dear listeners, I would like to make you aware of a few of the hindrances and deviations in the race so as to warn us against such hindrances. We read in 2 Timothy 2:5: "If anyone competes as an athlete, he does not receive the victor's crown unless he competes according to the rules." In Hebrews 12:1 we read: "Therefore, since we are surrounded by such a great cloud of witnesses, let us throw off everything that hinders and the sin that so easily entangles, and let us run with perseverance the race marked out for us." Yes, "fight the good fight of faith. Take hold of the eternal life to which you are called when you made good your confession in the presence of many witnesses" (1 Timothy 6:12). Dear friends, we can notice here that even if we run, we may still miss the prize. The text says, run so that you might take hold of it, or, as it has already been mentioned, even though someone strives, he will not be crowned unless he strives aright.

Our Saviour says the same thing to His disciples when they asked Him: "Lord, do you mean that only a few will be saved?" (Luke 13:23). He answered them by saying: "Make every effort to enter through the narrow door, because many, I tell you, will try to enter and will not be able to" (Luke 13:24). And why will they not be able to? The answer is only because they did not strive aright. Therefore, fight the good fight of faith. When God the Lord brought the masses of the people of Israel out of Egypt, He made no distinction, and anything that came from the seed He took under His leadership, with their destination Canaan. There they were to receive the promised inheritance, there they were to live as the people of God, as the chosen people, as the kingly priesthood, as people belonging to Him.

So now God brought them into the boundaries wherein they were to learn to run for the prize. They had to wander through the desert with the many deprivations and needs. Yet they were still under the marvellous leading of God. They were to be trained to be a people, who in firm faith and obedience were to be true to their God. They were to believe even though they did not see, they were to have, when they did not have. The desert was to be for them a fruitful pasture, for their God travelled with them into the desert. Through a firm faith and obedience each one was to prove that they were worthy to receive the inheritance promised to Abraham. To enter the desert they had to cross the Red Sea, which through God's marvellous provision he made it possible for them to pass through with dry feet. Then they were in the desert with the limitations, but they were to run for the prize. The people of Israel had not counted on wandering in the desert as a way of reaching their goal. They did not want to run under the restrictions of God, but wanted to follow their own lusts. In a short time they were murmuring against God about bread and water or meat. Soon they wanted to stone their God-appointed leaders, Moses and Aaron, and return to Egypt. Soon they let themselves be led into the lusts and depravity of the heathens living in the area. That is why, out of that great mass of people, only two entered the Land of Canaan. The others all died in the desert, and they lie buried there because of their unbelief, and as a result, they did not achieve the promise. They ran, but not in the right way and so they did not carry away the treasure.

Therefore, dear friends, let us run in the struggle that is ordained for us, toward the goal that has been set before us by our heavenly calling in

Christ Jesus. Let us fight the good fight of faith, so that we need not be left as the slain in the eternal wilderness. Therefore, let us think about what the Apostle Paul says: "Everyone who competes in the games goes into strict training" (1 Corinthians 9:25).

Yes, dear souls, all who are chasing after the heavenly treasure, let us think about it carefully and let it sink deeply into our hearts. "If anyone competes as an athlete, he does not receive the victor's crown unless he competes according to the rules" (2 Timothy 2:5). From this we can understand that if we do not run in the right way in the struggle that has been designated for us, we will not be crowned. No, then we, along with the five unwise maidens, will be turned away. They had prepared themselves to meet the bridegroom, but when their oil was lacking and their lamp of faith extinguished, the doors were locked and they could not enter to attend the wedding. And when they knocked and called out, "open the door for us," they received the frightening answer, "Go away, I don't know who you are" (Matthew 25:11–12).

Therefore, dear friends, let us run with patience the fight that is ordained for us, and as already mentioned, if anyone competes, he is still not crowned unless he competes according to the rules. But why do we so often struggle to compete the right way? The hardest, but the best way that we as Christians must fight is against ourselves, to conquer flesh and blood and to leave the sensual pleasures of this world. This is often very difficult, but if we do not want to leave the world and its attractions, we will not reach the treasure. Our text says to run in such a way as to get the prize, or run in such a way that you can take hold of it.

The Lord tells His disciples to think of Lot's wife. That is also written as a lesson and a warning for us. This is what the Saviour says to all His followers. Lot's wife ran out of Sodom so that the disaster that was to break out over the city would not swallow her up as well. Her beginning was good, but oh, on the way she stopped and looked back at Sodom. She still had a secret longing in her heart for Sodom. She could not so quickly separate herself from it, and so it came about that the vengeful arm of Jehovah so suddenly overtook her.

This is the way many Christians can begin their course. They make a good start. The Lord has called them and they have followed the call, moved out of Sodom to follow the Saviour, but their inward longings or thoughts tell them to go back to the lusts of Sodom, back to their self-love, self-righteousness. They look on others and forget what they are, and like the Pharisees they stand and thank God that they are better and more Christian. They think that they are doing God a greater service than other people do. That is why the Lord Jesus says in Luke 18 that those who think of themselves as righteous but despise others forfeit their treasure thereby. The poor tax collector stood from afar, and did not even want to lift his eyes to heaven, but beat on his breast and said: "God, be merciful to me, a sinner" (Luke 18:13). Such a penitent sinner will not throw away the treasure.

The Apostle Paul did not shy away from, or was ashamed of calling himself the greatest of all sinners or to call himself a miserable individual. He knew and acknowledged that in his flesh nothing good dwelt. That type of confession is already a race toward the goal. Honest and sincere anguish over your sins, sincere tears about your sins, acknowledging your sins before God and people, and the humble plea for forgiveness is also an appeal. If you call on the Lord in your weakness, that He might give you the strength and desire to carry on, if you strengthen yourself through prayer and God's word, you will make progress. If you also separate yourself from your former partners in sin, and tear all the bonds that have kept you tied to them, and humbly bow before the cross, you can go forth confident and happy, and run toward the treasure, which the heavenly calling holds before you.

So, dear brothers and sisters, those who say they are Christians, that they know God, they will keep His commands, and walk as He walked. And he who says he knows Him but does not keep His commands, is a liar and the truth is not in him.

A hindrance for many in the race for the heavenly treasure is self-love. So Satan, wherever possible, attacks them on the most vulnerable side, and mirrors for them great things in their understanding of Christianity. So whoever does not continue to be alert and pray, it can happen that he puts them to sleep with a false comfort, with a false solace about the forgiveness of sin, and lulls them to sleep in a false comfort of the peace of God.

If we now say we have no sin, we delude ourselves, and truth is not in us according to 1 John 1:8. Now, dear souls, it is quite sad in our day that so many people think so highly of their Christianity. Many a sinner has such strange ideas about overcoming the world, and of their denials, which cripple the strength of the spirit. These either require the languid rest of the flesh, or hinder the walk in humility and love, or the walk in spirit and truth.

We all stepped into certain restraints when we made our confession of faith before God and the congregation when we received holy baptism. Then we left Egypt, the house of service of the ruler of this world. We promised faithfulness to the Lord. We openly gave our testimony that we henceforth no longer would serve sin. Therefore, we are now all subject to one another out of reverence for Christ (Ephesians 5:21). So "Humble yourselves, therefore, under God's mighty hand, that He may lift you up in due time" (1 Peter 5:6). In Isaiah 2:11–12 we read: "The eyes of the arrogant man will be humbled and the pride of men brought low; the Lord alone will be exalted in that day. The Lord Almighty has a day in store for all the proud and lofty, for all that is exalted (and they will be humbled)."

From this, dear friends, we can understand that before God we have no right to praise ourselves, or to exalt ourselves above others, which nowadays happens frequently, so that people leave the fellowship, where they had promised God and the church to be faithful till death. They scorn or even persecute the church in which they were reared. But the Lord Jesus said if they have persecuted me, they will also persecute you according to John 15:20. O, let us humble ourselves under the cross of Christ, we who are sinners, and pray to the Lord with all our hearts that He would be gracious to us. May He have mercy on us. Let us continue with prayers and pleadings that we may attain grace, and not stay mired in our sins, and false dreams about our "good condition." O dear congregation, let us strengthen the sluggish hands, and lift up the stumbling knees, and pray for salve for the eyes so that we will be brave and not frivolously throw away our treasure. May we call out with blind Bartimaeus in Mark 10: "Jesus, son of David, have mercy on me" so that we too will be able to see. May He have pity on us. Yes, let us continue begging and pleading that we may receive grace, and not stay stuck in our sins, dreaming of our good conditions.

For God has also, dear listeners, marked out the course of our race. It is surrounded by His holy will, with His advice and His commandments.

On one hand, where in the commandments it says you shall go, there we have the surface on which we may run. On the other hand, where it says you shall not, there we are not to place our foot. Every "you shall not" is a barrier or a harness that God has brought out. The length of the course is our life. We do not know how long our course is, but God knows. He has set a goal before us, and we will not exceed that.

God has hidden from us the hour of death, so that each day we die to self and shall live to God and Christ. He has hidden the day from us, so that every day we will make His presence current. If the Lord had not hidden this day from us, wouldn't many, out of fear and sadness about the brief lifespan, begin the race? Or wouldn't many, in the confidence that they still had many years, think that they could begin running toward the goal in the cool evening hours of their life? Therefore, do not think to yourself, "I have lots of time, the day of death is far away. I will first be happy here on earth. When I become tired of life, then I will seek salvation. God will probably have mercy on me." The length of our course is unknown to us. Today or tomorrow, or any hour we may reach our destination, and that is why today is so important, because yesterday is gone, and we do not yet have tomorrow. So, as the Holy Spirit says: "Today, if you hear His voice, do not harden your hearts" (Hebrews 3:15). Therefore, think, dear congregation, that no one can begin his life again, and it is my heart's sincerest wish that no one might forfeit their inheritance.

If we do not go about proving with words and deeds that we are truly Christ's followers, then at the time of the great judgment day we will be considered as hopeless hypocrites and be thrown into outer darkness. Therefore, test yourselves as to what is the basis of your heart. For as sure as God lives, His word stands fast forever, and if we want to be saved we need to prepare ourselves to follow the God-appointed path, or we will never enter heaven.

The time is brief, O people, be wise
and exploit the present moment.
Only once you make this journey
Leave a good mark behind you.

See how quickly time passes for the fool
With eating, drinking, jesting, rest,
The wise one works and thus is the winner
He fills his time with doing good.

You cannot hold back a single hour
Before you notice, it is gone,
Wisdom tells you to be faithful
The faithful one will receive high payment.

So, Saviour, teach me to use my years
For Your services alone
From today until the end
To strew seeds for the life to come.

So what is it that constitutes the true walk of faith for the Christian to attain the treasure? Before all else, a sincere earnestness is needed. See, dear friends, what effort and what energy one puts into attaining worldly goods. We have been offered the inheritance of God, and the co-inheritance of Christ, eternal, unchanging goods that remain, which will not be eaten by rust or moths, which no one can pilfer. And yet only a few have the right earnestness to strive for it.

The Saviour holds the imperishable crown of life to the fighters, and says to them: "Be faithful unto death and I will give you the crown of life" (Revelation 2:10b). But only few heed His words. Many are thoughtless, others are weak and indolent, as though they are concerned only with minor things of the world. For the race to reach the heavenly treasure, real earnestness is needful. This earnestness pays off already, and how much more at the end. For he who valiantly strives may already receive here the great privilege that he can learn more and more to take certain steps so that he will be more and more united with the Spirit. So that more and more he tastes the comfort of the forgiveness of sins, and that he feels the peace with God, as we read in Isaiah 57:2. Those who have walked righteously will come to peace. "There remains, then, a Sabbath-rest for the people of

God" (Hebrews 4:9). The indolent, however, come to no peace, no rest, no strengthening, and what is the worst is that they fritter away their inheritance as the holy ones of the light.

Another requirement for the true run for the heavenly treasure is the love of truthfulness. Everyone on the side of truth listens to me, says the Lord, and this holds true for the beginning and the continuation of the run. To run within the bounds of the race requires the strengthening of brotherly love, and the love for the fellowship of God.

In earthly contests only one can win the prize. It is not that way in the spiritual. There all the contestants may achieve the crown that does not fade. Paul, who has worn his crown for a long time, admonishes us: "Join with others in following my example, brothers, and take note of those who live according to the pattern we gave you" (Philippians 3:17). Dear listeners, when we look at how Paul lived, and we take him as our example in order to walk in the same way, we will also achieve the victory with Paul, and carry away the imperishable crown of honour. The Apostle Paul says in Philippians 3:12: "Not that I have already obtained all this, or have already been made perfect, but I press on to take hold of that for which Christ Jesus took hold of me." Let us hold onto the confession of hope, and not waver, for He is faithful, who has predicted it. Let us together perceive one another by stimulating each other to love, and strengthening one another. Let us not leave our gatherings, as some have been doing, rather let us encourage one another—and all the more as you see the day approaching (Hebrews 10:23–25).

So finally, set diligently before your souls the treasure that we are to grasp. Yes, dear friends, let us run within the boundaries set for us, and not grow weary, and don't look behind you. Do not let anything lead you off the right way—not the world, and what is in the world, desires, property, honour, and the like. Do not be shocked when for a stretch of the road you have to wear the crown of thorns. The Lord Jesus also wore it, and it became for Him the victor's crown and the crown of honour, and it will be thus for you. Therefore, run in your bounds as long as you can run. If you slacken it will be worse than if you had not started.

When a righteous individual turns to evil, then the good that he has done before will no longer be considered (Ezekiel 18). Therefore, it says in Revelation 2:10: "Be faithful, even to the point of death, and I will give you the crown of life." So then let us continue in the struggle that has been prescribed for us, which holds before us the heavenly calling. Yes, let us be faithful, as the poet says: "Be Thou Faithful unto Death."

Be faithful even unto death, as you struggle for the crown of life;
Break confidently through distress, grasp the promised reward,
which out of grace is appointed for you, at the end of your race.

No one there will be crowned who did not bravely strive here;
Who has been scorned here on earth, suffered humiliation and hardship,
He there will receive a crown brighter than the rays of the sun.
If this treasure appeals to you, do not tire in the struggle
Only on Christ's path of suffering does one reach the wished for peace
For only sweat and toil brings us to the promised prize of Glory.

If at one time in the world you promised to follow Christ's banner
So do not leave the field, or else the victory is also lost.
Fight until the foe is beaten and your head carries the palms.
It is the duty of all Christians to believe and trust in God,
Do not depart from your faithfulness until you will see in the light
How for the fighters there is prepared the crown of righteousness.

Therefore, "let us fix our eyes on Jesus, the author and perfecter of our faith" (Hebrews 12:2), so that we, after the race is done, may not miss entering His rest, and out of grace we may receive the crown of righteousness through Jesus Christ. Amen.

Now, dear congregation, we want to prepare ourselves again for departure, but we do not want to leave unthankful, but want to praise and thank our God, and according to the Apostles' teachings, intercede for all people. So, let us pray together. Heavenly Father, we thank You that we have again been able to gather in peace. Continue to be with us. Be also with all those who have lost their way, so that they will once again be converted. Be also with our government, with the sick, the sad, with widows and orphans, and those who have spiritual problems. Be with travellers, and protect our country from devastation and ruin. Yes, be with all people in whatever sorrow they might be. Especially have mercy on the dying, and lead them all through a gentle and blissful death toward the joys of eternity, to be, and stay with you for all eternity. Amen.

Invitation to Participate in a Time
of Silent Congregational Prayer

For anyone who may still have something on their hearts for which they feel it necessary to pray, they can pray not only here in this hall, but also at home, evening or morning, yes, day and night, they may call on God the Lord in prayer.

The Lord hear our prayer and be gracious to us. The grace of our Lord Jesus Christ, the love of God the Father, and the comforting presence of His Holy Spirit be with us all. Amen. In Jesus's name, Amen.

Benediction/Dismissal

In connection with the public service I have nothing further to present to this worthy gathering at this time, except to say a hearty thank you for your love for the service. With the man of God, Moses, I say: "The Lord bless and protect you, the Lord let His face shine upon you and give you peace, yes He protects our coming and going from now on and into all eternity." Amen.

So go in the peace of the Lord.

Sermon #19

Two Praying at the Door of Grace:
The Pharisee and the Tax Collector

For the 11th Sunday after Trinity Sunday
Text: Luke 18:9–14
Written in July 1963 by Herman D. W. Friesen
I.N.J. (In the Name of Jesus)

Invocation/Collect

Praise be to the God and Father of our Lord Jesus Christ, who has saved us through His great mercy to a living hope through the resurrection of Jesus Christ from the dead, to an everlasting, undefiled, and unfading legacy that is kept for us in heaven. Amen.

Introductory Meditation

"How lovely are the feet of the messengers on the mountain who proclaim peace, preach good news, proclaim salvation, who say to Zion: 'Your God is king!'" (Isaiah 52:7). Thus, the prophet Isaiah prophesied in a difficult time to his humbled nation and in his spirit saw the messengers of peace coming over the mountains as God's angels to announce a time of grace and blessing to the earth. This prophecy was gloriously fulfilled in the new dispensation. The Apostles of Jesus, as messengers of peace from God, wandered over hill and dale, proclaiming good news and salvation to all peoples. The first and greatest messenger of peace and the good news of salvation, who preceded everyone, was the Prince of Peace, Jesus Christ. His first gracious call to peace was the Sermon on the Mount, with which He began His ministry among His people.

O, it must have been lovely to hear from Jesus in this way. Even though we do not stand on that mountain of blessing with material feet or hear with material ears the words of life from Jesus's lips, still there wafts to us a breath of mountain air like a breeze of peace from heavenly heights whenever we read or hear the Sermon on the Mount reverently. What lofty promises it announces, and what noble views it preaches? It is a lofty command of holy brotherly love that the preacher on the mountain speaks to our hearts, in that He leads us together before the altar of a Holy God, around whom we are to gather in unity as people of God.

Dear listeners, in Matthew 5:23–24 we read: "So if you are offering your gift at the altar, and remember that your brother has something against you, leave your gift there before the altar and go; first be reconciled to your brother, and then come and offer your gift." Truly this is a significant reminder for us as well, here in this holy place. We do not bring gifts of offering to this altar as the faithful in the Old Testament did, but the offering we should and would like to bring to the Lord as often as we are gathered in His house is the heart offering of our adoration, our thankfulness, and our vows. Also we would wish to receive, as we leave, the assurance of the grace of our God, with whom we are reconciled through the one eternally efficacious offering of our Lord Jesus Christ.

And now, dear ones, when we gather here in this holy place out of the clamour of the world, out of the hustle and bustle of daily life, when we gather before God as a congregation of the Lord, should we not from time to time be reminded of what we must not bring with us to this holy altar, what we must put off before our offering can be pleasing to God?

This altar is an offering altar of prayer. But, dear listeners, is our prayer the offering of Abel, of a childish purity, of a brotherly tender heart, or is it a Cain offering with hatred for the brother and envy that mixes into your worship, and robs you of God's blessing? According to the admonishment of the Lord, whoever is angry with his brother is worthy of judgment (Matthew 5:22). We have all, at one time, made a vow to walk according to the gospel, and to remain until the end in a loving relationship to God and our fellow human beings. Can we, dear listeners, look toward this altar with a good conscience? Does it not speak to us of broken promises, of forgotten intentions? Does it not also speak of a God and Saviour who holds against us that we left our first love? And what about the people who have something against us, or of parents whose love we have not returned, or of teachers whose admonishment we did not follow?

So dear congregation, we remember the crucified Saviour who loved us to His death, and gave us a new commandment. The Lord says "A new commandment I give you, that you love one another as I have loved you" (John 13:34). Here we receive the comfort of forgiveness of our sins through the power of Christ's reconciliation, and we lay down our offering of a new obedience. In due time death divides us, separates one from the other, a husband from his wife, leads the child to the grave of the parents, makes peace between adversaries. Often it is too late when one regrets that one has embittered someone else's life. The coarse husband looks for the last time on the pale face of his wife, for whom he has been the cause of so many tears, over whom now the coffin lid is being closed. The undutiful son would gladly have asked his good father's pardon, who took his heartache to the grave. The haughty daughter, who would not be warned, would gladly confess to her loving mother, who ended her life in sorrow. The upright teacher who was mocked in life, the faithful servant who was misused and counted unworthy any time he was in someone else's way. Now that they are gone, they appear in a different light. Now it is recognized what they were, and how they have been sinned against. But it is too late, and no wailing wakens the dead.

But what will happen when another wakes them, and us along with them? What will happen when those who were together here on the same road meet again before the throne of the eternal Judge? How many frightening meetings will there be, how many painful encounters, how many accusations might there be in the face of terror of eternity between souls, between perpetrators and their victims! And if the soul against whom you have sinned here on earth has long since forgiven you, will the righteous Judge also be silent forever and will the accuser in your own breast never awaken again?

O, in view of the eternal judgment, let not the admonition of the Lord be in vain. Make friends with your accuser quickly. Reconcile to one another and tolerate one another as long as you still are together, so that at the graveside there will be no late regrets or a terrible reunion in eternity! Yes, how many quarrels, how much strife would not happen, if we thought: "We are together on this path through this fleeting life"? How much more carefully we would treat each other in this life, if we rightly took to heart that we are together on the way to the grave, and no one knows how long it will be yet?

> O love as long as you can love
> The hour is coming, the hour is coming
> When you stand at the grave and mourn.

How much better it would be if we would apologize to each other for offences, forgive each other's mistakes, do good to one another. Oh, if only we wouldn't forget that we are together on the way to a holy and just Judge, who says with what measure you measure, you will be measured. "Blessed are the merciful, for they shall obtain mercy" (Matthew 5:7)! Now, dear ones, when in the pressures of life we often forget where we are going together, in our Lord's Sermon on the Mount we see the little things of this world, and before us a huge eternity. Here the heart should become still and the eyes bright. We need to understand again the words of Genesis: "Don't quarrel along the way" (Genesis 45:24).

Yes, here in the house of the Lord, here in the outer court of eternity, we should become more receptive to love and peace, and become quiet, reconciliatory, accommodating, gentle as we go home, because once more it has become clear to us. We are only pilgrims of this time, and want to reach eternity. The preacher not only places us before the gates of eternity, but he also places us on the mountain, in order to implant into our hearts the holy commandment of love, he leads us to the throne of grace of the heavenly Father, who is the original source and example of human love.

The Lord Jesus says: "You have heard that it was said: 'You shall love your neighbour and hate your enemy. But I say to you, love your enemy, bless those who persecute you, do good to those who hate you, pray for those who offend you and persecute you; so that you will be children of your Father in heaven. Because he lets the sun rise over the evil and the good, and lets it rain over the righteous and the unrighteous. For if you love those who love you, what will be your reward? Don't the tax collectors do the same? Therefore, you are to be perfect, just as your Father in heaven is perfect'" (Matthew 5:43–48). It is to the true, holy brotherly love that the Lord seeks to draw us upward. These are the most difficult trials of Christian understanding that he places in us here, in that he demands a love that does not haughtily give, but humbly gives in, and can gently forgive. Love like this not only works in a friendly way, but also is willing to suffer, which not only does good to friends, but also blesses the enemy.

O, dear listeners, it is to the highest step of holy love that the Lord calls His followers. But He also points us to the highest source of holy love, to the Father in heaven, who lets His sun rise over the bad as well as the good, and pours out His fertilizing rain on the just and the unjust. He is a God of love, and a Father of mercy, not only to the thankful and the obedient, but also to the unthankful and the disobedient.

And now, dear ones, if we think of the rich blessings that we have amply received although unearned, and still receive from the Father of love, then body and soul must testify to His grace. If we think of the great calling that we as Christians have been counted worthy to participate in, to be called children of the heavenly Father, created in His image, then we must try to be obedient to Him, to be like Him, as far as it is possible for frail humans. Then when we think of the glowing example of holy love given to us by the only begotten Son of the Father, who not only preached it on the mountain, but also fulfilled it in His whole life, and sealed it with His bloody death, be urged to love your enemies, bless those who persecute you, do good to those who hate you, and pray for those who offend you. If we let His word guide us, His blood cleanse us, and His spirit penetrate us, then should it be impossible to fulfill the high command of brotherly love? Then should not our hearts bubble at this blessed decision: yes, I will also love, will also forgive, also bless, as a child of my Father in heaven, as a disciple of my Saviour.

Now, dear congregation, to speak further to our edification, the words of our text provide further instruction. God is present. If we think of this every time we cross this threshold, then we will not come before Him other than with reverence. If we come with reverence before His holy face, everything in us that might distract and rob us of the blessing of the message will become silent. Then we will bow before Him confessing: "Speak, Lord,

Your servant is listening." Yes, Lord, grant us Your blessing, so that what is to be spoken by me, a weak, imperfect, and unworthy person, may be to Your honour, and may serve to our salvation. Amen.

Invitation to Participate in a Time of Silent Congregational Prayer

And so turn with me to our Lord and God for prayer.

The Lord hear our prayer and be gracious to us. If we have called to the Lord not only with our lips, but also with our hearts, we can comfort ourselves, and rejoice that He will hear us and bless this hour.

Reading of the Text

In this firm conviction, I turn, comforted, to the words of the text that are found in Luke 18:9–14, and reads: "He also told this parable to some who trusted in themselves that they were righteous and despised others: 'Two men went up into the temple to pray, one a Pharisee and the other a tax collector. The Pharisee stood and prayed thus with himself, "God, I thank thee that I am not like other men, extortioners, unjust, adulterers, or even like this tax collector. I fast twice a week, I give tithes of all that I get." But the tax collector, standing far off, would not even lift up his eyes to heaven, but beat his breast, saying, "God, be merciful to me a sinner!" I tell you, this man went down to his house justified rather than the other; for everyone who exalts himself will be humbled, but he who humbles himself will be exalted.'" Thus far the words of the text.

Homily

Dear friends! There is something lovely about a congregation gathered reverently in the house of the Lord, waiting for the grace of God, thirsting for the blessing of God's Word. As the Psalmist says: "How lovely is thy dwelling place, O Lord of hosts! My soul longs, yea faints for the courts of the Lord" (Psalm 84:2)! But, dear ones, if we want to receive the right benefit from our service, and take home the right blessing from the house of the Lord, then we also have to bring the right hearts before God's face, a heart open to receive God's grace, thirsty for God's Word as the seeded field thirsts for rain.

Already at the first service that the Bible speaks about, the offering of Cain and Abel, the service wasn't the same, and neither was the blessing the same. The Lord looked with favour on Abel and his offering, but He did not look with favour on Cain and his offering.

In the Scripture today we see two people at prayer before God in the same temple, at the same time, but only one brings a blessing home with him. Might there also be attenders in our churches in this day that do not please God with their offering, who leave without a blessing because they have locked out God's grace? There are many locks such as inattention, conceit, and a worldly mind. However, the worst and the strongest lock is self-righteousness and spiritual pride, which locks out the human heart from God's grace, here in church and outside in life. God opposes the arrogant, but gives grace to the humble. We have here an instructive example of this saying in the two prayers before the throne of grace.

Let us pray, "O Lord Jesus, You who alone are righteous before God, in Your grace send us the Holy Spirit, so that we are able to teach rightly and listen, so that this word will fall into all hearts as true manna to the soul. O great God, grant us grace for self-knowledge, and give us the self-love that does not blind us, since we are so prone to helping ourselves to the good that we can create with our own works seemingly. O grant that we may not appear before you hypocritically in our services, but forgive all our sins. Cleanse our souls from all guile, and our spirit from anything false. Grant us truth, purity, and innocence in all our actions, so that we may lead a pleasing life before You, O God, through Jesus Christ." Amen.

"He also told this parable to some who trusted in themselves that they were righteous and despised others" (Luke 18:9). Dear friends, if we apply this to our time and to Christianity today, which regretfully is very divided, and consists of so many divisions that each call out: "Here is Christ, there is Christ." One says: "We have the true, pure teaching," and the other says: "We have it." Each thinks they are justified, and therefore despise, condemn and damn others. We see that this can happen with what is right, but most of these people consider themselves righteous, and as a result despise others. In our day, isn't it true that almost everyone thinks about their belief system as better than this or that one, that he is a child of God, sitting in

God's lap, and the other is not, and so despises the others? We have good reason to guard against this error and deception.

Two people stand before us in our text, and they enter two different paths to salvation. How are we to appear before God's face, so that we may take a blessing home from His house? The tax collector in the temple teaches us to lower your eyes in pious self-examination and in humble confession of our unworthiness before God. Arrogance knocks in vain. The arrogant carries no blessing away with him, because he does not know himself, does not respect his brother, and does not need his God.

The tax collector stood afar, and did not want to raise his eyes to heaven. At the same time the Pharisee stood at the front of the temple, his head lifted to God, letting his eyes flit about the assembly, and with a haughty look at the tax collector, thanks God that he is not like other people, thieves, unrighteous, adulterers, or even like the tax collector.

The tax collector stands humbly close to the door, does not look at others to the left of him, because he senses his own unworthiness, so he lowers his eyes for silent reflection. Shouldn't we be able to learn from him? The many earthly things in the world that attract our attention and occupy our thoughts, the business concerns, the events of each day, the people with whom we associate, the anxieties and the joys of this world: all these, dear listeners, we are to leave behind when we step over this holy threshold and gather for worship. Here in God's house we are to give attention to ourselves, so that we can come to God. We should lower our eyes, so that with a concentrated heart, we can comprehend what God wants to say to us. But, dear ones, is that always the case with us? Are there some frivolous, superficial, distracted listeners, or conceited and self-righteous visitors in the house of the Lord? Are there visitors who come to see others and to be seen? Are there distracted listeners who cannot collect their thoughts, who, if not with their eyes, but with their thoughts, wander about during the singing, or the prayers or during the sermon to all the earthly things that Jesus wants to drive out of the temple? Are there those who are self-satisfied and self-righteous, who just look at others beside them, and judge them, quietly making side remarks, like the unloving judgment: I thank God that I am not like this tax collector, instead of beating their own breast and contemplating what is in their own heart and conscience. Oh, dear listeners, doesn't one often hear worldly conversations before the church service? Doesn't one often hear the conversations after the message, at the church door, that give no sign of the thought: God is present. Yes, there is no thought given to the entry of God's Word into one's heart. O dear listener, haven't you, from time to time and in the middle of the service, caught yourself with thoughts that shamed you and carried you far away from God and His Word, while you were sitting at your place with a devout demeanour? The Pharisee in the temple knows nothing of unworthiness or sin, he thinks he is clean from bad deeds, but also rich in good works. He fasts twice a week, when Moses only prescribed one fast day per year according to Leviticus 16:3. He gives a tenth of all he has, while according to the command of Deuteronomy 14:21–22, only the fruits of the field and of the herd were to be given as a tenth. He thanks God that he is better than other people, and he praises himself before God's face. Oh, how pride blinds a person's eyes, that he measures himself as pious, as faultless, and has no inkling of how much he is still lacking. By contrast, the tax collector didn't want to lift his eyes to heaven, but beat his breast and said: "God, be merciful to me, a sinner." He stands, with downcast eyes, before the holy One, the All-Knowing God, who sees into the secret places. Instead of praising himself before God, he accuses himself as a sinner. Instead of haughtily raising himself above others, he beats his breast in penitence and pleads for grace. Is that only appropriate for a tax collector, and not also for every Christian person? Is it only appropriate for a communion service, when we test our hearts and life before we step to the table of grace? Is it not also appropriate every time we approach God, to cast down our eyes in humble recognition of our unworthiness and our sin toward God?

When it says, God is present, the majestic, the all-powerful, the all-knowing, the only holy one, who then would be able to stand before him and praise himself for anything before God? When the holy figure, who has left us an example that we are to follow in His footsteps, appears before our eyes, who among us could brag about his Christianity before such a Lord and Judge? Would we not far more need to say with Daniel 9:7: "Lord, you are righteous, but this day we are covered with shame"?

When we, dear listeners, open our ears and our hearts to the Word of God, to comprehend the Word that is living and strong and sharper than a two-edged sword, a judge of thoughts and the disposition of our hearts, can we, then, rely on ourselves? Or can we, during the sermon, look self-righteously at others with the thought: "That applies to him or him, but it doesn't apply to me"? Instead we should humbly hear in our conscience: "You are the man!" and penitently beat our breast with the confession: "God, be gracious to me, a sinner!"

Dear ones, here before God's face, when we consider who God is and who we are, our pride and our arrogance and complacency will vanish. Then every Sunday must become a day of repentance, every sermon a repentance sermon, every prayer a prayer of penitence for us. Our place before God's face is here, next to the tax collector, and to each of us comes the reminder: "God, be gracious to me, a sinner." In this deep sigh, this heartfelt plea, the tax collector combines all his concerns. He gives to his God his sinful heart with all that burdened him and all he needed. He places it again before the gracious and compassionate God, for he knows: "The sacrifice acceptable to God is a broken spirit; a broken and contrite heart, O God, thou wilt not despise" (Psalm 51:17). And that, dear ones, is also how we should appear before the face of God our Saviour. We must lower our eyes before the holy and righteous One, and humbly stand, sending our sighs up to God, the gracious and compassionate one, not only to recognize the wrongs of our hearts, but also to long for and receive grace. That is why we are gathered in God's house. God's house is a place of mercy, placed into this world of sin and sorrow, so that people may receive grace upon grace. God's Word is a message of grace that invites the world to "Be reconciled to God!" God's table is a table of mercy for all those who hunger and thirst for righteous-ness, and the call goes out: "Come, all is prepared!" The hours of worship are hours of grace, where every soul searching for salvation shall experience that "The Lord is merciful and gracious, slow to anger and abounding in steadfast love" (Psalm 103:8). Therefore, do not flee from the face of God as if He were a consuming fire for sinners, do not avoid the house of the Lord, as if what you hear there is only disheartening for the spirit, or numbing for the will, only discouraging for the heart. No, give Him your heart again with the penitent plea: "God, be merciful to me, a sinner!" So that He will heal, and comfort, bless, and renew.

If your heart feels soiled by sin and depressed by guilt because you have forgotten God and have overstepped His ways, come before His face in penitence, and give your heart to Him again with the plea: "Cleanse me from my misdeeds and my sins" (Psalm 51:4). If your heart feels weak in faith, slow to do what is right, displeased with God's commands, give Him your heart again with the plea: "Lord, teach me to do Your will, create in me a pure heart, O God, and renew a steadfast spirit within me" (Psalm 143:10). If you feel your heart is burdened with cares, discouraged by afflictions, darkened because of the suffering of the day, and embittered by the evils of the world, give your heart to Him again with the plea that He comfort it through His Spirit, that He fill it with His peace, that He delight it with His grace, and that once more you may feel: "Lord, You refresh my soul and my body and spirit. Rejoice in the living God!"

For this reason everyone should let himself or herself be awakened, spread out your whole condition before the Lord at this moment, and with the Psalmist David sigh: "Search me, O God, and know my heart! Try me and know my thoughts! And see if there be any wicked way in me, and lead me in the way everlasting" (Psalm 139:23–24). Oh dear ones, let us not take this important subject matter lightly. Let us be concerned with being able to stand in God's sight, and not only about our standing before people. If we want to be acceptable not only to people, but also to God, then our hearts need to be changed and renewed through the grace of God.

In our Scripture portion we are introduced to two people, one a Pharisee, the other a tax collector. On the one hand, the Pharisee had a considerable glow of holiness and piety before people, he was considered righteous by people, he could boast about his good works, and he prayed with great frankness. On the other hand, the tax collector stood afar, and because of his sinfulness, did not feel worthy to lift his eyes to heaven, even less to enter the holy part of the temple. The Pharisee could not pass in God's eyes, because his heart was not righteous before God. For all his outer piety, he was full of self-love and pride, so that he could not please God, because God opposes the proud, but gives grace to the humble.

People generally look only at what is before their eyes, the outer respect-ability, piety, the diligence in godly works, and so on, but the Lord looks at the heart (1 Samuel 23:26). If the heart has not been changed by grace, cleansed and healed, then a person's Christianity cannot possibly count for anything. So those who count on their own selves for salvation cannot endure before God in their Christianity. This is the type of people that the Lord Jesus had before Him in this story, for He told this parable to some who considered themselves pious, who set their hope on themselves, who thought they were righteous, and despised others. Such a person is the Pharisee in the temple. "I thank God that I am not like other people, or like this tax collector." So speaks the proud man with a scornful side glance at his humble fellow worshipper. So scornfully he talks about a man, whom he in his pride, considers unrighteous.

The Pharisee speaks so haughtily about his fellow worshipper before the face of God, before whom we are all brothers in God's house. Let us be aware, dear ones, do we at times come into the holy place, here before God's face with loveless side glances and negative thoughts that seem to say: "I thank you, God, that I am not like this tax collector"? Oh dear listener, have you never caught yourself, during a sermon, when a sin was mentioned and God's judgment threatened, that you self-righteously thought of one of your neighbours, saying in your heart: "He's the one. Thank God that I am not like him"? People are so prone to this type of foolishness.

It must be said of them, what Paul said about the Jews in Romans 10:3: "Since they did not know the righteousness that comes from God and sought to establish their own, they did not submit to God's righteousness." Before God no other righteousness counts but the unexceptional righ-teousness of the bloody merit earned by Jesus Christ. These people don't want to accept, they don't want to be the sinners who crawl to the throne of grace poor and naked, in order to be cleansed there for free. They trust in themselves, they build on their good conduct and they base their hope on their virtues, on honesty and good works. They are not dependent on the righteousness of Christ. All this, dear ones, is pride, which thinks itself better than others. It is also like that with those whose service to God is purely out of habit. The text says that the Pharisee went up into the temple.

He stood and made his prayers with many words, but all this happened purely out of habit, and so could not please God. Dear ones, if in the temple the Pharisee with his "I thank you, God" had meant it in the way of the Pharisee whose name was Saul, later Paul, who writes: "I thank Christ Jesus our Lord, who has given me strength, that he considered me faithful, appointing me to his service. Even though I was once a blasphemer and a persecutor and a violent man, I was shown mercy" (1 Timothy 1:12–13). If it had been the humble thanks of a pardoned soul, which feels and confesses what I am because of God's grace, he would have been able to comfort himself with a gracious, favourable hearing, but that is not the way it is meant. It is not his God whom he thanks, but himself for his excellent status. He does not come before the Lord as a humble supplicant or with childlike thankfulness, but as one who needs nothing more from God's hand. So the penitent tax collector went to his house justified rather than the other. Only to where there is a hunger and thirst after righteousness can the Lord come with His spirit's power and grace. That is why those who are constantly comparing themselves with others, who might be worse than themselves, do not endure before the eyes of God.

The Pharisee's misfortunate deception was that he thanked God that he was not like other people, like thieves, the unrighteous, adulterers, or even like the tax collector. With this he complimented himself, and marvelled at how much more righteous he was than these people, when all the while this abomination lay in his heart. This is also the excuse of many people, even though they are persuaded by their conscience that they are not what they ought to be. They comfort themselves with the idea that they are not as bad as others, who are worse. But is one made godly when others are more godless? Is one cleansed of one's dirt, when others are deeper in unrighteousness?

No, dear ones, that will be no advantage on the day of judgment, because each one will have to give an account of himself before God, according to Romans 14:12. The Pharisee could boast: "I fast twice a week, and give a tenth of all that I have." But because it did not happen in good faith, because he did not remain humble, but sought his own glory, it became an abomination before God.

This principle applies to everything, even our best actions because whatever does not stem from faith is sin, according to Romans 14:23. Oh, dear listeners, how each one of us should examine ourselves, and learn to understand our condition. Just look at how bowed down the tax collector stands before the face of God. How he steps forth from afar, not daring to lift his eyes to God, but with a groan from his humble heart, storms heaven.

The Pharisee lifts his eyes up to God, of whose holy majesty he has no inkling. The tax collector does not dare to lift up his eyes in the face of all his unworthiness. The Pharisee looks with disdain at his neighbour. The tax collector has no time to judge others, but only beats remorsefully on his own breast. The Pharisee has no requests, he only brags. Before God the tax collector had nothing to brag about, but only to request: "God, be merciful to me, a sinner."

We may have importance before people. Before God the best of us are sinners, and happy is the person who can admit it penitently as the tax collector did. We hear in it the humility that not only rightly acknowledges poverty, but also honestly looks for grace in the phrase: "God be merciful to me, a sinner." Such a downcast soul is something precious before the Lord. The Lord wants to reveal his riches to such poor and humble souls. Such lowly plants will be illuminated with the loveliest rays from the Sun of Righteousness. Such who are poor in spirit will inherit the kingdom of heaven according to Matthew 5:3.

The tax collector smote his breast, accused himself as being a greatest sinner, and this came forth from his inner feelings of depravity. When a person realizes this, that he is not worthy to lift his eyes to God, to him God will be merciful. When sin has become so great, that one only feels totally sinful, then the grace of God becomes more powerful (Romans 5:20). He who judges himself and accuses himself will not be judged by the Lord (1 Corinthians 11:31). In the tax collector we are introduced to a sinner who comes to faith.

The concluding word of the Lord about the two prayers in the temple is thus: the Pharisee went back home as he had come. He did not lower himself, so God could not raise him up. He did not look for grace, therefore he could not find any grace. He brought along his own righteousness, so God did not give him His righteousness. He leaves, not as one blessed by the Lord, but as one about whom He says: "They serve me in vain, whose heart is far from me." The tax collector went home justified rather than the other. God gives grace to the humble. He who seeks Him with his whole heart will find Him. Be confident, your sins are forgiven. Go in peace, your faith has helped you. That is the response of the Lord to the tax collector's request: "God, be merciful to me," and he carried it home in his heart. Praise the Lord, my soul, and forget not all His benefits. He forgives all my sins and heals all my diseases. That was the psalm of praise that rang in his soul as he departed from the temple. And so, justified before God, as one blessed by the Lord, he came back to his house, and walked from then on among God's own.

Oh, dearest listeners, that we might all come to God's house as he did, with a humble, contrite heart that is yearning for salvation. Then, dear ones, we could also go home to our houses as the tax collector did, relieved of our worries, newly strengthened in our souls, made right before God as the blessed of the Father. O that all of us might not rest until we reach the point where in our hearts we have the testimony: "Be confident, your sins have been forgiven." May we, as often as we rise from prayer, as often as we come home from God's house, also go, made righteous as the humble tax collector, newly comforted and strengthened through the grace of our God and Saviour, until the time when we can exuberantly experience the phrase: "God gives grace to the humble, when the gates of grace in the heavenly Jerusalem will be opened to us in the upper holy place." To this end, may the Lord also bless this day, His day, in His house, and His Word. Yes, also all other days of grace and hours of grace. Amen.

The grace of our Lord Jesus Christ, the love of God the Father, and the comforting fellowship of the Holy Spirit be with us all. Amen. In the name of Jesus, Amen.

In conclusion, let us pray together: Heavenly Father, we thank You that You have once more allowed us to gather in peace in order to be edified by Your holy Word. Continue to be with us in the future and be gracious to us. May Your protecting hand be over us, and lead and guide us in Your ways and commands. Be with our ruling bodies, and grant that under their protection we may enjoy a quiet and peaceful life. Protect our land from devastation and destruction. Be also with all who have strayed from Your Word and will, and grant that they may again seek salvation. Be with all the sick and sorrowing, with those being tempted and longingly awaiting Your help. Be also with the widows and orphans, those who are travelling, and have mercy on all people in whatever distress or misery they may find themselves. In a special way be merciful to the dying, that they may end their lives in blessing.

Invitation to Participate in a Time
of Silent Congregational Prayer

In anything else that each one may have on their hearts, for which it is important to pray, they may call on the Lord at any time, not only in this place, but also at home, even day or night. So, join me in prayer to God the Lord.

May the Lord grant a favourable hearing to our prayer and be gracious to us.

Benediction/Dismissal

In connection with our public service I have nothing more to present, but only to thank you for your favourable acceptance of the message, and to say with the man of God, Moses: "The Lord bless you and keep you, the Lord make his face to shine upon you and be gracious to you, and protect our coming and going from now till eternity." Amen.

And so go in the peace of the Lord.

Sermon #54

For the Occasion of an Engagement Celebration

Written for the Glory of God and for the Well-Being of People
Written on June 29, 1963, by Herman D. W. Friesen
I.N.J. (In the Name of Jesus)

Invocation/Collect

The peace of God, which is higher than all human wisdom, protect all our hearts and minds in Christ Jesus for an eternal and blessed life. Amen.

Meditation on the Importance of Prayer

An important step has been taken. You have now entered the period of betrothal and of testing of your love; only a true and faithful love makes for a happy marriage, one that fate will not dampen. Will your love be the kind that stays faithful, engaged couple, in joy and in pain? Test yourself before God, and invite Him into this new union in order to unify your hearts. Then your period of engagement will be a blessing, and you will not regret your choice in your future married life. May the precious Lamb of God grant that the bride and the groom always give Him honour. Amen.

Dear friends, according to Christian custom we have gathered here in order to celebrate the promises of marriage of these two members, and to pray according to the Word of God and the commands of the Apostles. "Whatever you do, whether in word or deed, do it all in the name of the Lord Jesus, giving thanks to God the Father through Him" (Colossians 3:17). To this end, may the Lord grant us grace, and bless this celebration. How could there be a better beginning to a marriage than to call on the One in whom and through whom alone blessing and grace come? As we read in the Holy Scriptures, all believers, and children of God in the Old Testament, began and ended all of their important events and religious services with prayer. They believed they might load upon themselves the wrath of God if they began important tasks without asking for the help of God.

How much more then should we, who have the Word in our hands, begin in prayer? Those in the Old Testament looked to the distant future for the fulfillment of a dim forecast, whereas we, through Jesus Christ as the living Creator of heaven and earth, have learned to know Him and pray to Him as the reconciling, gracious Father who reaches down to us. While some looked from afar at the prediction of the beloved Saviour, how can we not at the beginning of such an earnest and holy state, before all else, draw near to God and call to Him for His support, protection, and blessing? As the Apostle says, "In him we live and move and have our being" (Acts 17:28). Truly, to every undertaking that God has not given His blessed agreement there will be an unholy ending. How much more then do we need to pray for His blessing in a marriage? After all, the greatest part of life's happiness depends on our marriage, and often not only our own happiness, but also that of our descendants.

Therefore, for people who want to enter marriage, and who begin, carry on, and end with prayer, it will mean that the man will be the head of the house. He will be able to give an accounting for his actions, and look after the nourishment and development of his family in a Christian manner. He will be able to look into the future and comfort himself with the words of the Apostle who says: "If God is for us, who can be against us?" (Romans 8:31). In a similar way for the bride, who often needs to leave her father and mother's home, and exchange what was near and dear to her in her home, with an unfamiliar environment. She can gladly enter her new destiny if she enters the marriage with God, and recognizes it as God's will for her.

Therefore, I would ask this couple to enter their engagement by sincerely calling on God, in the name of Jesus Christ, our Saviour and Sanctifier, just as the Apostle encourages us to do in the words quoted earlier (Colossians 3:17). The Apostle Paul says in Romans 15:4: "Everything that was written in the past was written to teach us." Therefore, we raise our hearts to God, the Lord, in order to pray for His blessing on this couple in the name of Jesus.

Prayer for the Couple

So pray with me: Faithful God and Father of our Lord and Saviour Jesus Christ, we bow before You in this hour and pray in the dust before Your feet. Yes, come, Lord Jesus, enter our midst and bless us, for we feel that without You we can do nothing. It is Your holy will that we pray to You to enter our midst, so grace us in this hour with Your blessed presence, which can only bring peace and joy to our hearts. Be in our midst and show us that You are the good Lord, as You so often have showed Yourself. Graciously lean toward us, come to us, because You gladly bless. We want to serve You. That is why we are here in this house. Give us, Lord, Your commands, and bless our souls, so that they will prosper in Your service. Instruct us from Your chair in Your Spirit's school. Give us open ears that in Your service we gladly note Your signs, and always carry Your light before us. Make Yourself sweeter to us, and day by day more sure and more essential. What the world has praised and raised as valuable, make it appear ever more dangerous to us. Lord, let Your gracious pleasure rest on us with blessing, so that we will end our life with You, and stand before Your throne. Amen.

Meditation on the Importance of Salvation in Jesus Christ

Dear friends in the Lord, we read in Acts 16 that the jailer was so frightened by the movement of the earth when the Apostle Paul and Silas were in prison because of their faith that he in his fright called out, "What must I do to be saved?" For this serious question he received the answer from the Apostle: "Believe in the Lord Jesus, and you and your house will be saved." This irrefutable truth is also written as a teaching for us, and I would wish with all my heart that this will also be your future stance, and remain with you, dear couple. For no one can lay any foundation other than the one already laid, which is Jesus Christ (1 Corinthians 3:11).

Salvation is found in no one else, for there is no name under heaven given to men by which they must be saved except the name of Jesus. May you often repeat the question of the jailer in your hearts: "What must I do to be saved?" You, too, will receive the answer of the Apostle: "Believe in the Lord Jesus Christ, and you and your house will be saved." Because our perverse hearts are so often inclined to other things, which are not able to make us happy and blessed, or give us peace and rest, so this message about the most necessary of all things, needs to be repeated again and again. And may that, dear couple, be the foundation for establishing your new home.

So many base their presumed luck on something futile instead of on the living God, on Jesus Christ, the foundation of all wholeness and blessing. "Seek first the kingdom of God, and all these things will be added to you," says our Lord. So the Holy Scriptures remind us not to look to temporal goods, not to set our confidence in worldly gains, or to set our eyes in that direction, but to seek always the better part, which shall not be taken from us. And this better part exists in the words: "Believe in the Lord Jesus Christ, and you and your house will be saved."

Those who begin marriage in the name of Jesus will experience the joy of the Lord, their Saviour, and remember the love with which God in Christ accepted them. He has led them since childhood, and they will acknowledge with Jacob: "Lord, I am unworthy of all the kindness and faithfulness you have shown me" (Genesis 32:10). With the Psalmist David (we might acknowledge): "Who am I, O Sovereign Lord, and what is my family, that you have brought me this far?" So those who sense their weakness and their unworthiness before the faithfulness and kindness of God, and bow before Him, in them will awaken the pious and sincere desire at the beginning of their marriage to be thankful for the life God has given them. As they make their pledge to one another, at the same time also make a genuine pledge to God and Saviour, whom they need to thank for their lives, they will no longer want to serve sin, but to live in the will of God. They will seek to establish a God-pleasing household so the Lord will be able to say of them as he said of Abraham in Genesis 18:19: "that he will direct his children and his household after him to keep that way of the Lord by doing what is right and just."

Yes, he will begin his marriage in a Christian way with the firm intention: "As for me and my household, we will serve the Lord" (Joshua 24:15). Because in every marriage that is made, in every household that is established, the church of God in Jesus Christ is to be built and promoted. If, then, the marriage is started in Christ Jesus and in faith, it will be easier to carry on in the mind and spirit of Jesus. In order that the good Spirit never departs from the engaged couple, it is necessary that you always look up in faith to Jesus in whatever you have at hand, and follow the advice of Tobias. All your life long, have God before your eyes and in your heart, and be careful not to agree to anything sinful, and do nothing against the commands of God.

Should misfortune come to you, God will give you the strength to carry it without complaining. Through godly faith in our Saviour, the bitter will become sweet, and the difficult, easier. You will be happy on good days, and take the bad as being for your good. For this you will strengthen yourselves with prayer. For in the state of marriage the Word of the Lord has special meaning, for "where two or three are gathered in My name, I am there in the midst of them" (Matthew 18:20). O, what a lovely and comforting promise, and further it also says, "anything they ask in My name, that they will receive from the Father" (John 14:13).

For this purpose, it is important that Christian couples faithfully attend public worship services and participate in holy services like Communion, in order to strengthen one another in our faith in the Saviour Jesus Christ, and in the love in which faith is active. In such fervour for the one thing that is important, you will notice among each other the encouragement to love and do good works, and not to leave the fellowship of believers as some have done. Be faithful to the church, love to be where a group of disciples are present in community to be refreshed by the Word of God.

When the hours come where the flesh wants to win over the spirit, where sin wants to rule over the mortal body, and fruit of sin announces itself in discord and bad moods, then the faith and love for Jesus, the Lord, will win through the humble bowing before Him, for He knows our hearts and will not break the crushed reed or extinguish the glimmering wick. Quickly the irritation will abate, and couples who are united in Christ will never let the sun go down on their anger. The marriage will be carried on happily because with faith all is easier, the hard times more pleasant, and the marriage responsibilities made into a gentle dew, and an easy burden, because the unity in Christ maintains nuptial love.

O, the demands made on the man when he gains the love of his wife, if he fears God and walks in His ways, who oversees his home well. Because he fears God, he need stand in awe of no man, and through piety he keeps his faithfulness. His wife then has a firm support, she keeps her respect for him, and continues to grow in love for him. How happy will the marriage be if it does not hang its heart and desire on the world, but has joy in God and its Saviour, and if they abide in faith and in love and in godliness and decorum. In such a marriage one does not know the unholy fear of anxiety by which a person thinks always of ruin, and eats his bread with worry. They know that each day will have its own troubles, but they also know that those who fear the Lord, will have no need, but will be able to say with the Psalmist David: "I will lie down and sleep in peace, for You alone, O Lord, make me dwell in safety" (Psalm 4:8).

Although even godly couples may experience different kinds of distress, with God they can bear it; yes, with God the burden will be lighter. If the dear Lord lays one on a bed of illness, the other prays for healing, and so they strengthen each other because they trust in the help of the Lord with patience and hope. When difficult times come, when the question is where will we get the bread we need, the Christian couple clings to the comforting promise of the Lord, "I will not leave you or forsake you" (Hebrews 13:5).

O, how many happy hours are experienced by Christian couples who are joined together in love, because they do not live with each other in quarrelling and jealousy, but in peace and love, and where peace and love dwell, the Lord promises a blessing forever, according to Psalm 133. We read in Ruth the story of Naomi returning to Judah. Ruth says to her mother-in-law: "Don't urge me to leave you or to turn back from you. Where you will go, and where you stay I will stay. Your people will be my people, and your God my God. Where you die, I will die, and there I will be buried. May the Lord deal with me ever so severely, if anything but death separate you from me" (Ruth 1:16–17). You are also to be so united in your stance, in order to live a Christian life of prayer. You are to look on each other's parents as "your people are my people" and "your God is my God." But it is even more important that your souls would be able to say with the poet:

Where you go, my Lord and my God
that is where I want to go.
No path shall be too steep or too difficult for me
If I may stand beside You,

And if it goes over steep heights
I will follow where You go.

And where You stay, O Lord, I will stay as well
If only I am with You.
For where You are, there will surely be
Only blessing and gain.
And if You stay in the vale of tears
To be with You is all my longing.

Your God and Father is also mine,
Through You He is that for me.
To love the Father was Your custom.
Therefore, I love Him as well.
How happy I may become,
I am permitted to call myself God's child.

Your people, my people, bought with Your blood,
To be owned by You
How I love those who have been baptized with Your Spirit
In order to proclaim Your honour.
I do not fear the derision of the enemy
I am a member of the congregation of the cross.

Lord, I am Yours, weak though I am
And yet in You I have much strength.
And You are mine, what You have in mind
Your Spirit within me works,
You will fully establish me
Into blessed eternity.

How good I have it, for time and eternity
That I am born now.
The name of Jesus creates confidence for me

That replaces everything else
In order to complete His work in me
So I rest quietly in His hands. Amen.

May you, dear bridal couple, also begin and carry on your marriage in the same way. But to attain this, it is necessary at the beginning, to again take into your hearts the One of whom it is written: "Salvation is found in no one else, for there is no other name under heaven given to men by which we must be saved as in the name of Jesus Christ" (Acts 4:12). Yes, take this One into your midst and into your home. It could be that in your hearts the question will often arise, and the answer will echo: "Believe in the Lord Jesus, so you and your house will be saved." To this end may the Lord grant you His blessing and assistance. Amen.

Now in conclusion I would ask that you test yourselves on this occasion of engagement, if you also stand with the Lord in a spiritual engagement, which the Lord says through the Prophet Hosea: "I will betroth you to Me forever; I will betroth you in righteousness and justice, in love and compassion. I will betroth you in faithfulness, and you will acknowledge the Lord" (Hosea 2:19–20).

Invitation to Participate in a Time of Silent Congregational Prayer

Therefore, beloved couple, look at the period of your engagement as a time that Tobias had designated as a time for prayer, as we read in Tobit 8:5–6 when he said to his bride: "We are children of saints, and we must not be joined together like heathen that know not God. So they both arose and prayed earnestly together that health might be given them." Because all blessing must be prayed for, we also all together want to bend our knees and with united hearts bring before the Lord any concern for this engaged couple, and entrust them to the Lord in prayer, that He might also in the future protect them and bless them. And so turn with me to the Lord in prayer.

The Lord hear our prayer and be gracious to us. That is the joy that we have in the Lord, says John. If we pray according to His will, our prayer will be heard.

Benediction/Dismissal

In connection with this engagement I have nothing further to present to this congregation, but only to thank you heartily for your favourable inclination and love.

Now I wish to give you the high priestly blessing from the man of God, Moses: "The Lord bless us and keep us, the Lord lift His countenance upon us and be gracious to us, the Lord protect our coming and our going to all eternity. In Jesus's name, Amen.

So go or stay in the peace of the Lord.

Sermon #50

FUNERAL SERMON FOR AN ADULT

Written in February 1964 by Herman D. W. Friesen
I.N.J. (In the Name of Jesus)

Invocation/Collect and Prayer

"Blessed are the dead who die in the Lord from now on. 'Yes,' says the Spirit, 'they will rest from their labour, for their deeds will follow them'" (Revelation 14:13). Grace, mercy, love, and peace I wish for this mourning gathering through Jesus Christ for a blessed and eternal life. Amen.

Let us pray together: Lord God, You are our refuge forever and ever, we turn to You for help with all our sorrows and complaints, just as a child turns to its mother when it is in pain. So, Lord, we ask You to send Your help to these sad and sorrowful hearts, because only with You is comfort and healing to be found, as well as pardon for our sins. Our lives are in Your hands also. So, grant Lord, that we be mindful of the fact that we too will die someday, so that we do not come to this hour without preparation, but that for us it will be an hour of deliverance from all evil. Amen.

Meditation

Dear mourning congregation, we have gathered here in this house of sorrow in order to lay to rest the deceased (sister) (brother) in the faith, which we as the living are obligated and indebted to perform as our last service of love. Every death reminds us and warns us to think about our end and its consequences. Will we reach the good portion, which has been earned for us by Christ, out of grace and mercy, through our faith, our life and walk, or not? O, let us be alert and pray and persevere therein to our end. Just as here at the (casket) (grave) of this (sister) (brother) (mother) (father) (grandmother) (grandfather) who has passed on, we are encouraged to think of our own ending and death.

This body is also a serious message of penitence that warns us that one day we too will be "counted and completed." How many enticements, physical and spiritual, has the heavenly Father already recommended to all of us? Everyone should ask themselves how we have spent our years; have we used the time of grace that the Lord has given us to God's glory? Or will it be said at the end that we have been weighed and found too light? Dear grieving assembly, whether short or long, eventually it will be said of all of us, give an account of your housekeeping, for you will no longer be a housekeeper.

The soul of this deceased person has completed its earthly career. (He) (she) ended the suffering and finished the struggle. But what about us? What might still be before us? Or when will it be our hour? Are we not prone to fall at any moment? Are we not prone to all kinds of dangers? Are we prepared to give an account at this time? Are we ready to pass on in faith, patience, and hope? Are we prepared to wait with patience and longing for the death of our flesh from this melancholy vale of tears? This body teaches us again how serious this earthly life is.

How will we be convinced that death does not respect who a person is or their age? How many people have become victims of death when they were still young? Yet for another it happens when a person is old, as the Psalmist says in Psalm 90:10: "The length of our days is seventy years—or eighty, if we have the strength; yet their span is but trouble and sorrow, for they quickly pass, and we fly away." For as soon as the Lord severs our lifeline, we wither away.

When we observe in the Holy Scriptures the witness and walk of our forefathers, the prophets, Apostles, and God-fearing people, it is obvious that they had a definite longing to leave this world in order to reach the heavenly Canaan. Our calling and our duty in this wicked world is very important and serious, namely to "work out your salvation with fear and trembling" (Philippians 2:12). "Make every effort to enter through the narrow door" (Luke 13:24).

Yes, it gives us a good opportunity to think about our own mortality as we are gathered here and see this soulless corpse completely motionless in (his) (her) casket. Let us be reminded that the hour will come for us when the spirit will separate itself from our perishable body, for "it has been appointed unto man to eventually die, and after that the judgment." Since we do not know when or how this might happen, or if before our death we may have to suffer through a period of illness, or if the pains may be so great that our thinking may be confused, we want to leave this to God because He knows what is best and beneficial for our souls. With sincere hearts we want to pray, "Lord, teach us to number our days aright, that we may gain a heart of wisdom" (Psalm 90:12). The proper wisdom will be when we prepare ourselves for death.

Let us hear the words from Psalm 28:7 where it says: "The Lord is my strength and my shield; my heart trusts in Him, and I am helped. My heart leaps for joy and I will give thanks to Him in song." Also this deceased one, now surrounded by mourning hearts, was allotted (his) (her) portion of time, which (he) (she) has now ended, and it was probably not an easy one. But we hope that (he) (she) had the comfort that we find in Psalm 68:20: "Our God is a God who saves; from the sovereign Lord comes escape from death." This is a precious comforting word for the depth of sorrow.

Oh, what is mankind for whom Jesus suffered in sorrow? People are devious, yet the Father, who is love, does not threaten, sometimes through illness or sorrow, often with kindness, continues to extend His grace, which knows no end. Scripture says that "there is joy in heaven when a penitent sinner repents," and with the prodigal son, who returns to restore the peace with his righteous father (Luke 15:10). He who wants to praise himself should praise because of the Lord. This is the way the Psalmist prayed in Psalm 86:11: "Teach me Your way, O Lord, and I will walk in Your truth; give me an undivided heart, that I might fear Your name."

Our life is nothing other than a journey—when we are born we begin the journey, and when we die the journey ends and we enter eternity. What counts on our journey here is which path we walked in this life. If we travel on the good path of faith and piety and in the fear of God, with humility, then it will end in the heavenly splendour. If, however, we travel the broad road of unbelief, ill nature, godlessness, or self-created righteousness, it will end in eternal ruin and condemnation. Therefore, let us constantly consider how we lead our lives so that we may always speak from the heart.

Yes, Lord, here I am. May Your good Spirit lead me on a smooth path. You, who brought Your people through the sea with dry feet, and led them through the desert to the chosen land, lead and guide us on Your ways, so that we do not rely on ourselves, but that again and again we might say with the Psalmist: "The Lord is my strength and shield; my heart trusts in Him, and I am helped. My heart leaps for joy and I will give thanks to Him in song" (Psalm 28:7). Therefore, we want to lift up our hearts and minds to the Lord, so that God may show grace to us all. God will comfort us and let His face shine upon us. That will heal us.

Yes, "blessed are the dead who die in the Lord. 'Yes,' says the Spirit, 'they will rest from their labour, for their deeds will follow them'" (Revelation 14:18). Thus, writes the Apostle John, after the voice of God from heaven revealed this to him and had given it into his heart. Hail to those who have reached the end, for whom this word might be the last and the finest gift we can call out to them at their gravesite. Happy are the sorrowing for whom this word may give comfort to their heart.

O, let us, while we are still well, go to Jesus with penitence and in faith and sincerely, from the heart, beg Him that He might wash away our sins with His blood, and receive us with favour, and grant us His grace. Then we will have a righteousness that can stand before the Lord's judgment. To attain this, let us engage all our strength of soul, as long as we wander here in this pilgrim life and hurry toward the fatherland because we are here only as strangers and pilgrims according to 1 Peter 2:11. So when in a storm of misery the weary pilgrim is assailed with spiritual attacks, he then seeks, with tears, to find strength in the wounds of Christ, so that in all the suffering and temptations he is not led astray.

Similar suffering and sorrows are what all true Christians may meet along their pilgrim way. These (sisters) (brothers) in the faith also received their share, but the days of suffering are measured, and in a short time we may be the ones who need to leave. We could come to the one who has said that where He is, those who are His will also come to be with Him. This prospect for those who are His, wherein they will be in the house of the Lord, can ease the burden and the difficulties of the final days of suffering. They know that their days are numbered and will soon end, for God speaks in the Holy Scriptures to all, and to individuals specifically, as also to you mourners.

God can, and will help, so cling to Jesus as your Saviour, so you will not be rejected. For the Lord says: "Can a mother forget the baby at her breast, and have no compassion on the child she has borne? Though she may forget, I will not forget you!" (Isaiah 49:15). Oh grieving congregation, may the passing on of this believing (sister) (brother) encourage us all to put our house in order, since we know that we have no abiding place here, but are seeking the future one. May all those gathered here accept this serious message of repentance preached by the body before us, so that it may serve to work a lasting blessing in our hearts through God's grace. He will accompany us until we, and all those souls entrusted to us, have overcome, and will be saved in eternity.

So we will attempt to encourage you, even if in simplicity and humility, and in weakness, with the words of our text, which reads: "The Lord is my strength and my shield; my heart trusts in Him, and I am helped. My heart leaps for joy and I will give thanks to Him in song" (Psalm 28:7). Our whole life is to be nothing other than prayer and thanksgiving. Namely, each day we are to call to God in prayer for His blessing, help, support, and grace, and if we have achieved this then to heartily thank Him for it.

In our God-fearing life's travels we should always be mindful that the Lord is our strength and our shield, our hearts hope in Him. But bad examples mislead and spoil the good, and according to Wisdom of Solomon, "the bewitching of vanity obscures good things, and the wandering of concupiscence undermines the innocent mind" (Wisdom of Solomon 4:12). Oh, pride and haughtiness, yes, the loveliest of what is worldly, will lead us to misery, and to call out alas. But the honest pilgrims cannot love this world, or consider this world their home. As the Lord says of His followers, "They are not of this world, just as I am not of this world" (John 17:14).

Dear grieving assembly, let us pay attention. Today, through this believing (sister) (brother) in the faith who has passed away, if we think of the many years they lived submitted to human things, they may often have felt deep in their souls that it was all frivolous. So many hot tears may have run down their cheeks, but we hope sincerely that their clothes have been made bright through the blood of the Lamb. Now they will be resting in the bosom of Abraham, and they could do no other than through prayers and petitions, turn to the merciful love of God for which the wounds of Jesus stand open for all penitent sinners. As we sincerely hope (she) (he) will have entered the house of rest through the grace and mercy of God, where (she) (he) will have attained the imperishable crown of eternal life.

All people must pass through the wall of death because of sin. That is why the preparation for the hour of departure is so very important: as the Apostle John says, in the time of grace, "we must carry out our tasks as the night comes, and no one can work any longer" (John 4:9). For only God knows the number of our days. He alone knows how or when we will give up our spirit, and that whether our end could come suddenly. Our life or our death rests alone in God's hands. As David says in Psalm 139:16: "Your eyes saw my unformed body. All the days ordained for me were written in Your book."

Therefore, dear souls, it is most necessary that in all our doing or leaving, in as far as we are able, we should seek to live in such a manner as we would have wished to have lived when death comes near to us. For nothing in this wretched world can shackle us or restrain us, that we would not daily find a reason to humble ourselves, and not only ourselves, but with all our hearts to serve and love God alone. Jesus's teaching and His conduct requires that we also live pious lives, after which we will be legitimate, specially chosen heirs—to which all people are called.

People have many obstacles to struggle against. The road is narrow that leads to life, and only a few find it. Often a person feels they need to pray with the Psalmist: "Show me, O Lord, my life's end and the number of my days; let me know how fleeting is my life. You have made my days a mere handbreadth; the span of my years is as nothing before You" (Psalm 39:4–5). Thus, the body here warns us, and shows us that we too will need to leave, so that we might call out that all people are as nothing, even though they live so securely. They go about like a shadow and create much unnecessary work and unease (according to Psalm 39).

How happy will those be, who in this world, have sought to follow the teachings of Jesus, and who have taken up their cross and sought to follow the way of affliction. Of them it will be said that these are the ones who have come out of great tribulation and have washed their clothes and made them bright in the blood of the Lamb. For the person who needs to leave the world loses only what has brought him anxiety and sorrow. All the heartaches, misery, cares, and sorrows are covered by the grave's mound. But then he wins what a person is created for, namely eternal and secure rest, and bliss, and we hope that this departed one will have reached this goal through the grace of Jesus Christ.

Dear mourning assembly, just as this (sister) (brother) in the faith has parted from us in death, all of us at one time will also depart this world, and may God grant that at that time we also may be given a place at the right hand of God. We trust that this believing (sister) (brother) has departed from the desert of this world, and through the grace of God has entered eternal rest. For there remains a Sabbath rest for the people of God, and all who believe may enter this rest.

The longing during the painful suffering, of which these departed ones experienced so much during their grave illness, was terrible to watch, so that it was pathetic to see, and even the relatives were prompted to wish the soul could be released from the ties to the body.

Reading of Obituary

So, you grieving ones, do not be overly sad at the passing of your (mother) (father) (loved one), but think that whatever God lets happen to them is to serve for the best of those who love God. Comfort each other with the words that the Lord Jesus spoke: "If a man keeps My word, he will never see death" (John 8:51). He who does not believe will die. It follows then that the death of a believer is only a sleep. Jesus said to His disciples about the death of Lazarus: "Lazarus, our friend is sleeping" (John 11:11). And David says: "Precious in the sight of the Lord is the death of His saints" (Psalm 116:15). In Revelation 14:13 the Spirit also says: "Blessed are the dead who die in the Lord. 'Yes,' says the Spirit, 'they will rest from their labour, for their deeds will follow them.'"

When a soul during their healthy life gives into sin and thus to judgment, if then they have many struggles to endure from the adversary by God's permission, (she) (he) clings to the cord of promise once grasped, that God would not leave them or forsake them. With the words of the poet, I say:

There all my complaints will be silent!
There my pious song of praise
Brings to You, for the trials of life,
My thanks, with happy feelings.
Joyously I say, they are done,
The Lord has made everything well.

As a mother comforts her child,
So Your goodness comforts me,
As one in the bliss of the redeemed
With complete satisfaction.
Then it will become obvious
How great His leading was.

My Saviour, who Yourself on earth
Bore the yoke of pain and sorrow,
Should I become weary of suffering
And feel the burdens of the day
Then strengthen mightily my spirit
That it will tear itself away from disgruntlement.

Grant that in the hope of yonder rest,
Which is the inheritance of the pious,
I will gladly do the Father's will
As you there will be my Father.
So my time of testing will be followed
By certain, perfect everlasting bliss. Amen.

The Lord leads us, often in a marvellous way. He does not always let us look into His secrets, but still He only has good intentions for us. He does not want anyone to be lost, but that everyone be saved and live, even though His paths for us often may seem dark, so that we do not know which way to turn for the pain and afflictions, but this only may be to draw us closer to Him. Job also complained about this when he says: "But my mouth would encourage you; comfort from my lips would bring relief. Yet if I speak, my pain is not relieved; and if I refrain, it does not go away" (Job 16:5–6). And how often will this believing (sister) (brother) have brought their pain before the Lord, and kept clinging to the Lord until the end, for the Lord alone helps us to live securely. Now (his) (her) complaints have come to an end and (he) (she) has entered (his) (her) fatherland where there are no more temptations. There God will wipe away all tears from (her) (his) eyes, which they wept here under the burden of the cross. So if God's leading sometimes seems hard, basically they are no different than paths of refining and compassion, whose aim is blessing and salvation.

Now, dear grieving congregation, we will accompany this soulless body to the silent lodging of the grave, where they rest to the end of days. In our imagination, we also want to step into our own grave, to see our own mortal body being entrusted to the earth, and remind ourselves of our own mortality. In this way we can see ourselves put on the new person created in the image of God, in integrity, righteousness, and holiness. May the Lord grant that the hour of death will not overtake us when we are unprepared, so that we will not be relegated to the left side of the Lord, but will be made holy through God's grace. For this, may God and Jesus Christ grant us strength to that end. Amen.

Concluding Prayer

In conclusion, let us pray: O almighty and holy God and Father, we thank You that You loved us poor, sinful people so much that You gave up Your only begotten Son to do away with our sin, to save us and make us righteous, so that we do not need to mourn as those who have no hope. When we take our loved ones to the grave, we can comfort ourselves that there will be a resurrection and a reunion for all souls seeking God. So we pray, be gracious to us and grant us Your Holy Spirit to lead us in all truth, so that when death draws near to us, we also may die blessed in the Lord. Yes, Lord, comfort these sorrowing hearts, be with them and do not remove Your hand from them, but help them in all their needs, and lead them, and us all, toward the joys of eternity, to be with You and stay with You into eternity. Amen. In Jesus's name, Amen.

Conclusion

Nothing is so sure as that one day we will die and need to leave this world; in Isaiah 38 we read that when King Hezekiah was ill the Lord sent the prophet to him to tell him: "Put your house in order, because you are going to die." King Hezekiah prayed fervently to God, where at the Lord let him know that he had heard his prayer and had seen his tears, and had added another fifteen years to his life. So how many of us have already received several years of grace in the hope that we will accept salvation; have we made use of them to that end? How often have we been in danger of death, but the Lord has saved us? How often have we been sick, but the Lord helped us again? When the allotted years had elapsed for King Hezekiah, he had to bid farewell to this world. It will be no different for us. Therefore, be sure to put your house in order.

Sermon #45

For the Preparation of
Baptismal Candidates: Part 1

Written for the Praise of God and the Instruction of Youth
and for the Blessing of the Congregation
Written in 1965 by Herman D. W. Friesen

Opening Prayer

My God, in your wisdom, after Adam's fall and sin locked the gates of paradise, you nevertheless gave your children another kind of paradise out of your fatherly grace, and this garden is called your church.

Introductory Meditation

Dear friends in Christ Jesus, together with you dear young people and devout listeners. As we all know, there are friends here today who by their testimony declare that by hearing God's Word according to Romans 10 have, together with believers, tasted the good Word of God and the vitality of the future (heavenly) world to come. They bow their shoulders in obedience to the truth and take upon themselves the yoke and light burden of Christ so that they might find rest for their souls according to Matthew 11:28–29.

Dear youth, think about and give careful consideration to what you are about to do. Through baptism you want to be joined with Jesus our Saviour for the rest of your life. May this good resolution reflect a holy earnestness and not merely a performance. But in all earnestness strive, with a committed and upright heart, to unite in your spirit with Jesus. You must preserve this union by earnest watching and praying, otherwise it is of no use. Don't think that an external water baptism brings salvation in and of itself. Oh no—if you don't repent with all your heart and by true faith seek forgiveness in the blood of Christ, external water baptism or joining the congregation simply doesn't suffice.

Oh my dear young people you must deeply repent when being baptized and convert to God with your whole heart. That is to say you must fully acknowledge your sinfulness and disobedience before God, and with bitter tears pray that for the sake of Jesus's blood all previous sins are forgiven and through grace obliterated by Christ.

In Romans 6 the Apostle Paul writes: "Or don't you know that all of us who were baptized into Christ Jesus were baptized into his death? We are therefore buried with him in baptism and through baptism into death in order that, just as Christ was raised from the dead through the glory of the Father, we too may live a full life" (Romans 6:3–4).

With these words dear young people, the Apostle indicates that all who allow themselves to be baptized in the name of Jesus must imitate his holy life and lifestyle. They must walk as he walked: in meekness, humility, love, peace, holiness, and righteousness. In baptism you must lay aside the old man, that through lust debases in error, and put on the new man, created in the image of God in true righteousness and holiness (Ephesians 4).

So dear young people, let this be our foremost concern that you whole-heartedly strive to conduct a righteous life and walk before the all-seeing God. Don't think that you can fool God by hypocrisy, or that you can confess and acknowledge him with your mouth, but deny him in your heart. Publicly you say that you believe in God the Father, Son, and Holy Spirit and promise to serve him in holiness and righteousness but in your lifestyle demonstrate that you serve the world and sinful lusts and desires, sin and unrighteousness. You cannot hide from the almighty God and Creator. His all-knowingness and all-seeing eyes penetrate the hidden, including the innermost parts of our heart.

Therefore, I plead with you believing young people, for God's sake and the sake of your soul's salvation, that your undertaking is heartfelt and that you did earnestly and rightly with your God lay aside all deceit and hypocrisy and serve God with your whole heart. Live your allotted lifespan in holiness and righteousness. You are not only being accepted into the congregation as members, but God will write your name in the book of life and graciously accept you into his heavenly kingdom. Your reward will be great in heaven and you will be filled with inexpressible and glorious joy (1 Peter 1:8). May God the Father, Son, and Holy Spirit, praised to all eternity, steer us toward this joy. Amen.

Now I turn to you believing congregation. On this special occasion let us scrutinize and earnestly examine ourselves whether we have really kept our promises and been obedient to God's commands. Have we kept them, done heartfelt repentance and have truly converted to God? Or have we been disobedient and lived in sin and unrepentance? Oh it would be so desirable that there was no one among us who still needed to repent, but rather that we all are truly converted Christians. May we all have firm trust and hope in the Lord so that we can say with the Psalmist: "but God will redeem my soul from the grave, he will surely take me to himself" (Psalm 49:15).

Yet it is of deep concern that many of us still have no such confidence, a deep inner confidence and assurance that God in his grace has accepted us, and that our sins are forgiven. We have good reason to admonish one another with the words of John [the Baptist]: "Produce fruit in keeping with repentance" (Matthew 3:8). Therefore, you unrepentant who are still unconverted, who until now have heard the voice of the Lord and his servants with deaf ears, let me, an imperfect messenger, warn you. From now on seek to better your life and walk. "Today, if you hear his voice, do not harden your hearts" (Hebrews 4:7). Today, the divine command to repent is directed to you via my weak and insignificant strength. Do not harden your hearts. Today, while the words of salvation are presented to you, words calling for true repentance. Today, the Lord still gives time and opportunity to repent and convert. Allow his goodness and long suffering to lead you to repentance.

Think about it you unrepentant. How often have you heard both the most loving and earnest repentance sermons? But have they changed you for the better? How often have you heard God's categorical command to repent? But have you responded and offered obedience? How often have you heard of the unmerited grace and long suffering of our Saviour who sustains unrepentant sinners year after year? Have you allowed yourself to be convinced?

O my dear ones—the works—yes the works that one intended to do often result in the opposite. Has our Lord God complained about us until this hour, as he once did about disobedient Israel when he says: "I stretch forth my hand all day towards a disobedient people who follow their own thoughts on a pathway that is not good" (Isaiah 65:2)? All you who have been disobedient to the voice of God call upon the name of the Lord our

God with a humble voice. It is high time you repent. Woe to you if you procrastinate. You don't know how long God will offer you his grace. It is still the time of grace and the Lord calls to you, "Come to me all you who are weary and burdened and I will give you rest, for I am gentle and humble in heart and you will find rest for your souls" (Matthew 11:28–29). Oh convert from your evil ways. "Seek the Lord while he may be found; call on him while he is near. Let the wicked forsake his way and the evil man his thoughts. Let him turn to the Lord and he will have mercy on him and to our God for he will freely pardon" (Isaiah 55:6–7).

But you dear young people who profess that you have begun to walk in God's ways and have been reconciled to God through true repentance and conversion—it is my heart's desire and prayer that this indeed has happened. Do not hesitate to move forward with your resolve, for if you don't you have already begun to go backwards. Seek to pursue holiness in the fear of God, hold to God's Word and follow the same. So the Lord God, not through your merit, but through the merit of his Son Jesus Christ will receive and accept you into his kingdom of grace. I wish that all of us might, by grace, achieve this. Amen.

Invitation to Participate in a Time of Silent Congregational Prayer

Before we continue, we want to bend our knees before the Lord our God and in the name of Jesus ask for the gracious presence of the Holy Spirit that all that we do here today may be to the praise and honour of his holy name and contribute to our soul's salvation and edification. Amen. Join me in a prayer of faith to the Lord God.

The Lord hear our prayer and be gracious to us.

Catechetical Recitation and Examination

I request that the young people will be so good and stand in order to answer the questions from the *Catechism*. You, O Lord, permit and bless all our proceedings to the honour of your holy name. For Jesus's sake. Amen.

Lord, show us the way of your statutes so that we observe them to the very end. Teach us to observe your law with all our hearts. Lead us on the pathway of your precepts for we delight in them. Yes Lord, show us your way and teach us to daily cling to you. For whoever fears the Lord will be instructed in the right way. Therefore, oh Lord we love the place of your home and the place where your glory resides. Let your face shine over us all, especially over our dear young people who stand here before you and this congregation. Strengthen your insignificant servant for this important act and teach us your precepts. Before your face we beseech you from the bottom of our hearts, be gracious to us according to your word, you merciful God and Saviour Jesus Christ. Amen.

Concluding Challenge to Baptismal
Candidates and Congregation

Much beloved young people, you have now answered the questions. Now as stated in 2 John 1:8, "Watch out that you do not lose what you have worked so hard to achieve. Be diligent so that you receive your full reward." Remember the words of Jesus that the pathway to heaven is narrow and the portal of eternal life small. There is no other way to the life of eternal joy than the way of struggle, the path of death and suffering that Jesus, the author and finisher of our faith, together with his disciples and followers walked.

If you want to follow God faithfully, the Lord Jesus Christ says that beginning with his baptism by John the Baptist, the Kingdom of Heaven suffers violence. We see this happening in the life of our dear Lord Jesus Christ in Matthew 4. As soon as he was baptized by John in the Jordan River, he was led by the Spirit into the desert to be tempted by the devil. The devil tried various tactics to bring about his fall, but the Lord Jesus resisted every attack so that the deceiver finally left him. The holy angels came and ministered to him. Much beloved souls! If that happened to the Lord Jesus Christ, how much more will the tempter (namely Satan) try to overcome you? As the Apostle Peter warns in 1 Peter 5:8, "the devil prowls around like a roaring lion looking for someone to devour."

Oh that we might all run the race ordained for us with patience and look upon Jesus, the author and finisher of our faith. Always remember the covenant you made with God, and how you have given yourself to Jesus's banner of the cross—that you want to serve him in holiness and righteousness. Yes, dear young people, make every effort to resolutely follow your calling and election until your blessed end. Yes, earnestly strive that you do not lose what you have worked for so that you receive your full reward. Not the one who made a good beginning in the struggle, but the one who endures will be saved.

Oh dear friends in Christ! It would be so desirable if we, not alone, but all together not only begin on the good path but also steadfastly remain on the good pathway. It is not enough just to begin with good intentions, but we must steadily practise it in order to be blessed by it. What would a good beginning help if the end were evil? It would help us as little as it did Lot's wife when she left Sodom. She had a good beginning, but her heart desired the pleasures of Sodom by which she partook in its sins and so perished (Genesis 19).

It is essential to strive after the good and continue in it by God's power, to daily desire sanctification and strive after it. It will require a determined earnestness. The world and our sinful lusts will hinder us in doing good, and hinder us on the pathway of virtue, and ever seek to overcome us. Therefore, we must always persistently and energetically bond with Jesus, the bridegroom of our soul who will steadfastly offer us a word of comfort. "So, do not fear for I am with you; do not be dismayed for I am your God. I will strengthen you and help you. I will uphold you with my righteous right hand" (Isaiah 40:10).

We should not think to rely on our own natural strength in order to reach the end of our days and persevere in the way of virtue. Otherwise we would not only fail daily, but even miss entirely the right pathway. Yet if we are constantly united with Christ our Saviour through faith and love it will not necessarily save us from all evil. We need the power by which he overcame sin and death in order to ultimately usher us into eternal bliss. Amen.

𝔖ermon #1

"But the Lord God Called Out, 'Adam, Where Are You?'"

This Sermon Is Written to Honour God and Nurture the People
Text: Genesis 3:9
Written in April 1966 by Herman D. W. Friesen
I.N.J. (In the Name of Jesus)

Invocation/Collect

May grace, mercy, love, and peace from God the Father and our Lord Jesus be with you. Through the power that is at work through the Holy Spirit, I, a humble servant of God's Word, with heartfelt sincerity, wish these blessings for all assembled here. Amen.

Introductory Meditation

In the Genesis creation account we read that God created man in His own image to live righteous and holy lives (Ephesians 4:24). Then God ordered man to live in the Garden of Eden to tend and care for it. Then God commanded and said: "You are to eat of every fruit in the garden, but you are not to eat from the tree of knowledge of good and evil, for when you eat of it you will surely die" (Genesis 2:16–17). This was the only command God gave to mankind that they were not to transgress against.

But evil had already entered the world, for God had created angels and some of the angels had departed from God. They resented the well-being of humans and tried to mislead mankind into renouncing God. It was precisely to keep sin out of paradise that man was to guard it. With faithful obedience to the holy will of God, man was to overcome this satanic temptation so that he might live happily in paradise in faithful obedience to God's commands. And to make sure that His simple commands might be obeyed, the loving God provided a threat with specific consequences that would apply if His commands were violated, namely, that the day humans ate of the forbidden fruit they would die.

How contentedly Adam and Eve lived in paradise. Their consciences were clean and unsoiled by sin. With childlike faith they trusted in God their Father, until they transgressed against His commands. This is the human condition. As long as we avoid sin, we too have peace in our hearts and are contented. When we transgress God's holy laws, we become conflicted and restless. Sin destroys joy and innocence.

Therefore, my beloved, this great blessing that mankind enjoyed in its innocence awakened Satan's jealousy. His wicked intent was to secure man's eternal damnation. From the beginning he was a murderer and could not endure truth (John 8:44); hence, he strove for man's eternal destruction. Satan used a scheming snake as his accomplice to corrupt the innocent, childlike faith of Adam and Eve. Satan questioned God's motivation in denying them the fruit. The issue raised was this: Do we really need to take God at His Word? Is it not reasonable to think that we should enjoy more of what this world has to offer? And Satan asked them, "Did God really say you were not to eat of this tree?" See my beloved, the Tempter found entrance with our first parents with this cunning question: "Did God really give you that command?" In this way Satan continues to tempt, deviously forcing the question: "Is there really any harm in this or that practice?" Does God really expect His commands to be obeyed precisely?

Because our natural inclinations tend this way, the Tempter is often successful in luring people into sin. Often Satan points us to people who are involved in worldly activities, people who also profess to be religious, but do not take God's Word seriously. And we ask: Is it not preferable for people to be a little more indulgent, and to pay less attention to the smaller moral issues so they can live more peacefully and indulgently? Such accommodations will result in the eternal destruction of our souls. And for this reason my beloved, we must not yield to the Tempter's allurements. We are to resist Satan so that he flees from us (James 4:7).

Avoid the passing allurements of this world so that you will not lose your faith unexpectedly (2 Peter 1:4). In the hour of her temptation, Eve was enticed by the beautiful fruit and she rationalized that the "forbidden fruit" would make her wise. So she reached for this fruit, ate some, and then offered the same to her husband who then ate of it. Immediately following this act of disobedience, sin was completed. At once the bitter consequences of sin set in. Adam and Eve suffered the consequences of their sinful behaviour, namely personal and eternal death. Yes, eternal death was the result of this first sin. Owing to their desecrated condition, Adam and Eve could no longer stay in paradise. Henceforth the entrance was barred by an angel armed with an unsheathed sword to block access to the tree of life (Genesis 3:23–24).

But God in His mercy did not permanently consign man to such misery. Immediately after meting out their punishment, He provided a way of escape, promising a way for all who are born of women to overcome the death penalty. For this reason we want to praise Him in faithful obedience, for in Christ Jesus is fulfilled the promise He made to our first parents. The atoning work of God's Son therefore frustrated the plans of Satan (1 John 4:9). "For the grace of God has appeared that offers salvation to all people" (Titus 2:11). No longer does the angel (Cherub) bar entry to paradise. With the crushing of the snake's head, the entry to paradise has again been opened to us. The wrongdoers on the cross who humbly and sincerely confessed Christ received the promise at once: "today you shall be with me in paradise" (Luke 23:43).

"This is how God showed His love among us: He sent His one and only Son into the world that we might live through Him" (1 John 4:9). Jesus tells us that He has come to call sinners, not righteous people, to repentance. And lovingly now He offers to all repentant sinners these words of comfort and hope: "Come to me, all you who are weary and burdened, and I will give you rest" (Matthew 11:28).

Invitation to Participate in a Time of Silent Congregational Prayer

Now to add more encouragement to this occasion, let us pay close attention to the words of our text. However, before I continue, let us kneel together in childlike trust, praying to the Giver of every good and perfect gift. And in the quietness of this moment ask for God's blessing on us, and that with His encouragement everyone present here will find eternal salvation. Amen. And now will you join me in a humble prayer.

May the Lord hear our prayer and be gracious to all.

Reading of the Text

On a well-grounded conviction that God in His grace has heard our prayer, let us now return to explore the deeper meaning of our Genesis text. "But the Lord God called to the man, 'Where are you?'" (Genesis 3:9). Thus far the reading of the text.

Homily

With this story as background, let us consider the first human encounter with sin. It is for all people a mirror of their own moral depravity, so much so that each can recognize their own inner need and poverty. As Adam tried to hide himself in the garden from the all-seeing eyes of God, to cover his nakedness with fig leaves, and then blame Eve for his moral fall, so mankind attempts to avoid personal moral responsibility by shifting blame to others. And if people manage to conceal their sins publicly, they cannot escape God's eyes. No one can escape hearing the indistinguishable words of God: "Soul, where are you?"

Let us pray: Holy Father of heaven and earth, we see and feel eternity rapidly approaching. Who knows how near that moment may be, for even in mid-life death surrounds us. Oh Lord, let this awareness constantly be before us. So much of the temporal world seems so important to us. We pray that our living will not be consumed by these attachments, for we know that this world and all its pleasures will perish. Give us a deep sincerity so that with fear and trembling one day we shall find our blessed eternal destiny. Please answer these our prayers for the sake of your great love. Amen.

Further to Genesis Chapter 3, after Adam and Eve had eaten the forbidden fruit, in the cool of the evening, they heard the voice of God, and Adam and his wife hid themselves among the trees to escape the presence of the Lord. If we reflect on our own condition, we discover that our experience often parallels that of Adam and Eve. When our infatuation with evil has faded and our inflamed passions have cooled, sober reflection sets in and we discover that the sunshine of our joy has dimmed.

In this condition, man seeks escape among the trees of innocence, leaving the feeling that a dark night of reproach is at hand. Owing to their transgressions, Adam and Eve became aware of their nakedness and sought to cover themselves with braided fig leaves. Similarly for us, a troubled conscience leaves us feeling naked before the all-seeing eyes of God. Then we look for excuses or extenuating circumstances to excuse ourselves from the consequences of our action, as though we can cover our vices with fig leaves. Or when we approach the evening of our lives and we sense our earthly pilgrimage nearing its end, then our conscience accuses us of having transgressed God's commands. Or when we are gathered in the house of the Lord, we hear God's servants admonishing us with the words of Hebrews 3:7–8: "So, as the Holy Spirit says: 'Today, if you hear His voice, do not harden your hearts as you did in the rebellion, during the time of testing in the desert.'" Or when in unguarded moments the reading of God's Word informs us that "we must all appear before the judgment seat of Christ, that each one may receive what is due him for the things done while in the body, whether good or bad" (2 Corinthians 5:10). My beloved, on all of these occasions we repeatedly hear the voice of the Lord our God, encouragingly admonishing us and calling: "Soul, where are you?"

And although we, like Adam, try to hide and distance ourselves from the admonition of the Lord, even so God is omnipresent. No one can hide from the presence of God as we read in Psalm 139:11: "If I say, surely the darkness will hide me and the light become night around me." Therefore, let us make sure that we do not neglect the invitation of God. Rather let us humbly and with repentance in our hearts come into the light of His presence, to confess our sins and desire our Lord Jesus. Like Adam, we cannot hide from God.

And now my beloved, let us consider the call of God to Adam "where are you" as a call to each of us personally. Like Adam we often cast up all manner of excuses and lies to satisfy our consciences. People are frequently inclined to satisfy themselves with earthly pleasures and participate in lustful adventures. These, along with the ever-present flowering gardens of lust, all too often cause guilty consciences and entice us to obliterate the voice of God. And people frequently drown the voice of their conscience by occupying themselves with earthly concerns as a means of avoiding dealing with the sin in their lives, and refusing to consider the consequences of death.

In this way people often prefer participating in worldly places of entertainment, such as playing ball, more often than church attendance, which only indulges in what God opposes. Add to this an attitude of pride in what we wear and the result is fleshly temptations without number.

Oh dear soul, if you participate in these transgressions, do you not hear the voice of God calling: "Soul, where are you?" And when you are filled with worldly pleasures, do you not hear in the quiet hours of night the voice of your conscience asking: "Where have you been?" and "Whom have you served?" And as you wake up in the morning after a peaceful sleep what does your conscience say to you then about the gracious protection of God in your life, that once again the sunshine of God's love has been provided for you? And what if you repeatedly persist in hiding in the garden of lust? Soul, where are you? Wake up and consider your condition.

Adam yielded to his temptation, and so it will be with you. The autumn of your life approaches. The roses of your indulgence will wilt. The leaves of your joy will be shed. Cold doubts will destroy your self-confidence. You will lose hope for the future when the world with all its allurements will perish. When the joys of this world have disappeared and life is over, how do you propose to stand before the judgment throne of God? Adam had no choice but to appear before the presence of God, without a single valid excuse for his sins. In the same way you too will stand before God impoverished and pitiable. If in this life you have been indifferent toward your eternal destiny, you too will stand in terror before God when He summons you and asks: "Soul, where are you? Why did you not do what I bade you to do?" With the pressures of life upon us, we often forget what our priorities ought to be. But Matthew 6:33 teaches us "to seek first His kingdom and His righteousness, and all these things will be given to you as well."

How often do we hear the admonishing voice of God, but have no time for His Word, or to assemble in His house? We hide behind our earthly business, such as the farmer in his field, the mother in her kitchen, the housewife with her domestic tasks. As we read in Luke Chapter 10, where Jesus visits Mary and Martha, Mary sat at the feet of Jesus to hear His teaching. However, Martha busied herself serving Jesus and confronted Him asking if He did not care that Mary was leaving all of the household work for her. Jesus responded in a way that caught her attention. "Martha, Martha," the Lord answered, "you are worried and upset about many things, but only one thing is needed. Mary has chosen what is better, and it will not be taken away from her" (Luke 10:41–42). The lesson Jesus teaches us is that our earthly encumbrances must not become an excuse for ignoring our eternal well-being. Rather seek first the kingdom of God, for the angel of death can call us at any moment and we must leave this world and all that we have accumulated. If at this moment we have no eternal investments, then for us will be fulfilled the words of Jesus in Matthew 23:28: "In the same way, on the outside you appear to people as righteous but on the inside you are full of hypocrisy and wickedness." Soul, where are you?

And further, another way of avoiding the appeal of the Holy Spirit are the many youthful activities that produce a sense of superiority. Such people unreservedly come into the presence of God and can only talk about themselves and their work. Such was also the attitude of the temple Pharisee when in Luke 18 he paraded his human self-righteousness. No one with such an inner disposition will prevail before God, whose eyes can detect the inner motivations of the heart. Luke 7:21: "The kingdom of God does not come with your careful observation." So, "Do not deceive yourselves. God is not mocked" (Galatians 6:7). For Jesus tells us in Matthew 7:21: "Not everyone who says to me, 'Lord, Lord,' will enter the kingdom of heaven, but only he who does the will of my Father who is in heaven."

How often do people emulate Martha? How many people expend energy in fading endeavours, and think they are serving God in these ways? Such service does not proceed from a humble heart. No, such service desires to be seen by people and receive their approval. When our expression of faith is a means of impressing others then our righteousness is based on our own good works. As such, our hope is grounded on self-righteousness, which leaves us with no solid basis to stand before God.

However, my beloved, there are people who use all kinds of excuses to hide from God. These people appear pious. They do not trust their own righteousness. They confess to being sinners and acknowledge falling short of the grace of God. But these people offer all kinds of excuses to avoid proper self-examination. They may say that they are old and have deeply ingrained habits, which they cannot let go. An aged, deeply rooted tree is hard to dislodge. Others harbour feelings that life has become so difficult because others have unjustly treated them. Close friends have misled them and they are to blame for misfortunes. However, they can derive much comfort from their advocate Jesus Christ, who came into the world to bear their sins, for He has taken their sins upon Himself.

See, my beloved, many try to hide from God. They try to hide behind common human weaknesses. Adam sought to excuse himself by saying, "The woman whom you gave to be with me, she gave me of the tree, and I did eat" (Genesis 3:12). And Eve responded to God, saying, "The serpent deceived me, and I ate" (Genesis 3:13). When we try to excuse ourselves by appealing to our human weaknesses, then let us hear the admonition of Paul in Galatians 5:16: "So I say, walk by the Spirit, and you will not gratify the desires of the flesh." And the Lord Jesus counsels us in Matthew 16:24: "If anyone would come after me, he must deny himself and take up his cross and follow me." Therefore, we need continually to acknowledge responsibility for our own actions. We bear personal responsibility for the conduct of life. And if only we had persisted in prayer and self-discipline we could do this. God has done all He can do. Just as Adam had to face God, so we cannot escape the brilliance of God's presence. No excuses will prevail for us to cover our excuses and sins, or to minimize them. Oh that we might avoid making excuses for our failures.

Along with the prodigal son, I counsel you to genuine repentance: "Father, I have sinned against heaven and against You. I am no longer worthy to be called Your son" (Luke 15:21). Yes, let all of us come before our God with genuine repentance and plead for His mercy. The holy Apostle Paul too knew this human struggle, when he called out: "O wretched man that I am! Who shall deliver me from the body of this death?" (Romans 7:24). But Paul adds: "But thanks be to God! He gives us the victory through our Lord Jesus Christ" (1 Corinthians 15:57). And in Romans 5:19, Paul teaches us: "For just as through the disobedience of the one man the many were made sinners, so also through the obedience of the one man the many will be made righteous." All who seek after God, accept these words from John: "On the last and greatest day of the festival, Jesus stood and said in a loud voice, 'Let anyone who is thirsty come to Me and drink'" (John 7:37).

Therefore, my beloved, let us fight on valiantly. But never assume that if we have parted with an evil habit, or have ceased committing some sin, that we have conquered all. For the closer we get to heaven, higher are the mountains we must climb. For this reason the Lord Jesus encourages us to watch and pray: "Be alert and of sober mind. Your enemy the devil prowls around like a roaring lion looking for someone to devour" (1 Peter 5:8). We must, therefore, entrust ourselves entirely to the loving arms of God: "It is because of Him that you are in Christ Jesus, who has become for us wisdom from God—that is, our righteousness, holiness and redemption" (1 Corinthians 1:30). Only in Him will we find a righteousness that prevails with God, entirely His accomplishment through the holy shed blood of our Saviour, which is more efficacious than the blood of Abel (Hebrews 12:20).

> Jesus's blood and His righteousness
> That is my beauty and coat of honour
> With this I will prevail before God
> When I enter the heavenly kingdom.

Let us constantly look to Jesus the founder of our faith (Hebrews 12:2). Let us never forget His martyr's death, His bloody and painful sufferings, and His death on the cross. Let us surrender ourselves to our heavenly Father in childlike obedience, for He is loving toward His children. Let us be confident in the presence of enemies, humble toward God, patient in suffering, resolute against all ungodly living, eager to embrace the better part, looking to Jesus as our example. These virtues we have lost through our sins. Let us follow the footsteps of Jesus, steadfastly facing the cross as we are encouraged in Philippians 2:5.

> Jesus go before us on life's road
> We do not want to neglect
> To speed after You
> Take our hands, until we are in our fatherland.

Yes, in Him we have a leader on the journey to holiness. For when we surrender ourselves entirely to Jesus, the Holy Spirit takes up residence in us so that He can progressively cleanse us from all sin and strengthen us in doing good. In this way we can be more valiant in our fight against sin, and more joyful in carrying our own cross so that we can affirm what Paul says: "I can do all this through him who gives me strength" (Philippians 4:13).

Only through Him and no one else will we find the door to paradise. Through Adam we lost paradise; through Christ we have rediscovered it. And at the entrance to the lost paradise stands the armed Cherubim, with his unsheathed, threatening sword. But at the entrance to the reawakened paradise stands our advocate Jesus Christ, our Saviour and Redeemer, with the victory palm in His hand, lovingly calling to us: "Come to me, all you who are weary and burdened, and I will give you rest" (Matthew 11:28). Again He says: "Whoever serves Me must follow Me; and where I am, My servant also will be. My Father will honour the one who serves Me" (John 12:26).

And that, my beloved, is the blessed hope with a holy promise that comforts us in our greatest travails. We know with certainly that heaven awaits with an open door for all repentant sinners. Therefore, I admonish all of my listeners to pay heed to our text, which still calls to us: "Soul, where are you?" In the same manner, He still calls to all who have not turned to the Lord. Let us not search for excuses and hide from our hearing the inviting, loving voice of Lord who loved us unto death, and who with heavenly patience and great forbearance carries us along. Our compassionate Saviour is standing at our heart's door and knocking to seek admission. My beloved, let us consider the fate that awaits us at that great judgment day. What will be the fate of unrepentant sinners who have ignored the Word of God? Then such people will remember every opportunity for repentance that was rejected and regret every occasion that the great question "where are you" was ignored (Jeremiah 4:4). But it will be too late.

It is a sobering truth that many of us may be standing at the edge of eternity. Many die suddenly without an opportunity to reflect on life after death. And some God allows to experience a hospital bed with an extended illness, and be reminded of this burning question: "Soul, where are you?" All illnesses and instances of death are wake-up calls for godly repentance.

Let us remember the huge price Jesus paid on the cross to secure our salvation and how He was cursed to become our Redeemer. How many people prefer to indulge in fleshly lusts and the accumulation of possessions rather than accumulate heavenly riches? How quickly it is that earthly gains fade away and we pass from time into eternity. How tragic it is when people have been concerned only with the accumulation of earthly treasures while remaining spiritually impoverished. This is why Jesus asked the question in Luke 9:25: "What good is it for someone to gain the whole world, and yet lose or forfeit their very self?" And again, Jesus warns us: "Whoever is ashamed of Me and My words, the Son of Man will be ashamed of them when He comes in His glory and in the glory of the Father and of the holy angels" (Luke 9:26).

Therefore, my beloved, when we perceive the voice of God asking us, "Soul, where are you?" let us avoid gathering fig leaves to cover our spiritual nakedness. Rather, let us approach God with humble repentance, and say, "Lord, here am I." "Teach me to do Your will. For You are my God. Your Spirit guides me on the path of life." He will be merciful to us, for Jesus said that He had come to seek and save the lost. And that is why lovingly He still calls to us: "Come to Me all who are burdened. And I will give you peace" (Matthew 11:28). He wishes to impart His peace. Let us all purpose to find this peace, given to us by a Holy God: Father, Son, and Holy Spirit, praised in all eternity.

And now may the grace of the Lord Jesus Christ, the love of God the Father, together with the comforting presence of His Holy Spirit be with you all. Amen. In the name of Jesus, Amen.

Invitation to Participate in a Time
of Silent Congregational Prayer

Now my beloved, let us end this admonition and conclude with gratitude to God, and pray that henceforth God will accompany us with His grace, that we may win the salvation of our souls. And so let me invite you one more time to join me in prayer.

May God hear our prayer and be gracious to all.

Benediction/Dismissal

Finally, I have no more to say to you other than to thank you for this opportunity to speak to you today, and conclude with the blessing of Moses: "The Lord bless you and keep you, may His countenance shine upon you" (Numbers 6:24). May He preserve us until we enter eternity.

Depart in Christ's peace.

Notes

Introduction

1   The term *Kanadier* is now often used in a broader international sense to identify the descendants of the original immigrants to Canada who later relocated to parts of Central and South America, creating a transnational Low German "village among nations." Royden Loewen, *Village among Nations: "Canadian" Mennonites in a Transnational World, 1916–2006* (Toronto: University of Toronto Press, 2013).

2   For a helpful overview of the circumstances and motivations surrounding the exodus of almost twenty thousand Mennonites from southern Russia during the late nineteenth century, see Ernest N. Braun, "Why Emigrate?" *Preservings* 34 (2014): 4–10; and James Urry, *Mennonites, Politics, and Peoplehood: Europe—Russia—Canada 1525–1980* (Winnipeg: University of Manitoba Press, 2006).

3   Henry Schapansky, *The Old Colony (Chortitza) of Russia: Early History and the First Settlers in the Context of Mennonite Migrations* (Rosenort, MB: Country Graphics and Printing, 2001); and John J. Friesen, "Reinländer Mennoniten Gemeinde," in *Old Colony Mennonites in Canada, 1875–2000*, ed. Delbert Plett (Steinbach, MB: Crossway Publications Inc., 2001), 13.

4   For a copy of the order-in-council authorizing the formation of this reserve, see Leonard Doell, ed., *Mennonite Homesteaders on the Hague-Osler Reserve, 1891–1999* (Saskatoon: Mennonite Historical Society of Saskatchewan, 1999), 6.

5   Another reserve was organized for a group of Mennonites from Kansas and Oklahoma in 1905 by the Saskatchewan Valley Land Company. It became known as the Quill Lakes Mennonite Reserve.

6   "Editorial," *The Daily Phoenix* (Saskatoon), 5 January 1909.

7   "Mennonite Mob," *Fifth Estate*, CBC, 10 March 1992, https://www.youtube.com/watch?v=6Buf-yaN_tE; Andrew Mitrovica and Susan Bourette, "The Wages of Sin: How God-Fearing Old Colony Mennonites—'the plain people'—Have Become Some of Canada's Biggest and Most Dangerous Drug Smugglers," *Saturday Night*, April 2004, 28–36; and *Pure*, season 1, episodes 1–6, directed by Ken Girotti, created by Michael Amo, first aired 9 January 2017, CBC, http://www.cbc.ca/pure/.

8   C. Henry Smith, *The Story of the Mennonites* (Berne, IN: Mennonite Book Concern, 1941), 650; Cornelius Krahn, "Old Colony Mennonites," in *Mennonite*

Encyclopedia (Hillsboro, KS: Mennonite Brethren Publishing House, 1955–1990). See also the negative portrayal in Wolfgang W. Moelleken and Melita A. Moelleken, "Language Conflicts of Low German-Speaking Mennonites in Southern Ontario, Canada," in *Plurilingua: Language Conflict and Minorities*, ed. P. H. Nelde (Bonn, Germany: Dümmler, 1990), 95–108.

9   See Frank H. Epp, *Mennonites in Canada, 1786–1920: The History of a Separate People* (Toronto: University of Toronto Press, 1974); and Frank H. Epp, *Mennonites in Canada, 1920–1940: A People's Struggle for Survival* (Toronto: Macmillan, 1982).

10   Ted Regehr, *Mennonites in Canada: A People Transformed, 1939–1970* (Toronto: University of Toronto Press, 1996), 127–32.

11   See, for example, E. K. Francis, *In Search of Utopia: The Mennonites in Manitoba* (Altona, MB: D. W. Friesen and Sons Ltd., 1955); J. Winfield Fretz, *Colonization in Mexico: An Introduction* (Akron, PA: Mennonite Central Committee, 1945); Calvin W. Redekop, *The Old Colony Mennonites: Dilemmas of Ethnic Minority Life* (Baltimore: Johns Hopkins Press, 1969); and Henry Leonard Sawatsky, *They Sought a Country: Mennonite Colonization in Mexico* (Berkeley: University of California Press, 1971).

12   See the helpful annotated bibliography in Royden Loewen, *Horse-and-Buggy Genius: Listening to Mennonites Contest the Modern World* (Winnipeg: University of Manitoba Press, 2016), 231–36.

13   David M. Quiring's recent work highlights the often tense relations and conflicting interests of Mennonites in Canada and Mexico (*The Mennonite Old Colony Vision: Under Siege in Mexico and Canadian Connections* [Steinbach, MB: Crossway Publications Inc., 2003]). Notable also is Benjamin Nobbs-Thiessen's assessment of the often ambivalent way that North American Mennonites viewed Old Colony Mennonites living in Mexico and South America ("Mennonites in Unexpected Places: Sociologist and Settler in South America," *Journal of Mennonite Studies* 28 [2010]: 203–24).

14   His anthology, *Old Colony Mennonites in Canada, 1875–2000*, is a valuable contribution. In addition, the pages of *Preservings*, a publication by the Hanover Steinbach Historical Society, contain numerous items written by Plett.

15   See, for example, Delbert Plett, "The Lonely Ohm—Myth and Reality: The Pastoral Vision and Challenges of the Conservative Mennonite Ministerial Lehrdienst," *Preservings* 21 (December 2002): 94–108.

16   For a more nuanced theological defense of Old Colony Mennonites, see John J. Friesen, "Old Colony Theology, Ecclesiology and Experience of Church in Manitoba," *Journal of Mennonite Studies* 22 (2004): 131–44. He portrays the Old Colony Mennonite theological system as a particular version of an Anabaptist vision that, like others, has had its successes and failures.

17   An excellent example is the extensive, and often highly collaborative, work of Royden Loewen. See Loewen's *Horse-and-Buggy Genius* and *Village among*

Nations: "Canadian" Mennonites in a Transnational World, 1916–2006 (Toronto: University of Toronto Press, 2013), as well as *Hidden Worlds: Revisiting the Mennonite Migrants of the 1870s* (Winnipeg: University of Manitoba Press, 2001).

18 Exceptions include Leo Driedger, "A Sect in a Modern Society: A Case Study, the Old Colony Mennonites of Saskatchewan" (MA thesis, University of Chicago, 1955); and Richard Friesen, "The Old Colony Mennonite Settlements in Saskatchewan: A Study in Settlement Change" (MA thesis, University of Alberta, 1975). Worthy of mention also is the mammoth volume of information compiled by Leonard Doell and Jacob G. Guenter in *Hague-Osler Mennonite Reserve 1895–1995* (Saskatoon: Hague-Osler Reserve Book Committee, 1995).

19 Royden Loewen, "A Village among the Nations: Low German Migrants and the Idea of Transnationalism in the History of Mennonites in Canada," *Conrad Grebel Review* 33, no. 1 (Winter 2015): 31.

20 Some historians consider biography an inferior way of exposing the past, while others question the premise that any coherence can be extracted from individual lives. See Barbara Caine, *Biography and History* (New York: Palgrave Macmillan, 2010), 5–7.

21 See, for example, Daniel Aaron, ed., *Studies in Biography* (Cambridge, MA: Harvard University Press, 1978).

22 Michael Armstrong Crouch, *Prepared for the Twentieth-Century? The Life of Emily Bonnycastle Mayne (Aimée) 1872–1958* (Newcastle, UK: Cambridge Scholars Publishing, 2015), 36.

23 Margaret S. Archer, *Being Human: The Problem of Agency* (Cambridge: Cambridge University Press, 2000), 18.

24 Hans Werner, *The Constructed Mennonite: History, Memory, and the Second World War* (Winnipeg: University of Manitoba Press, 2013).

25 William F. Brewer, "What Is Recollective Memory?" in *Remembering Our Past: Studies in Autobiographical Memory*, ed. David C. Rubin (Cambridge: Cambridge University Press, 1995), 19–66.

26 Ulrich Neisser, "Memory with a Grain of Salt," in *Memory: An Anthology*, eds. Harriet Harvey Wood and A. S. Byatt (London: Vintage, 2009), 88.

Chapter 1

1 See John Dyck, ed., *Bergthal Gemeinde Buch, 1843–1876* (Steinbach, MB: Hanover Steinbach Historical Society, 1993), 283; Doell and Guenter, *Hague-Osler Mennonite Reserve 1895-1995*, 40; and Doell, *Mennonite Homesteaders*, 110.

2 See Dyck, *Bergthal Gemeinde Buch, 1843–1876*, 332; and John Dyck and William Harms, eds., *1880 Village Census of the Mennonite West Reserve, Manitoba, Canada* (Winnipeg: Manitoba Mennonite Historical Society, 1998), 48.

3 Historians and archeologists continue to examine evidence that suggests these
   nomadic communities were descendants of Asiatic peoples who made their
   way across Beringia thousands of years ago. See, for example, J. Víctor Moreno-
   Mayar et al., "Terminal Pleistocene Alaskan Genome Reveals First Founding
   Population of Native Americans," *Nature* 553 (January 2018): 203–7; and
   Mikkel W. Pedersen et al., "Postglacial Viability and Colonization in North
   America's Ice-free Corridor," *Nature* 537 (September 2016): 45–49. In contrast,
   the creation stories of many Indigenous peoples place their origins within North
   America. For a comprehensive overview of the history of Canada's original
   inhabitants, see Olive Dickason with David T. McNab, *Canada's First Nations:
   A History of Founding Peoples from Earliest Times*, 4th ed. (Don Mills, ON:
   Oxford University Press, 2008).

4 John Milloy, *The Plains Cree: Trade, Diplomacy and War, 1790–1870* (Winnipeg:
   University of Manitoba Press, 1988).

5 John Webster Grant, *Moon of Wintertime: Missionaries and the Indians of
   Canada in Encounter since 1534* (Toronto: University of Toronto Press, 1984),
   143–66.

6 See James Daschuk, *Clearing the Plains: Disease, Politics of Starvation, and the
   Loss of Aboriginal Life* (Regina: University of Regina Press, 2013).

7 Gerald Friesen, *The Canadian Prairies: A History* (Toronto: University of
   Toronto Press, 1987), 242–73.

8 See the provocative work of Roger Epp, a contemporary Mennonite who
   explores Mennonite complicity with the Canadian government's colonizing
   project, *We Are All Treaty People: Prairie Essays* (Edmonton: University of
   Alberta Press, 2008).

9 See, for example, Howard Palmer, "Strangers and Stereotypes: The Rise of
   Nativism, 1880–1920," in *The Prairie West: Historical Readings*, 2nd ed., eds. R.
   Douglas Francis and Howard Palmer (Edmonton: University of Alberta Press,
   1992), 320–21.

10 See, for example, the stories and presentations from the "History of Aboriginal-
   Mennonite Relations Symposium," featured in *Journal of Mennonite Studies* 19
   (2001): 9–179. Particularly notable is the story of Leonard Doell's advocacy
   among Mennonites currently living on land that became part of the Hague-
   Osler Mennonite Reserve in 1897. The belated addition was land that had
   been granted to the Young Chippewayan Band as part of Treaty 6, but then
   taken from the band without its knowledge or consent. While the incoming
   Mennonite settlers were unaware of the actions by which the thirty square
   miles of prime agricultural land came to be included in the reserve, they became
   beneficiaries of this governmental transgression. Doell encouraged Mennonites
   to act on a moral obligation to participate in rectifying this injustice ("Young
   Chippewayan Reserve No. 107 and Mennonite Farmers in Saskatchewan,"
   165–67).

11 Leonard Doell, "The First Mennonite Settlers in Alberta," *Preservings 33* (2013): 42–54.

12 Doell and Guenter, *Hague-Osler Mennonite Reserve 1895–1995*, 21; Leonard Doell, "Klaas Peters: A Pioneer Entrepreneur," in *Historical Sketches of the East Reserve, 1874–1910*, ed. John Dyck (Steinbach, MB: The Hanover Steinbach Historical Society, 1994), 295; and *Old & New Furrows: The Story of Rosthern* (Rosthern, SK: Rosthern Historical Society, 1977), 19, 385–86, 555–56.

13 Doell, *Mennonite Homesteaders*, 114, 260; and Doell and Guenter, *Hague-Osler Mennonite Reserve 1895–1995*, 40.

14 Richard Friesen, "Saskatchewan Mennonite Settlements: The Modification of Old World Settlement Patterns," *Canadian Ethnic Studies 9*, no. 2 (1977): 78.

15 The villages in the Hague-Osler Reserve used one of four models: (1) seventeen villages were organized using the traditional linear Strassendorf plan, along with its method of land allocation (for example, Neuanlage, Neuhorst); (2) the "unorganized" village was more of a grouping of individual farmers who used the Strassendorf layout (for example, Kronsthal); (3) the four-corner hamlet (for example, Blumenort); and (4) a district with settlers in proximity making efforts to collaborate in matters such as organizing a school (see Friesen, "Saskatchewan Mennonite Settlements," 72–90; Doell, *Mennonite Homesteaders*, 19–22; and Doell and Guenter, *Hague-Osler Mennonite Reserve 1895–1995*, 31–33).

16 David L. and Elizabeth Friesen received a homestead patent on SW 32-39-3-W3, their children David and Anna Friesen on SE 30-39-3-W3, Herman B. and Maria Friesen on NE 30-39-3-W3, Johann B. and Katharina Friesen on NW 30-39-3-W3, Franz B. and Margaretha Friesen on NW 32-39-3-W3, and Jakob K. and Elizabeth Reddekopp on NW 36-39-4-W3 (see Doell, *Mennonite Homesteaders*, 110–11, 113, 116, 231). Anna's parents, Jacob P. and Katherina (Rempel) Wiebe, along with some of Anna's siblings, joined the Friesen families in Saskatchewan in 1902 (Doell, *Mennonite Homesteaders*, 290–91).

17 The Department of the Interior discontinued the "Hamlet privilege" in 1907 in order to encourage settlers to take up residence on their homestead (Doell, *Mennonite Homesteaders*, 27–28). The two quarters on which Blumenheim was located were eventually subdivided into forty-acre strips in 1925 (Doell, *Mennonite Homesteaders*, 40).

18 See Doell and Guenter, *Hague-Osler Mennonite Reserve 1895–1995*, 579; Abram Janzen and Leonard Doell, "Blumenheim Village," in Doell and Guenter, *Hague-Osler Mennonite Reserve 1895–1995*, 41; and Dennis Stoesz, "A History of the Chortitzer Mennonite Church of Manitoba, 1874–1914" (MA thesis, University of Manitoba, 1987), 74. The Rosthern group tried to organize a church and wrote to several Ältesten in Russia and Manitoba seeking advice. For a list of excommunicated families, see Doell and Guenter, *Hague-Osler Mennonite Reserve 1895–1995*, 21.

19 Of the thirteen children born to David and Anna Friesen, two died as one-year-old infants (one in 1894 prior to the move to Saskatchewan, and one in 1905 after the move).

20 *Wichtige Dokumente betreffs der Wehrfreiheit der Mennoniten in Canada: Im Selbstverlage der Canadischen Mennonitengemeinden* (Gretna, MB: B. Ewerts Drukerei, 1917), 10–11.

21 Two of David's children (Marie and Wilhelm) eventually married two of Katarina's children (David and Katherina).

22 See Leonard Doell, "The Mennonite Private Schools," in Doell and Guenter, *Hague-Osler Mennonite Reserve 1895–1995*, 635–67; and Jake Peters, *Mennonite Private Schools in Manitoba and Saskatchewan, 1874–1925* (Steinbach, MB: Mennonite Village Museum, 1985) for a good description of these schools.

23 *Wichtige Dokumente betreffs der Wehrfreiheit der Mennoniten in Canada*, 10–11.

24 Adolf Ens, *Subjects or Citizens? The Mennonite Experience in Canada, 1870–1925* (Ottawa: University of Ottawa Press, 1994), 17; and William Schroeder, *The Bergthal Colony* (Winnipeg: CMBC Publications, 1974), 85–91.

25 Kelly Lynn Hedges, "Plautdietsch and Huuchdietsch in Chihuahua: Language, Literacy, and Identity among the Old Colony Mennonites in Northern Mexico" (PhD dissertation, Yale University, 1996).

26 Friesen, "Reinländer Mennoniten Gemeinde," 13.

27 James Urry, *None but Saints: The Transformation of Mennonite Life in Russia, 1789–1889* (Winnipeg: Hyperion Press, 1989), 153–54.

28 Doell, "The Mennonite Private Schools," 636.

29 Jakob W. Goerzen, *Low German in Canada, A Study of "Plautditsch"* (Edmonton: self-published, 1972).

30 An insightful glimpse into the life of a village teacher is offered by Johan I. Wiens, "Light and Shadows of the Teaching Profession" (1917), cited in Doell and Guenter, *Hague-Osler Mennonite Reserve 1895–1995*, 644–46. See also Peters, *Mennonite Private Schools*, 23–28; Doell and Guenter, *Hague-Osler Mennonite Reserve 1895–1995*, 401–3, 635–44; and "Schulverordnung: General School Regulations of the Chortitzer Mennonite Church ca. 1880," in *Working Papers of the East Reserve Village Histories, 1874–1910*, ed. John Dyck (Steinbach, MB: Hanover Steinbach Historical Society, 1990), 125–26.

31 Negative perceptions about the educational quality of the German private schools were created in part by the political prejudices of those trying to pressure the Mennonites to accept the English-language public schools, and in part from the gradual educational stagnation that occurred over time as teachers who had received some training in Russia were replaced by local men who had not received any training. The absence of any teacher training programs for the teachers in the Old Colony Mennonite schools gradually diminished the quality of education. See Francis, *In Search of Utopia*, 164.

32   In 1915, the teacher in Blumenheim was paid $30 a month for six months, along with one hundred bushels of oats.

33   Doell and Guenter, *Hague-Osler Mennonite Reserve 1895–1995*, 41, 656.

34   See Ken Horseman, "Education," in *The Saskatchewan Encyclopedia: A Living Legacy* (Regina: Great Canadian Research Center, 2005), 280.

35   Francis, *In Search of Utopia*, 233.

36   Doell and Guenter, *Hague-Osler Mennonite Reserve 1895–1995*, 650–53.

37   For an overview and analysis of this conflict, see the work of Ens, *Subjects or Citizens?* 105–70; and William Janzen, *Limits of Liberty: The Experience of Mennonite, Hutterite and Doukhobor Communities in Canada* (Toronto: University of Toronto Press, 1990).

38   See Alan M. Guenther, "'Barred from Heaven and Cursed Forever': Old Colony Mennonites and the 1908 Commission of Inquiry Regarding Public Education," *Historical Papers: Canadian Society of Church History* (2007): 129–48; Doell and Guenter, *Hague-Osler Mennonite Reserve 1895–1995*, 583, 648–49; and William Janzen, "The 1920s Migration of Old Colony Mennonites from the Hague-Osler Area to Mexico," *Mennonite Historical Society of Saskatchewan Occasional Papers* (2006): 2–5.

39   Guenther, "'Barred from Heaven and Cursed Forever,'" 143.

40   E. H. Oliver, "The Country School in Non-English Speaking Communities in Saskatchewan," address delivered to the Saskatchewan Public Education League, Regina, SK, September 22, 1915 (published as a pamphlet). It is worth noting that the provincial government's official responses to Oliver's campaign were more moderate than Oliver's report (Janzen, "The 1920s Migration of Old Colony Mennonites," 6).

41   Guenther, "'Barred from Heaven and Cursed Forever,'" 133.

42   See Horseman, "Education," 277–91.

43   The new districts included Scarpe (in Blumenhoff), Passchendaele (near Hochfeld), Venice (in Blumenthal), Pembroke (in Neuanlage), Renfrew (near Blumenheim), LaBassee (in Reinland), Steele (southeast of Hepburn), and Embury (in Gruenfeld). Public school districts already in existence included Saskatchewan School (1888), Rosthern (1899), Hague (1903), Osler (1905), Clark's Crossing (Penner School) (1905), Warman (1906), Lily (near Aberdeen) (1911), River Park (near Aberdeen) (1912), Heidelberg (north of Hague) (1913), and Reinfeld (north of Hague) (1914).

44   Ens, *Subjects or Citizens?* 147–53.

45   Janzen, "The 1920s Migration of Old Colony Mennonites," 9; and Ens, *Subjects or Citizens?* 147–53.

46   In 1920, Johan F. Peters of Neuanlage wrote a letter to Premier Martin, describing the dilemma facing Old Colony parents with school-aged children: "If we send our children to public schools we violate God's commands in not holding to that which we promised our God and Saviour at holy baptism. If we do not

send them, we offend against your laws. Does Mr. Martin want us to transgress God's laws in order to keep his? Oh how difficult it is to be a true Mennonite." Cited in Doell and Guenter, *Hague-Osler Mennonite Reserve 1895–1995*, 657.

47 Ens, *Subjects or Citizens?* 131–38; and Doell and Guenter, *Hague-Osler Mennonite Reserve 1895–1995*, 41, 656.

48 Ens, *Subjects or Citizens?* 156.

Chapter 2

1 Services were also conducted for a short time in the late 1890s in Rosthern.

2 For a brief description of a typical service, see Doell and Guenter, *Hague-Osler Mennonite Reserve 1895–1995*, 582–83.

3 For a discussion of stratification, class structure, and distribution of power among Old Colony Mennonites, see Calvin W. Redekop, *The Old Colony Mennonites: Dilemmas of Ethnic Minority Life* (Baltimore: Johns Hopkins Press, 1969), 93-102.

4 See James Urry, "The Ältesters: The Position of Elder in Mennonite Congregational Communities," *Preservings* 21 (2002): 3–5.

5 Johann Wiebe, *Die Auswanderung von Russland nach Kanada* (Cuauhtemoc, Chihuahua, Mexico: Campo 6½, Apartado 297, 1972). Wiebe settled with his family in the village of Rosengart, south of Winkler, until his death in 1905. See Peter D. Zacharias, "Ältester Johann Wiebe (1837–1905)," in *Church, Family and Village: Essays on Mennonite Life on the West Reserve*, eds. Adolf Ens, Jacob E. Peters, and Otto Hamm (Winnipeg: Manitoba Mennonite Historical Society, 2001), 53–66; Peter D. Zacharias, *Reinland: An Experience in Community* (Altona, MB: Reinland Centennial Committee, 1976), 185–202; and "Part Two: Aeltester Johann Wiebe," in Plett, *Old Colony Mennonites in Canada*, 45–72.

6 For a comprehensive list of Old Colony Mennonite ministers and Ältesten who served in the Hague-Osler region, see Doell and Guenter, *Hague-Osler Mennonite Reserve 1895–1995*, 591–99; and John Janzen, ed., *As I Remember It… Neuanlage, 1895–1995* (Hague, SK: self-published, 1995), 20–22.

7 Leonard Doell, "Ältester Jakob Wiens (1855–1932)," *Preservings* 29 (2009): 15.

8 Doell, "Ältester Jakob Wiens (1855–1932)," 15–17; and Loewen, *Village among Nations*, 134.

9 Plett, *Old Colony Mennonites in Canada*, 143. The ministers included Johann Wall, Peter Klassen, Peter H. Klassen, Abram Wall, Peter Wiens, and Johann P. Wall (Janzen, *As I Remember It…Neuanlage*, 20).

10 Cited in Loewen, *Village among Nations*, 14–15.

11 Sawatsky, *They Sought a Country*, 37; Quiring, *The Mennonite Old Colony Vision*; and Adolf Ens, "A Second Look at the Rejected Conservatives,"

Mennonite Reporter, November 25, 1974, 36–37, reprinted in *Preservings 16* (June 2000): 3–8.

12 Isaak M. Dyck, "Emigration from Canada to Mexico, Year 1922," trans. Robyn Dyck Sneath (unpublished manuscript), cited in Loewen, *Village among Nations*, 14.

13 Loewen, *Village among Nations*, 14–17; and Loewen, "A Village among the Nations," 29–48.

14 Janzen, "The 1920s Migration of Old Colony Mennonites," 19. The pressure to conform was keenly felt by church members: my paternal grandfather, Frank B. Guenter, described how four out of six siblings in his father's family (Jacob F. Guenter) participated in the migration to Mexico. He recalls how those who did not participate were chastised and rejected as *heiden* (heathen). Frank B. Guenter, interview with author, November 22, 1994.

15 This is explicitly spelled out by Johann P. Wall, one of the ministers leading the migration. Johann P. Wall, letter to C. B. Dirks, September 10, 1933, Herman D. W. Friesen personal papers. See also Titus F. Guenther, "Theology of Migration: The Ältesten Reflect," *Journal of Mennonite Studies* 18 (2000): 164–76.

16 Abram G. Janzen, *Ältester Johan M. Loeppky, 1882–1950: As I Remember Him* (Hague, SK: self-published, 2003), 4–5.

17 Katarina is the niece, as well as a first cousin once removed, of Ältester Jacob Wiens, which may have added some pressure to join the migration to Mexico. It is worth noting that the connection between Herman Friesen and Ältester Wiens's family is later strengthened through marriage: Helena Wall, Ältester Wiens's wife, and Anna Hildebrand, the mother of Margaretha Banman, Herman's wife, were first cousins.

18 Janzen, "The 1920s Migration of Old Colony Mennonites," 13; and Sawatsky, *They Sought a Country*.

19 The individuals associated with the Sommerfelder Mennonite Church migrated to southern Manitoba from the Bergthal Colony in Russia during the 1870s, along with other Mennonites from the Chortitza Colony. Despite initial settlement on the East Reserve, by 1880 most members of this group had relocated to the West Reserve. Internal conflict resulted in the formation of the Sommerfeld Mennoniten Gemeinde, led by Ältester Abraham Doerksen, as well as the more culturally accommodating Bergthaler Mennonite Church of Manitoba. Sommerfelder Mennonites from Manitoba began moving to new settlements in the Swift Current and Herbert areas of Saskatchewan during the late 1890s and early 1900s. In Saskatchewan, this group eventually became known as the Bergthaler Mennonite Church (see Peter Bergen, *History of the Sommerfeld Mennonite Church, that is, the Background and First One Hundred Years of the Sommerfeld Mennonite Church* [Altona, MB: Sommerfeld Mennonite Church, 2001]; and Leonard Doell, *The Bergthaler Mennonite Church of Saskatchewan, 1892–1975* [Winnipeg: CMBC Publications, 1987]).

The Bergthalers eventually established congregations in the Hague-Osler region as well, some of whom migrated to Mexico and Paraguay during the 1920s.

20   Johann P. Wall, a former ministerial colleague, denounced Loeppky for his "devious behavior," and accused him of "striving for the prestige of high position" (Johann P. Wall, letter to C. B. Dirks, September 10, 1933). See also Johann Loeppky, "Journal on a Trip to Mexico—1921," *Preservings* 26 (2006): 37–44; Loewen, *Village among Nations*, 27–33; Janzen, "The 1920s Migration of Old Colony Mennonites," 19; and Janzen, *Ältester Johan M. Loeppky*, 6.

21   "Elbing Catechism," *Global Anabaptist Mennonite Encyclopedia Online*, http://gameo.org/index.php?title=Elbing_Catechism. Robert Friedman notes the *Catechism* reflected Lutheran and Pietistic influences in *Mennonite Piety through the Centuries: Its Genius and Its Literature* (Sugarcreek, OH: Schlabach Printers, 1980), 134–37.

22   The *Confession of Faith* reflects the considerable influence of several older Anabaptist-Mennonite confessions that have served as major theological landmarks in the Anabaptist-Mennonite tradition, including the *Dordrecht Confession* (1632), the *Ris Confession* (1766), the *Prussian Confession* (1660), the *Prussian Confession* (1792), and the *Rudnerweide Confession* (1853), the latter of which was widely used by Mennonites in Russia, particularly in the Molotschna Colony. See Karl Koop, ed., *Confessions of Faith in the Anabaptist Tradition, 1527–1660* (Kitchener, ON: Pandora Press, 2006); Howard John Loewen, *One Lord, One Church, One Hope, and One God: Mennonite Confessions of Faith* (Nappanee, IN: Institute of Mennonite Studies, 1985); and Dennis Stoesz, "The Religious Literature of the Chortitzer Mennonite Church, 1878–1903" (unpublished paper, 1981).

23   The *Confession of Faith* contains thirteen articles that are identical to the *Prussian Confession* (1792), written and published by Gerhard Wiebe who was the Ältester of the Flemish congregation at Elbing and Ellerwald, but it also contains some notable differences. Dennis Stoesz speculates that geographic and social differences between the different Mennonite colonies in Russia may account for the presence and use of multiple confessions. Given the isolation of the Fuerstenland Colony, where Johann Wiebe first served as Ältester, it is possible that church leaders in this colony modified the *Prussian Confession* (1792), which Ältester Johann Wiebe then brought with him to North America. Given the fact that Ältester Wiebe was a capable writer, and that he wrote a short preface for the *Confession of Faith*, it is possible that he saw the move to Canada as a new opportunity to include revisions to several articles. Without any records of the Mennonite Church in the Fuerstenland Colony, or any documentation of the Old Colony Mennonite Church in Manitoba going through a deliberate process of doctrinal revision, we may never know the circumstances around the origin of this rather unique Anabaptist-Mennonite confession.

24 Article 8, "Of Holy Baptism," is four pages in length in the *Confession of Faith*, in contrast to only several sentences in the *Dordrecht Confession* and a paragraph in the *Rudnerweide Confession*.

25 The other Anabaptist-Mennonite confessions mentioned above specify that an experience of regeneration is a necessary prerequisite for baptism. Individuals who "hear the teaching of the Holy Gospel, believe, and with penitent heart gladly accept it, must be baptized" (Article 7, "Concerning Christian Baptism," *Rudnerweide Confession*). Another important variation in nuance between the *Confession of Faith* and the *Dordrecht Confession* is the notion of "worthiness." The latter prescribes baptism to be done "in the most worthy name of the Father, and of the Son, and of the Holy Ghost, according to the command of Christ," whereas the former expresses "the wish and hope that almighty God will prosper all those who are contemplating [baptism] and will find them worthy and qualified in their hearts." In one, worthiness is a quality attached to God, and, in the other, worthiness must be achieved in order to be accepted by God. More comparative work needs to be done to assess the degree of theological consistency between the *Confession of Faith* and the confessions that have served as major landmarks in the Anabaptist-Mennonite tradition.

26 See the explanation offered by Ältester Wiens to government officials during the 1908 hearings in Guenther, "'Barred from Heaven and Cursed Forever,'" 134.

27 Article 9, "Of the Lord's Supper," *Confession of Faith*.

28 See Redekop's description of how baptism, church membership, and marriage serve as rites of passage within the community (*The Old Colony Mennonites*, 33).

29 Hans Werner, "'A mild form of deviancy': Premarital Sex among Early Manitoba Mennonites," *Journal of Mennonite Studies* 26 (2008): 146–47.

30 Werner, 151–52.

31 Werner, 153.

32 Werner, 148–49.

33 Werner, 144.

34 Doell and Guenter, *Hague-Osler Mennonite Reserve 1895–1995*, 584.

35 See Abe Rempel, "The Reorganization of the Old Colony Mennonite Church," in Ens, Peters, and Hamm, *Church, Family and Village*, 243–47; and Doell and Guenter, *Hague-Osler Mennonite Reserve 1895–1995*, 585–86.

36 See Janzen, *Ältester Johan M. Loeppky*, 13.

37 Plett, *Old Colony Mennonites in Canada*, 156–57.

38 See Dawn S. Bowen, "The Transformation of a Northern Alberta Frontier Community" (MA thesis, University of Maine at Orono, 1990).

39 Doell and Guenter, *Hague-Osler Mennonite Reserve 1895–1995*, 442.

40 Robert Loewen, "Prespatou Old Colony Mennonite Church," in Plett, *Old Colony Mennonites in Canada*, 160.

41 For example, the Old Colony in La Crete retained the use of the *lange Wiez*, melodies with a slower tempo (Robert Loewen, "La Crete Old Colony

Mennonite Church," in Plett, *Old Colony Mennonites in Canada*, 158). Those in northern British Columbia were particularly appreciative of the way their isolation prevented participation in elections (Doell and Guenter, *Hague-Osler Mennonite Reserve 1895–1995*, 444–45). A similar observation is made by Cornelius Krahn and Henry Leonard Sawatzky; see "Old Colony Mennonites," Global Anabaptist Mennonite Encyclopedia Online, http://www.gameo.org/encyclopedia/contents/O533ME.html.

42   Janzen, "The 1920s Migration of Old Colony Mennonites," 20.

43   Brian Cousins, "Transportation," in *The Saskatchewan Encyclopedia*, 946.

44   Doell and Guenter, *Hague-Osler Mennonite Reserve 1895–1995*, 587–88. It is worth noting that the Old Colony Mennonite leaders repeatedly rejected offers of assistance from both the General Conference Mennonite Church in Neuanlage and the Mennonite Brethren Church in Hepburn, Saskatchewan.

Chapter 3

1   Heinrich was born in Russia in 1871 (the first child in a family of fourteen children). His parents, Cornelius and Margaretha (Vogt) Banman, immigrated to Canada in 1877, arriving in Quebec City on the SS *Sarmatian* on June 30, 1877. The family homesteaded in Manitoba on the West Reserve near Gruenfeld, south of Winkler, Manitoba. See "Passenger Lists of Mennonite Immigrants to Manitoba: 1874–1880," in Dyck, *Bergthal Gemeinde Buch, 1843–1876*, 326–27.

2   Anna was born in Russia in 1877 (the tenth child in a family of ten children). Her parents, Isaac and Katherina (Bergen) Hildebrand, immigrated to Canada in 1878, arriving in Quebec City on the SS *Peruvian* on June 30, 1878. The family homesteaded in Manitoba on the West Reserve near Blumenhoff, southeast of Winkler, Manitoba, before moving further west. See "Passenger Lists of Mennonite Immigrants to Manitoba," 327.

3   The legal land descriptions were NW18-39-3-W3 and NW34-38-3W3. Doell, *Mennonite Homesteaders*, 31–32.

4   Leonard Doell, "Kronsthal Village," in Doell and Guenter, *Hague-Osler Mennonite Reserve 1895–1995*, 141–42.

5   A typical wedding is described by Jacob G. Janzen, "Wedding in the Early Days," in Janzen, *As I Remember It…Neuanlage*, 25–28.

6   See Doell and Guenter, *Hague-Osler Mennonite Reserve 1895–1995*, 674–76.

7   Kerry L. Fast, "Religion, Pain, and the Body: Agency in the Life of an Old Colony Woman," *Journal of Mennonite Studies* 22 (2004): 103–29.

8   Werner, "'A mild form of deviancy,'" 146.

9   For an extended discussion of Old Colony Mennonite family life, see Loewen, *Horse-and-Buggy Genius*, 131–59.

10   Friesen, *The Canadian Prairies*, 382–417.

11   For a family of five, relief was limited to $20.20 per month, minus 20 per cent if
      the applicant had access to meat and dairy products. Doell and Guenter, *Hague-
      Osler Mennonite Reserve 1895–1995*, 395.

12   The Old Colony Mennonite Church had a long-established practice of using the
      attic of church buildings as a "store house of the Lord" (Malachi 3:10). Members
      would bring extra vegetables, dried fruits, smoked meat, and grain that could
      be distributed by the deacons. The system was not adequate to meet the needs
      created by the economic conditions during the 1930s, and, as a result, this
      tradition of sharing and distributing food was discontinued.

13   For a first-hand account of village life during the 1930s and 1940s, see J. M.
      (Jack) Driedger, *Growing Up in Blumenheim: Life in an Old Colony Mennonite
      Village during the Thirties and Forties* (Saskatoon: self-published, 1998).

14   Ronald S. Love, "Telecommunications," in *The Saskatchewan Encyclopedia*,
      927–28.

15   This was unlike the Amish, who have been much more reflective and intricately
      intentional in assessing the impact of technology on their community and
      navigating their interaction with technology. See Donald B. Kraybill, *The Riddle
      of Amish Culture* (Baltimore, MD: Johns Hopkins University Press, 2001),
      141–87.

16   Several of Margaretha's relatives were part of the migration to Mexico, including
      her father's sister Margaretha (married to Isaac Thiessen) and her mother's
      brother Cornelius (married to Eleanor Sawatsky). Two uncles later joined
      migrations to La Crete and Bolivia.

17   Harold S. Bender, "Hymnology of the North American Mennonites," *Global
      Anabaptist Mennonite Encyclopedia Online*, http://gameo.org/index.php?
      title=Hymnology_of_the_North_American_Mennonites&oldid=113433.

18   The Ziffersystem uses numbers rather than notes, with the numbers from
      one to seven representing the notes of the scale in a manner similar to the
      syllables of the sol-fa system familiar in the Anglo-Saxon world. The system
      was developed in Europe during the eighteenth and nineteenth centuries as a
      way of teaching people who were unfamiliar with conventional musical notation
      to sing. Heinrich Franz introduced this musical innovation to Mennonites
      in Russia when he came to teach in Gnadenfeld. See Johann Peter Klassen,
      Elizabeth Horsch Bender, and Harold S. Bender, "Ziffersystem Numerical
      Musical Notation," *Global Anabaptist Mennonite Encyclopedia Online*, http://
      www.gameo.org/encyclopedia/contents/Z544ME.html.

19   Regehr, *Mennonites in Canada*, 353.

20   Patricia A. Kaufert, Penny Gilbert, and Robert Tate, "The Manitoba Project: A
      Re-examination of the Link between Menopause and Depression," *Maturitas*
      14, no. 2 (January 1992): 143–55; and N. E. Avis et al., "Longitudinal Study
      of Hormone Levels and Depression among Women Transitioning through
      Menopause," *Climacteric* 4, no. 3 (2001): 243–49.

21   Leonard Doell, email to author, August 22, 2014. Margaretha felt free to talk
      to Leonard Doell about her experience in North Battleford because his own
      grandmother had been hospitalized in the same institution during the 1930s.

22   See C. Stuart Houston, *Steps on the Road to Medicare* (Montreal: McGill-
      Queens University Press, 2002).

23   C. Stuart Houston and John A. Boan, "Health Care: Saskatchewan's
      Leadership," in *The Saskatchewan Encyclopedia*, 433–35.

24   Sadly, this is often still the case. See, for example, Stephen P. Hinshaw, "The
      Stigmatization of Mental Illness in Children and Parents: Developmental
      Issues, Family Concerns, and Research Needs," *The Journal of Child Psychology
      and Psychiatry* 46, no. 7 (July 2005): 714–34; and Caroline E. Mann and Melissa
      J. Himelein, "Factors Associated with Stigmatization of Persons with Mental
      Illness," *Psychiatric Services* 55, no. 2 (2004): 185–87.

25   The extensive and sensitive research by Judith C. Kulig and her colleagues
      among Low German–speaking Mennonites, many of whom are Old Colony
      Mennonite women, is very helpful for understanding the relationship between
      mental health and illness and religious beliefs. See, for example, Judith C. Kulig
      and HaiYan (LingLing) Fan, *Mental Health Beliefs and Practices among Low
      German Mennonites: Application to Practice* (Lethbridge, AB: University of
      Lethbridge, 2016).

26   Judith C. Kulig et al., "Being a Woman: Perspectives of Low-German-Speaking
      Mennonite Women," *Health Care for Women International* 30, no. 4 (2009):
      324–38.

27   Also commonly used were passages such as Proverbs 19:18, 22:15, 23:13–14,
      29:15, and Hebrews 12:6–7.

28   For a moving story of an Old Colony Mennonite boy living near the village of
      Neuanlage who repeatedly experienced whippings at the hands of his father, see
      Jacob G. Janzen, "My Tender Years," an eleven-part serialized autobiography in
      Western People 14 (September 17–November 26, 1981).

29   "Schulverordnung," 125–26.

30   Margaret married Ben Goertzen in 1951 (at age twenty), Annie married John
      Klassen in 1952 (at age twenty-two), Dave married Betty Neudorf in 1954
      (at age twenty-one), Tena married Peter Loewen in 1957 (at age twenty-two),
      Mary married Bill Wiebe in 1958 (at age twenty-one), Elizabeth married
      Cornie Guenther in 1958 (at age nineteen), Jake married Katharina Dyck in
      1962 (at age twenty-two), Helena married John Enns in 1964 (at age twenty-
      two), Judith married Peter Ginther in 1963 (at age nineteen), Eva married Pete
      Zacharias in 1966 (at age eighteen), Wilhelm (Bill) married Stella Harms in
      1969 (at age twenty-three), and Justina married Abe Peters in 1970 (at age
      twenty-one).

31   Dave Friesen's wife Betty Neudorf was the daughter of Peter P. Neudorf, an
      Old Colony Mennonite minister elected in 1935; Judith married Peter Ginther,

son of Johan Ginther who became an Old Colony Mennonite minister in 1963; Helena married John Enns, son of Jacob L. Enns who became an Old Colony Mennonite minister in 1963; Eva married Peter Zacharias, son of Peter Zacharias who was elected an Old Colony Mennonite minister at the same time as Herman Friesen; Wilhelm (Bill) married Stella Harms, daughter of John Harms who was a General Conference Mennonite minister in Burns Lake, British Columbia; and Justina married Abram Peters, son of Jacob D. Peters who was a Bergthaler Mennonite minister. In addition, Tena's husband Peter Loewen (son of Ältester Abram Loewen) became an Old Colony Mennonite minister in 1970, and Elizabeth's husband Cornie Guenther became a minister in a Chortitzer Mennonite congregation in Osler, Saskatchewan, in 1976.

32   It is worth noting that several of Herman's nephews did join the military during the Second World War. For more on the larger story of the Canadian Mennonite response to the war, see A. J. Klassen, ed., *Alternative Service for Peace in Canada during World War II, 1941–1946* (Abbotsford, BC: MCC [BC] Seniors for Peace, 1998); and Nathan Dirks, "The Mennonites Go to War: Revisiting Canadian Soldiers during the Second World War," *Journal of Mennonite Studies* 34 (2016): 63–87.

33   Some of the land sold by the Old Colony Mennonite members who migrated away from the Hague-Osler region, and some of the available land surrounding the Hague-Osler Reserve, was purchased by Mennonites arriving from Russia during the 1920s and 1930s (see Epp, *Mennonites in Canada*, 94–186), thereby reducing the farmland available for use by the children of those Old Colony Mennonites who opted not to migrate.

34   See Karen Warkentin's summary of interviews with Old Colony Mennonite men in South America for a window into the persistence of the agrarian-based sense of identity in "'Emma jedohne': Memories and Old Colony Mennonite Identity," *Journal of Mennonite Studies* 31 (2013): 131–34.

35   Herbert Peters, "Martensville: Halfway House to Urbanization," *Mennonite Life* 23, no. 68 (October 1968): 164–68.

36   A similar observation is made by Janzen, "The 1920s Migration of Old Colony Mennonites," 20.

37   Peter A. Elias, an original member of the Old Colony Mennonite Church in Manitoba, describes those who transferred to other denominations as "adulterers/divorcers (*Ehebrechers*)" in *Voice in the Wilderness: Memoirs of Peter A. Elias (1843–1925)*, trans. and ed. Adolf Ens and Henry Unger (Winnipeg: Manitoba Mennonite Historical Society, 2013), 64.

38   Janzen, "The 1920s Migration of Old Colony Mennonites," 18.

39   Also in the region were several Mennonite Brethren congregations, but Old Colony Mennonites generally did not consider them because of their belief that immersion was the only true mode of baptism. As a result of this view, they insisted on rebaptizing those who had been sprinkled or poured.

The unwillingness to recognize and accept the Old Colony Mennonite understanding and practise of baptism as legitimate was perceived as an offensive expression of spiritual elitism. The Mennonite Brethren adjusted their practice during the 1960s, but the damage done to their reputation among the Old Colony Mennonites lasted much longer.

40 Doell, *The Bergthaler Mennonite Church of Saskatchewan.*

41 Jack Heppner, *Search for Renewal: The Story of the Rudnerweider/EMMC, 1937– 1987* (Winnipeg: Evangelical Mennonite Mission Conference, 1987), 98–111. John D. Friesen was the son of Herman Friesen's first cousin, David I. Friesen.

42 Jake Buhler, "Jacob H. Pauls: Orphan, Minister, Father, Missionary," *Saskatchewan Mennonite Historian* (Fall 2011): 12.

43 Bruce L. Guenther, "The Road Less Traveled: The Evangelical Path of Kanadier Mennonites Who Returned to Canada," *Journal of Mennonite Studies* 22 (2004): 155–56. Both this article, and Bruce L. Guenther, "The Convergence of Old Colony Mennonites, Evangelicalism and Contemporary Canadian Culture—A Case Study of Osler Mission Chapel (1974–1994)," *Journal of Mennonite Studies* 14 (1996): 96–123, discuss in more detail the reasons why some Old Colony Mennonites opted for more evangelical Protestant denominations.

Chapter 4

1 Russian Mennonites used a limited number of given names (primarily names taken from the Bible). The repeated use of the same given name, especially within the same family or others with the same surname, often created instances of mistaken identity. To avoid such confusion, particularly after becoming involved in public leadership roles, Herman added two initials (D and W) to his name at some point in his adult life. He took the first initial from the first letter of his father's first name (David), and the second initial from the first letter of his mother's maiden name (Wiebe).

2 *Saskatchewan School Minute Book, 1937–1960*, Mennonite Historical Society of Saskatchewan Archives, Saskatoon. It was not possible to verify from the Minute Book the exact date Herman began his public involvement as a school board trustee. Given that trustees were elected for three-year terms, and given that Herman's term ended in December 1938, it is likely that he was elected in early 1936. It seems unlikely that he would have served the previous 1933–35 term given that he would have been only twenty-five years of age in 1933, that he did not have any school-aged children at that time, and that he and Margaretha experienced significant loss during these years with the death of their oldest son and both of Margaretha's parents, which left them with the responsibility for the entire farm.

3 Bob Wahl, *Contending with the Horses* (Denver, CO: Outskirts Press, Inc., 2009), 55–59; Bob Wahl, *The Story of Saskatchewan School, No. 99: The Lives and*

Times of Pioneers on the South Saskatchewan River (Victoria, BC: Friesen Press, 2014); and Maryanne Caswell, *Pioneer Girl* (Toronto: Tundra Books, 2001).

4   See Doell and Guenter, *Hague-Osler Mennonite Reserve 1895–1995*, 654.

5   In his memoirs, Peter A. Elias identifies the various activities that were prohibited by Ältester Johann Wiebe during the 1880s as inconsistent with the teaching of Jesus Christ. These included the purchase of fire insurance, the use of buggies with rooftops, running for public office and participation in elections, use of bicycles, and marriage to someone who was not a member of the Old Colony Mennonite Church. Lack of compliance often resulted in excommunication, but, over time, some of these prohibitions were abandoned and others, like participation in elections, were unevenly enforced (*Voice in the Wilderness*, 60–65).

6   This was the only English-language schooling he obtained. I was not able to determine either the specific school at which he took English classes (probably either Renfrew or Saskatchewan School), or the exact date. It is likely he took these classes before he was married rather than after, and therefore Renfrew is the more probable location.

7   *Saskatchewan School Minute Book*, May 25, 1938.

8   Doell and Guenter, *Hague-Osler Mennonite Reserve 1895–1995*, 517.

9   See, for example, *Saskatchewan School Minute Book*, November 5, 1937; January 15, 1938; January 17, 1938; April 7, 1938.

10   Wahl, *The Story of Saskatchewan School*, 163–69.

11   *Saskatchewan School Minute Book*, January 17, 1938; February 3, 1938.

12   For correspondence from Peter Paul Lepp and Superintendent E. Crough discussing the issue, see Wahl, *The Story of Saskatchewan School*, 187–94.

13   I was not able to locate extant records of the East Osler Government Aided School Board.

14   The Evangelical Mennonite Brethren Conference (now known as the Fellowship of Evangelical Bible Churches) was started by a group of Kanadier Mennonites in Minnesota in 1889. Its theological emphases and missionary orientation reflect the influence of American evangelical Protestantism.

15   M. P. Scharf, "An Historical Overview of the Organization of Education in Saskatchewan," in *A History of Education in Saskatchewan*, ed. Brian Noonan, Dianne Hallman, and Murray Scharf (Regina: Canadian Plains Research Center, 2006), 3–20.

16   Doell, *Mennonite Homesteaders*, 404–5; and Doell and Guenter, *Hague-Osler Mennonite Reserve 1895–1995*, 513–20. Herman did not pursue renomination at the end of 1959 and was succeeded as a councillor by Peter Unger.

17   Rural Municipality of Corman Park Records, Saskatoon.

18   Bob Wahl, interview with author, August 6, 2013.

19   Jacob G. Guenter, ed., *Osler… The Early Years and the One Room School #1238 (1905–1947): Reminiscences Past and Present* (Saskatoon: Osler Historical Museum, 1999), 394–95.

20 Herman kept a private ledger of loans he had made to individuals. Margaretha eventually destroyed the ledger after his death because she did not want others to know who had repaid loans and who had not.

21 *Gesangbuch: Eine Sammlung geistlicher Lieder zur Allgemeinen Erbauung und zum Lobe Gottes (Songbook: A Collection of Spiritual Songs for General Edification and to the Glory of God)*, 7th ed. (Elkhart, IN: Mennonitischen Verlagshandlung, 1912). The first edition of the hymnal was compiled in 1767. It contained 505 songs and 150 Psalms derived from selections taken from two early-eighteenth-century hymn books prepared by the Lutheran Pietists, Johann Freylinghausen and Friedrich Rogall, and from the Dutch *Veelerhande Schriftuerlijke Liedekens*, which had been in use in Holland by Mennonites since the days of the Reformation. The Psalms came from a Psalter published by Ambrosius Lobwasser. The hymnal went through numerous editions, and, over time, the Psalms were removed and other songs from a variety of sources were added. The hymnal has the distinction of being the Mennonite hymnal that was second only to the *Ausbund*, which dates back to 1564, in the longevity of its continuous usage. See Peter Letkemann, "The German Hymnody of Prussian Mennonites: A Tale of Two Gesangbücher," *Preservings 18* (June 2001): 120–30.

22 Letkemann, 120.

23 Judith Klassen, "Under the Bed and Behind the Barn: Musical Secrets and Familial Vitality in Mennonite Mexico," *Journal of Mennonite Studies* (2009): 246.

24 Wesley Berg, "Old Colony Singing: Old Songs in a New Land: Russian Mennonite Hymns Come to Manitoba," *Preservings 16* (June 2000): 44–45.

25 Doell and Guenter, *Hague-Osler Mennonite Reserve 1895–1995*, 588; and Rempel, "The Reorganization of the Old Colony Mennonite Church," 248.

26 Zacharias, *Reinland*, 191–92.

27 Loewen, "Prespatou Old Colony Mennonite Church," 160.

28 At the time of his election, six of his children were already married, and another married several months afterward. The youngest five ranged in age from eleven to twenty. Most of his children observed the impact of Friesen's election as a minister in the church from a distance.

29 Werner, "'A mild form of deviancy,'" 149–50.

30 Bob Wahl, interview with author, August 6, 2013.

31 "Inaugural Sermon (Jeremiah 1:7; Romans 15:30–33)," 1962, Sermon #5. All of the sermons referenced in this book are a part of Herman D. W. Friesen's personal papers.

32 For multiple, first-person examples, see Plett, "The Lonely Ohm—Myth and Reality," 98–99.

33 Sermon #5.

34 Joseph C. Liechty, "Humility: the Foundation of Mennonite Religious Outlook in the 1860s," *Mennonite Quarterly Review* 54 (1980): 5–31; and Robert

Friedmann, "Gelassenheit," *Global Anabaptist Mennonite Encyclopedia Online,*
http://gameo.org/index.php?title=Gelassenheit&oldid=119963.

35 Johannes Bachman, *"Unser Täglich Brot": Biblische Betrachtungen auf alle Tage
im Jahre* (Cleveland, OH: Central Publishing House, 1894). A revised second
edition was published in 1895, and a third edition was published in 1964, with
a foreword by Ältester Jacob Froese (Winkler, Manitoba). This devotional book
was given as a gift by Herman and Margaretha to some of their adult children
during the 1960s. At some point in their married life, Herman and Margaretha
began the practice of reading a short section of scripture every morning at
breakfast with family members. This habitual custom remained a priority, even
when other demands were pressing for time.

36 "An Accounting of Your Personal Household (Luke 16:1–9)," August 1962,
Sermon #34. The Kronsthal congregation heard Sermon #19 ("Two Praying
at the Door of Grace: The Pharisee and the Tax Collector [Luke 18:9–14],"
July 1963) four times, and the Neuanlage congregation heard Sermon #25
("If We Say that We Have Fellowship with Him [Jesus] While We Walk in
Darkness, We Lie and Do Not Live According to the Truth [1 John 1:16],"
November 1963) four times (twice within a six-month period in late 1968 and
early 1969).

37 A good example of this are the Old Testament texts used in Sermon #25.

38 Cornelius J. Dyck, "The Role of Preaching in the Anabaptist Tradition,"
Mennonite Life 17 (January 1962): 21–25; and O. C. Edwards Jr., *A History of
Preaching* (Nashville, TN: Abingdon Press, 2004).

39 See "For the Preparation of Baptismal Candidates: Part 1," 1965, Sermon #45;
and "For the Preparation of Baptismal Candidates: Part 2," 1966, Sermon #11.

40 "Articles of Faith #1," April 1963, Sermon #44.

41 Sermon #45.

42 Article 8, "Of Holy Baptism," *Confession of Faith.*

43 Sermon #45.

44 "About the Horror of the Devastation of Jerusalem (Matthew 24:15–28),"
March 17, 1965, Sermon #10; Sermon #19; and "The Wicked Servant: How Do
I Learn the Difficult Art of Forgiving my Debtors from the Heart? (Matthew
18: 23–35)," January 15, 1963, Sermon #36.

45 "Funeral Sermon for an Adult," 1964, Sermon #50.

46 Sermon #36.

47 For Herman, the benchmark for Christian living is Jesus's Sermon on the
Mount ("Run in Such a Way as to Get the Prize [Matthew 5–7; 1 Corinthians
9:24–27]," July 1962, Sermon #12), along with one of Jesus's great
commandments, namely to love our neighbours as ourselves (Sermon #36).

48 John Friesen observes that Old Colony theology is often more implicit than
explicit due to the lack of interest or ability on the part of ministers. As a
result, "one looks in vain for a well-articulated Old Colony theology" ("Old

Colony Theology, Ecclesiology and Experience of Church," 132). The inability to articulate clearly their theological convictions left them vulnerable to misunderstanding and at a disadvantage when engaging other denominations. See Guenther, "The Convergence of Old Colony Mennonites," 100.

49 Sermon #50.

50 Sermon #50.

51 Questions 1–4 in Chapter 3, "Faith in Christ," Catechism.

52 Sermon #12.

53 Sermon #36. Herman does recognize the tension between God as righteous Judge and God as loving Father ("Flee from the Midst of Babylon, Let Every Man Save His Life [Jeremiah 51:6]," February 1965, Sermon #28); however, in most sermons, the former is much more prominent than the latter.

54 Sermon #10. Even his funeral sermons are not eulogistic but are focused on motivating a response from the living (for example, Sermon #50).

55 Although believers are encouraged to remain faithful to God out of love for Him, it is generally the fear of facing God the Judge that serves as the primary motivation for obedience (Sermon #25).

56 Sermon #50.

57 David Schroeder, "Evangelicals Denigrate Conservative Mennonites— Understanding the Conservative Wing of the Mennonite Church," Preservings 15 (December 1999): 47; and David Schroeder, "Salvation: 'You Will Know Them by Their Fruits,' Matthew 7:16," Preservings 18 (June 2001): 32–35.

58 For example, Herman alludes to biblical references such as Matthew 6:5 and Luke 18:11 in his warning about spiritual pride in Sermon #12.

59 For a fuller discussion of the theological and psychological impact of the evangelical Protestant emphasis on "assurance of salvation" among Kanadier Mennonites, see Guenther, "The Road Less Traveled," 155–57.

60 The Anabaptist idea that faith only becomes operative if there is obedience that is expressed in works of faith is more consistent with medieval Catholicism than Protestantism. See Walter Klaassen, Anabaptism in Outline: Selected Primary Sources (Waterloo, ON: Herald Press, 1981), 41–42.

61 Redekop, The Old Colony Mennonites, 35. For an insightful look at how such a communal understanding of soteriology can impact the personal lives of individual church members, see Fast, "Religion, Pain, and the Body," 116–18.

62 "But the Lord God Called Out, 'Adam, Where Are You?' (Genesis 3:9)," April 1966, Sermon #1; and "The Harvest is Plentiful, But Few Are the Labourers (Matthew 9:35–38, Luke 15:1–10)," January 1969, Sermon #26.

63 Redekop, The Old Colony Mennonites, 210. He notes also the limitations of the decision-making systems within many Old Colony Mennonite communities for addressing the inevitable cultural dilemmas that will be encountered.

64 Warkentin, "'Emma jedohne,'" 134. See also Friesen, "Old Colony Theology, Ecclesiology and Experience of Church," 135.

65 Titus F. Guenther explores the relationship between the Old Colony Mennonite theological understanding of the church and the motivation for migration in "Theology of Migration," 164–76. See also Abe Peters, "Spiritual Challenges Facing Colonies in Mexico," December 4, 1998, MCC Canada Office, Winnipeg, MB, for an excellent explanation of the theological foundation undergirding Old Colony Mennonite opposition to change.

66 Loewen, *Hidden Worlds*, 5.

67 Sermon #25; and "Parable of the Pharisee and Tax Collector (Luke 18:9–14)," October 1962, Sermon #37.

68 Donald Stoesz, "Historical Origins of the Church Lectionary," *Preservings* 33 (2013): 64–72. A useful model for further study of Old Colony Mennonite sermon collections is Donald Stoesz, "Sermons and Services of the Sommerfelder Stoeszs," unpublished manuscript, Donald Stoesz Fonds, Mennonite Historical Society of Alberta. See also Donald Stoesz, *Canadian Prairie Mennonite Ministers' Use of Scripture: 1874–1977* (Victoria, BC: Friesen Press, 2017).

69 Donald Stoesz, "Analysis of Five Worship Schedules," in "Sermons and Services of the Sommerfelder Stoeszs."

70 For example, "Palm Sunday (Matthew 21:1–9)," April 1964, Sermon #30; "Good Friday (John 19:31–42)," January 1964, Sermon #32; and "Christmas (Luke 2:1–14)," December 1965, Sermon #29.

71 For example, Sermon #1; Sermon #28; and "Last Sunday of the Year (Genesis 32:10)," November 27, 1963, Sermon #24, and Sermon #25.

72 Sermon #36.

73 Sermon #44; and "New Year's Sermon (1 Peter 1:22–23)," December 1962, Sermon #43. See chart in Stoesz, "Analysis of Five Worship Schedules," 9.

74 Old Colony Mennonites living in La Crete initiated several migrations to British Honduras and Bolivia during the 1960s. See Dawn S. Bowen, "To Bolivia and Back: Migration and Its Impact on La Crete, Alberta," *Journal of Mennonite Studies* 22 (2004): 59–82.

75 Writing about Old Colony Mennonites in Saskatchewan during the 1950s, Leo Driedger suggests that, after the exodus of members to Mexico during the 1920s, the group lacked the resolve and strength to rebuild its "village life," and, therefore, those who remained in Canada were forced to accept cultural changes for fear of losing members to other denominations ("A Sect in a Modern Society," 116–17).

76 The six trips to southern Manitoba took place in December 1962, January 1964, November 1966, November 1967, January 1969, and August 1969; the three trips to La Crete and Fort St. John took place in February 1963, December 1965, March 1969; a trip directly to Fort St. John took place in September 1964; and, in June 1968, he travelled to Aylmer in Ontario.

77 Abram G. Janzen, *Memories of an Old Colony Waisenamt Manager* (Hague, SK: self-published, 2004), 26–28; Royden Loewen, "Roots in Medieval Flanders:

Searching for the Genesis of Mennonite Inheritance Practices," *Preservings* 26 (2006): 17–19. See also "Old Colony Waisenamt By-Laws and Regulations," File 1, Vol. 5643, Mennonite Heritage Centre, Winnipeg, Manitoba.

78 Doell and Guenter, *Hague-Osler Mennonite Reserve 1895–1995*, 589–90; Abram Buhler, "Walking Worthy of the Vocation—Abram Buhler, 1903–1982: Farmer, Family Man and Bishop of the Saskatchewan Bergthaler Church," *Preservings* 22 (June 2003): 98–103.

79 Sermon #1.

80 Sermon #26.

81 Eva Hoffman, *Lost in Translation: Life in a New Language* (New York: Penguin Books, 1989), 242.

82 Jill Ker Conway, *When Memory Speaks: Exploring the Art of Autobiography* (Toronto: Random House, 1998), 177.

Appendices

1 The sermon collection may well have contained more sermons at the time of Herman's death in 1969. Family members indicate Margaretha occasionally agreed to lend some of Herman's sermons to other ministers, some of which were never returned.

2 Of the sixty-five sermons that remained in the Herman D. W. Friesen sermon collection, at least thirteen, and possibly several others, were not written by Herman. His collection includes sermons written by Cornelius Hamm (a Bergthaler Mennonite Ältester), Abram J. Buhler (a Bergthaler Mennonite Ältester), Jacob W. Neufeld (an early-twentieth-century minister), Isaac J. Goertzen (an Old Colony minister in La Crete, Alberta, who later moved to Bolivia, where he became an Ältester), Cornelius Krahn (a minister in La Crete, Alberta), as well as several written by ministerial colleagues Julius Ens and Abram J. Loewen, who had both migrated from the Hague-Osler region to Prespatou, British Columbia.

3 This sermon is of particular personal significance to me because it was used in Neuanlage on July 12, 1964, at the funeral of my paternal great-grandfather, Jacob F. Guenter.

Selected Bibliography

Books

Bennion, Janet. *Desert Patriarchy: Mormon and Mennonite Communities in the Chihuahua Valley*. Tucson: University of Arizona Press, 2004.

Bergen, Peter. *History of the Sommerfeld Mennonite Church, that is, the Background and First One Hundred Years of the Sommerfeld Mennonite Church*. Altona, MB: Sommerfeld Mennonite Church, 2001.

Camden, Laura L., and Susan Gaetz Duarte. *Mennonites in Texas: The Quiet in the Land*. College Station: Texas A&M University Press, 2006.

Cañás Bottos, Lorenzo. *Old Colony Mennonites in Argentina and Bolivia: Nation Making, Religious Conflict and Imagination of the Future*. Leiden, the Netherlands: Brill, 2008.

Doell, Leonard. *The Bergthaler Mennonite Church of Saskatchewan, 1892–1975*. Winnipeg: CMBC Publications, 1987.

Doell, Leonard, ed. *Mennonite Homesteaders on the Hague-Osler Reserve, 1891–1999*. Saskatoon: Mennonite Historical Society of Saskatchewan, 1999.

Doell, Leonard, and Jacob G. Guenter, eds. *Hague-Osler Mennonite Reserve 1895–1995*. Saskatoon: Hague-Osler Reserve Book Committee, 1995.

Driedger, Leo. *Mennonites in the Global Village*. Toronto: University of Toronto Press, 2000.

Elias, Peter A. *Voice in the Wilderness: Memoirs of Peter A. Elias (1843–1925)*. Translated and edited by Adolf Ens and Henry Unger. Winnipeg: Manitoba Mennonite Historical Society, 2013.

Ens, Adolf. *Subjects or Citizens? The Mennonite Experience in Canada, 1870–1925*. Ottawa: University of Ottawa Press, 1994.

Ens, Adolf, Jacob E. Peters, and Otto Hamm, eds. *Church, Family and Village: Essays on Mennonite Life on the West Reserve*. Winnipeg: Manitoba Mennonite Historical Society, 2001.

Epp, Frank H. *Mennonites in Canada, 1786–1920: The History of a Separate People*. Toronto: University of Toronto Press, 1974.

———. *Mennonites in Canada, 1920–1940: A People's Struggle for Survival*. Toronto: Macmillan, 1982.

Francis, E. K. *In Search of Utopia: The Mennonites in Manitoba*. Altona, MB: D. W. Friesen and Sons Ltd., 1955.

Fretz, J. Winfield. *Colonization in Mexico: An Introduction*. Akron, PA: Mennonite Central Committee, 1945.

Goerzen, Jakob W. *Low German in Canada, A Study of "Plautditsch."* Edmonton: self-published, 1972.

Good Gingrich, Luann. *Out of Place: Social Exclusion and Mennonite Migrants in Canada*. Toronto: University of Toronto Press, 2016.

Guenter, Jacob G. *"Men of Steele": Saskatchewan Valley Mennonite Settlers and Their Descendants*. Saskatoon: self-published, 1981.

Hedburg, Anna Sofia. *Outside the World: Cohesion and Deviation among Old Colony Mennonites in Bolivia*. Uppsala, Sweden: Uppsala University, 2007.

Hershberger, Aaron, and Elmina Hershberger, eds. *Called to Mexico: Bringing Hope and Literacy to the Old Colony Mennonites*. Nappanee, IN: Old Colony Mennonite Support, 2011.

Janzen, Abram G. *Ältester Johan M. Loeppky, 1882–1950: As I Remember Him*. Hague, SK: self-published, 2003.

———. *Memories of an Old Colony Waisenamt Manager*. Hague, SK: self-published, 2004.

Janzen, John, ed. *As I Remember It…Neuanlage, 1895–1995*. Hague, SK: self-published, 1995.

Janzen, William. *Build One Another Up: The Work of MCCO with the Mennonites from Mexico in Ontario, 1977–1997*. Kitchener: MCC Ontario, 1998.

———. *Why Did They Leave Canada? The Mennonite Migration to Mexico and Paraguay in the 1920s*. Ottawa: The Ottawa Office of Mennonite Central Committee Canada, 2007.

Klassen, Doreen. *Singing Mennonite: Low German Songs among the Mennonites*. Winnipeg: University of Manitoba Press, 1989.

Kouwenhoven, Arlette. *The Fehrs: Four Centuries of Mennonite Migration*. Leiden, the Netherlands: Winco Publishing, 2013.

Kraybill, Donald B., and James P. Hurd. *Horse-and-Buggy Mennonites: Hoofbeats of Humility in a Postmodern World*. University Park: Pennsylvania University Press, 2007.

Kulig, Judith C., and HaiYan (LingLing) Fan. *Death and Dying Beliefs and Practices among Low-German-Speaking Mennonites: Application to Practice*. Lethbridge, AB: University of Lethbridge, 2013.

———. *Mental Health Beliefs and Practices among Low German Mennonites: Application to Practice*. Lethbridge, AB: University of Lethbridge, 2016.

Loewen, Royden. *Diaspora in the Countryside: Two Mennonite Communities in Mid-20th Century America*. Toronto: University of Toronto Press, 2006.

———. *Hidden Worlds: Revisiting the Mennonite Migrants of the 1870s*. Winnipeg: University of Manitoba Press, 2001.

———. *Horse-and-Buggy Genius: Listening to Mennonites Contest the Modern World*. Winnipeg: University of Manitoba Press, 2016.

———. *Village among Nations: "Canadian" Mennonites in a Transnational World, 1916–2006*. Toronto: University of Toronto Press, 2013.

Martens, Hildegard M. *Mennonites from Mexico: Their Immigration and Settlement in Canada*. Waterloo, ON: Conrad Grebel College, 1975.

Plett, Delbert, ed. *Old Colony Mennonites in Canada, 1875–2000*. Steinbach, MB: Crossway Publications Inc., 2001.

Quiring, David M. *The Mennonite Old Colony Vision: Under Siege in Mexico and Canadian Connections*. Steinbach, MB: Crossway Publications Inc., 2003.

Redekop, Calvin W. *The Old Colony Mennonites: Dilemmas of Ethnic Minority Life*. Baltimore: Johns Hopkins Press, 1969.

Rempel, Herman. *Kjenn jie noch Plautdietsch? A Mennonite Low German Dictionary*. Rosenort, MB: PrairieView Press, 1995.

Roessingh, Carel, and Tanja Plasil, eds. *Between Horse & Buggy and Four-Wheel Drive: Change and Diversity among Mennonite Settlements in Belize, Central America*. Amsterdam, the Netherlands: VU University Press, 2009.

Sawatsky, Henry Leonard. *Sie Suchten Eine Heimat: Deutsch-Mennonitische Kolonisierung in Mexiko, 1922–1984*. Marburg, Germany: N. G. Elwert Verlag, 1986.

———. *They Sought a Country: Mennonite Colonization in Mexico*. Berkeley: University of California Press, 1971.

Schapansky, Henry. *The Old Colony (Chortitza) of Russia: Early History and the First Settlers in the Context of Mennonite Migrations*. Rosenort, MB: Country Graphics and Printing, 2001.

Schmiedehaus, Walter. *Die Altkolonier-Mennoniten in Mexiko*. Winnipeg: CMBC Publications and *Die Mennonitische Post*, 1982.

———. *Ein feste Burg ist unser Gott: Der Wanderweg eines christlichen Siedlervolkes*. Cuauhtémoc, Mexico: G. J. Rempel, 1948.

Stoesz, Donald. *Canadian Prairie Mennonite Ministers' Use of Scripture: 1874–1977*. Victoria, BC: Friesen Press, 2017.

Thiessen, Jack. *Mennonite Low German Dictionary/Mennonitisch-Plattdeutsches Wörterbuch*. Madison, WI: Max Kade Institute for German-American Studies, 2003.

Towell, Larry. *The Mennonites: A Biographical Sketch*. London: Phaidon, 2000.

Wahl, Bob. *The Story of Saskatchewan School, No. 99: The Lives and Times of Pioneers on the South Saskatchewan River*. Victoria, BC: Friesen Press, 2014.

Waisenverordnung der Reinlander Mennoniten Gemeinde in Canada. Winnipeg: Nordwesten Publishing Company, 1914.

Wessel, Kelso L., and Judith A. Wessel. *The Mennonites in Bolivia—An Historical and Present Social-Economic Evaluation*. Ithaca, NY: Cornell University, 1967.

Zacharias, Peter D. *Reinland: An Experience in Community*. Altona, MB: Reinland Centennial Committee, 1976.

Journal Articles and Chapters in Books

Allen, Gordon, and Calvin W. Redekop. "Old Colony Mennonites in Mexico: Migration and Inbreeding." *Social Biology* 34, no. 3 (Fall–Winter 1987): 166–79.

Berg, Wesley. "Hymns of the Old Colony Mennonites and the Old Way of Singing." *Musical Quarterly* 80 (1996): 77–117.

———. "Old Colony Singing: Old Songs in a New Land: Russian Mennonite Hymns Come to Manitoba." *Preservings* 16 (June 2000): 44–45.

Bowen, Dawn S. "*Die Auswanderung*: Religion, Culture and Migration among Old Colony Mennonites." *The Canadian Geographer* 45, no. 4 (2001): 461–73.

———. "Preserving Tradition, Confronting Progress: Social Change in a Mennonite Community, 1950–1965." *American Review of Canadian Studies* 25, no. 1 (1995): 53–77.

———. "Resistance, Acquiescence, and Accommodation: The Establishment of Public Schools in a Conservative Old Colony Community." *Mennonite Quarterly Review* 74, no. 4 (October 2010): 551-581.

———. "To Bolivia and Back: Migration and Its Impact on La Crete, Alberta." *Journal of Mennonite Studies* 22 (2004): 59–82.

———. "Two Governments and a Railway: Old Colony Mennonite Relocation to Central British Columbia in the 1940s." *Journal of Mennonite Studies* 36 (2018): 209-235.

Buhler, Abram. "Walking Worthy of the Vocation—Abram Buhler, 1903–1982: Farmer, Family Man and Bishop of the Saskatchewan Bergthaler Church." *Preservings* 22 (June 2003): 98–103.

Buhler, Linda. "Mennonite Burial Customs—Part One." *Preservings* 7 (1995): 51–52.

———. "Mennonite Burial Customs—Part Two." *Preservings* 8 (1996): 48–50.

———. "Mennonite Burial Customs—Part Three." *Preservings* 10 (1997): 78–80.

Burkhart, Charles. "The Church Music of the Old Order Amish and Old Colony Mennonites in Mexico." *Mennonite Quarterly Review* (January 1953): 34–54.

———. "Music of the Old Colony Mennonites in Mexico." *Mennonite Life* (January 1952): 20.

Büscher, Wolfgang. "Mennoniten: Gottes Fahrendes Volk." *Geo*, no. 2 (February 1996): 128–43.

Cañás Bottos, Lorenzo. "Marrying the Brother's Wife's Sister: Marriage Patterns among Old Colony Mennonites in Argentina." *Journal of Mennonite Studies* 31 (2013): 75–86.

———. "Transformations of Old Colony Mennonites: The Making of a Trans-statal Community." *Global Network* 8, no. 2 (2008): 214–31.

Castro, Pedro. "The 'Return' of the Mennonites from the Cuauhtemoc Region to Canada: A Perspective from Mexico." *Journal of Mennonite Studies* 22 (2004): 25–38.

Cox, Christopher. "The Resilient Word: Linguistic Preservation and Innovation among Old Colony Mennonites in Latin America." *Journal of Mennonite Studies* 31 (2013): 51–74.

Driedger, Leo. "Early Mennonite Settlement in Saskatchewan: Hague-Osler Settlement." *Mennonite Life* 13, no. 1 (January 1958): 13–17.

———. "Mennonite Change: The Old Colony Revisited, 1955–1977." *Mennonite Life* 32, no. 4 (1977): 4–12.

———. "Old Colony Mennonites Are Moving Again: From Mexico to British Honduras." *Mennonite Life* 13, no. 4 (October 1958): 160–66.

———. "Saskatchewan Old Colony Mennonites." *Mennonite Life* 13, no. 2 (April 1958): 63–66.

Enns, Katherine. "Old Colony Mennonites of Mexico: A Separate People." *California Mennonite Historical Society Bulletin* (Spring 2009): 1–6.

Ens, Adolf. "A Second Look at the Rejected Conservatives." *Mennonite Reporter*, November 1974, 36–37. Reprinted in *Preservings* 16 (June 2000): 3–8.

Epp, Reuben. "Plautdietsch: Origins, Development and State of the Mennonite Low German Language." *Journal of Mennonite Studies* 5 (1987): 61–72.

Erb, Peter C. "Critical Approaches to Mennonite Culture in Canada: Some Preliminary Observations." In *Visions and Realities: Essays, Poems, and Fiction Dealing with Mennonite Issues*, edited by Harry Loewen and Al Reimer, 203–11. Winnipeg: Hyperion Press Ltd., 1985.

Fan, HaiYan (LingLing), and Judith Kulig. "Diversity in Rural Communities: Palliative Care for the Low German Mennonites." *Journal of Rural and Community Development* 9, no. 4 (2014): 246–58.

Fast, Kerry L. "Religion, Pain, and the Body: Agency in the Life of an Old Colony Woman." *Journal of Mennonite Studies* 22 (2004): 103–29.

———. "Why Milking Machines? Cohesion and Contestation of Old Colony Mennonite Tradition." *Journal of Mennonite Studies* 31 (2013): 151–66.

Felt, Judy Clark, Jeanne Clark Ridley, Gordon Allen, and Calvin Redekop. "High Fertility of Old Colony Mennonites in Mexico." *Human Biology* 62, no. 5 (October 1990): 689–700.

Francis, E. K. "The Mennonite School Problem in Manitoba, 1874–1919." *Mennonite Quarterly Review* 27, no. 3 (July 1953): 204–37.

Fretz, J. Winfield. "Mennonite in Mexico." *Mennonite Life* (April 1947): 24–27. Reprinted in *Preservings* 23 (December 2003): 68–70.

Friesen, John J. "Old Colony Theology, Ecclesiology and Experience of Church in Manitoba." *Journal of Mennonite Studies* 22 (2004): 131–44.

———. "Reinländer Mennoniten Gemeinde." In Plett, *Old Colony Mennonites in Canada*, 3–19.

Friesen, Richard. "Saskatchewan Mennonite Settlements: The Modification of Old World Settlement Patterns." *Canadian Ethnic Studies* 9, no. 2 (1977): 72–90.

Good Gingrich, Luann, and Kerry Preibisch. "Migration as Preservation and Loss: The Paradox of Transnational Living for Low German Mennonite Women." *Journal of Ethnic and Migration Studies* 36 (2010): 1499–1518.

Guenther, Alan M. "'Barred from Heaven and Cursed Forever': Old Colony Mennonites and the 1908 Commission of Inquiry Regarding Public Education." *Historical Papers: Canadian Society of Church History* (2007): 129–48.

Guenther, Bruce L. "The Convergence of Old Colony Mennonites, Evangelicalism and Contemporary Canadian Culture—A Case Study of Osler Mission Chapel (1974–1994)." *Journal of Mennonite Studies* 14 (1996): 96–123.

———. "Evangelicalism within Mennonite Historiography: The Decline of Anabaptism or a Path towards Dynamic Ecumenism?" *Journal of Mennonite Studies* 24 (2006): 35–53.

———. "Osler Mission Chapel (1974–1994): The Convergence of Old Colony Mennonites with Evangelical Protestantism in 20th-Century Canadian Society." *Mennonite Historical Society of Saskatchewan Occasional Papers* (2006): 1–37.

———. "The Road Less Traveled: The Evangelical Path of Kanadier Mennonites Who Returned to Canada." *Journal of Mennonite Studies* 22 (2004): 145–66.

Guenther, Titus F. "Theology of Migration: The Ältesten Reflect." *Journal of Mennonite Studies* 18 (2000): 164–76.

Hall, Barry L., Judith C. Kulig, Robert Campbell, Margaret Wall, and Ruth C. A. Babcock. "Social Work and Kanadier Mennonites: Challenges and Rewards." *Journal of Religion and Spirituality in Social Work: Social Thought* 24, no. 3 (2005): 91–104.

Harder, David. "Schools and Community: Remembrances of School Teacher David Harder (1894–1968), Eichenfeld, Mexico." *Preservings* 23 (December 2003): 9–23.

Hedberg, Anna Sofia. "Speaking of 'Peter Money' and Poor Abraham: Wealth, Poverty and Consumption among Old Colony Mennonites in Bolivia." *Journal of Mennonite Studies* 31 (2013): 87–104.

Hiebert, Martha. "Stories of Betrayal and Hope among 'Horse and Buggy' Mennonite Women in Bolivia." *Journal of Mennonite Studies* 31 (2013): 193–201.

Hostetler, John, and Calvin Redekop. "Education and Assimilation in Three Ethnic Groups." *The Alberta Journal of Educational Research* 8 (December 1962): 189–203.

Janzen, William. "The 1920s Migration of Old Colony Mennonites from the Hague-Osler Area to Mexico." *Mennonite Historical Society of Saskatchewan Occasional Papers* (2006): 1–21.

———. "Government Pressure, Mennonite Separateness, and the 1920s Migration to Mexico and Paraguay." *Preservings* (2008): 5–10.

Jaquith, James R. "Multilingualism among the Old Colony Mennonites." *Mennonite Life* (July 1969): 137–42.

Jaworski, M. A., A. Severini, G. M. Mansour, K. Hennig, J. D. Slater, R. Jeske, J. Schlaut et al. "Inherited Diseases in North American Mennonites: Focus on

Old Colony (Chortitza) Mennonites." *American Journal of Medical Genetics* 32 (1989): 158–68.

Klassen, Doreen Helen. "'I wanted a life of my own': Creating a Singlewoman Mennonite Identity in Mexico." *Journal of Mennonite Studies* 26 (2008): 49–68.

Klassen, Judith. "Under the Bed and Behind the Barn: Musical Secrets and Familial Vitality in Mennonite Mexico." *Journal of Mennonite Studies* (2009): 229–47.

Kulig, Judith, and Barry Hall. "Health and Illness Beliefs among Southern Alberta Kanadier Mennonites." *Journal of Mennonite Studies* 22 (2004): 185–204.

Kulig, Judith C., Barry L. Hall, Ruth C. A. Babcock, Robert Campbell, and Margaret Wall. "Childbearing Practices in Kanadier Mennonite Women." *Canadian Nurse* 100, no. 8 (2004): 34–37.

Kulig, Judith C., and HaiYan (LingLing) Fan. "Suffering: Is the Concept Significant among Low German-Speaking Mennonites?" *Journal of Mennonite Studies* 29 (2011): 153–65.

Kulig, Judith C., Ruth C. A. Babcock, Margaret Wall, and Shirley Hill. "Being a Woman: Perspectives of Low German-Speaking Mennonite Women." *Health Care for Women International* 30, no. 4 (2009): 324–38.

———. "Childbearing Beliefs among Low-German-Speaking Mennonite Women." *International Nursing Review* 55, no. 4 (2008): 420–26.

Letkemann, Peter. "The German Hymnody of Prussian Mennonites: A Tale of Two Gesangbücher." *Preservings* 18 (June 2001): 120–30.

Loewen, Royden. "Competing Cosmologies: Reading Migration in an Ethno-Religious Newspaper." *Histoire sociale/Social History* 47 (2015): 87–105.

———. "To the Ends of the Earth: Low German Mennonites and Old Order Ways in the Americas." *Mennonite Quarterly Review* (2008): 427–48.

———. "A Village among the Nations: Low German Migrants and the Idea of Transnationalism in the History of Mennonites in Canada." *Conrad Grebel Review* 33, no. 1 (Winter 2015): 29–48.

Martens, Helen. "The Music of Some Religious Minorities in Canada." *Ethnomusicology* 16, no. 3 (1972): 360–71.

Milner, Cameron. "Valley Christian Academy: Promoting Diversity and Assimilation." In *A History of Education in Saskatchewan*, edited by Brian Noonan, Dianne Hallman, and Murray Scharf, 109–23. Regina: Canadian Plains Research Center, University of Regina, 2006.

Nobbs-Thiessen, Ben. "Mennonites in Unexpected Places: Sociologist and Settler in South America." *Journal of Mennonite Studies* 28 (2010): 203–24.

Peters, Abe. "Old Colony Communities Face Difficult Challenges." *Canadian Mennonite* 3, no. 10 (May 1999): 6–8.

Peters, Herbert. "Martensville: Halfway House to Urbanization." *Mennonite Life* 23, no. 68 (October 1968): 164–68.

Peters, Jacob. "Mennonites in Mexico and Paraguay: A Comparative Analysis of the Colony Social System." *Journal of Mennonite Studies* 6 (1988): 198–214.

Plasil, Tanja. "Community and Schism among the Old Colony Mennonites of Belize: A Case Study." *Journal of Mennonite Studies* 33 (2015): 251–73.

Quiring, David M. "Intervention and Resistance: Two Mennonite Visions Conflict in Mexico." *Journal of Mennonite Studies* 22 (2004): 83–102.

Redekop, Calvin W. "Decision Making in a Sect." *Review of Religious Research* 2 (1960): 79–86.

———. "The Old Colony: An Analysis of Group Survival." *Mennonite Quarterly Review* 40, no. 3 (July 1966): 190–211.

Redekop, Paul. "The Mennonite Family in Tradition and Transition." *Journal of Mennonite Studies* 4 (1985): 77–93.

Rempel, Abe. "The Reorganization of the Old Colony Mennonite Church." In Ens, Peters, and Hamm, *Church, Family and Village*, 243–50.

Roessingh, Carel, and Tanja Plasil. "From Collective Body to Individual Mind: Religious Change in an Old Colony Mennonite Community in Belize." *Journal of Mennonite Studies* 24 (2006): 55–72.

Schmiedehaus, Walter. "Mennonite Life in Mexico." *Mennonite Life* (April 1947): 28–38. Reprinted in *Preservings* 23 (December 2003): 71–76.

Schroeder, David. "Evangelicals Denigrate Conservative Mennonites— Understanding the Conservative Wing of the Mennonite Church." *Preservings* 15 (December 1999): 47–48. Reprinted in Plett, *Old Colony Mennonites in Canada*, 33–34.

———. "Salvation: 'You Will Know Them by Their Fruits,' Matthew 7:16." *Preservings* 18 (June 2001): 32–35.

———. "Sommerfelder Sermons and Literature." Paper presented at the Manitoba Mennonite Historical Society, November 1995. Published as "Worship and Teaching in the Sommerfeld Church." In Ens, Peters, and Hamm, *Church, Family and Village*, 125–36.

Stoesz, Dennis. "The Religious Literature of the Chortizer Mennonite Church, 1878–1903." Unpublished paper, 1981.

Stoesz, Donald. "Historical Origins of the Church Lectionary." *Preservings* 33 (2013): 64–72.

———. "Sermons and Services of the Sommerfelder Stoeszs." Unpublished manuscript. Donald Stoesz Fonds. Mennonite Historical Society of Alberta Archives, Calgary.

Tracie, Carl J. "Ethnicity and the Prairie Environment: Patterns of Old Colony Mennonite and Doukhobor Settlement." In *Man and Nature on the Prairies*, edited by Richard Allen, 46–65. Regina: Canadian Plains Research Center, University of Regina, 1976.

Warkentin, John. "Going on Foot: Revisiting the Mennonite Settlements of Southern Manitoba." *Journal of Mennonite Studies* 18 (2000): 59–81.

Warkentin, Karen. "'Emma jedohne': Memories and Old Colony Mennonite Identity." *Journal of Mennonite Studies* 31 (2013): 129–49.

Werner, Hans. "'A mild form of deviancy': Premarital Sex among Early Manitoba Mennonites." *Journal of Mennonite Studies* 26 (2008): 143–59.

Theses and Dissertations

Anderson, Alan B. "Assimilation in the Block Settlements of Northern Saskatchewan: A Comparative Study of Identity Change among Seven Ethno-Religious Groups in a Canadian Prairie Region." PhD dissertation, University of Saskatchewan, 1972.

Bowen, Dawn S. "The Transformation of a Northern Alberta Frontier Community." MA thesis, University of Maine at Orono, 1990.

Burkhart, Charles. "The Music of the Old Order Amish and the Old Colony Mennonites: A Contemporary Monodic Practice." MA thesis, Colorado College, 1952.

Driedger, Leo. "A Sect in a Modern Society: A Case Study, the Old Colony Mennonites of Saskatchewan." MA thesis, University of Chicago, 1955.

Friesen, Richard. "The Old Colony Mennonite Settlements in Saskatchewan: A Study in Settlement Change." MA thesis, University of Alberta, 1975.

Görzen, Jakob Warkentin. "Low German in Canada, a Story of 'Ploudîts' as Spoken by Mennonite Immigrants from Russia." PhD dissertation, University of Toronto, 1952.

Hedges, Kelly Lynn. "Plautdietsch and Huuchdietsch in Chihuahua: Language, Literacy, and Identity among the Old Colony Mennonites in Northern Mexico." PhD dissertation, Yale University, 1996.

Klassen, Judith Marie. "Encoding Song: Faithful Defiance in Mexican Mennonite Music-Making." PhD dissertation, Memorial University of Newfoundland, 2008.

———. "'Well wie noch een poa Leeda singen?' Family Music-Making and Particular Experience among Mennonites in Southern Manitoba." MA research paper, York University, 2003.

Kliewer, Victor. "Nonresistance or Pacifist? The Peace Stance of the Conservative Kanadier Mennonites, 1874–1945." MA thesis, University of Manitoba and University of Winnipeg, 2011.

Lanning, James Walter. "The Old Colony Mennonites of Bolivia: A Case Study." MS thesis, Texas A&M University, 1971.

Letkemann, Peter. "The Hymnody and Choral Music of Mennonites in Russia, 1789–1915." PhD dissertation, University of Toronto, 1985.

Nobbs-Thiessen, Benjamin. "Mennonites in Unexpected Places: An Authentic Tradition and a Burdensome Past." MA thesis, University of British Columbia, 2009.

Quiring, David Menno. "Mennonite Old Colony Life under Siege in Mexico." MA thesis, University of Saskatchewan, 1997.

Stoesz, Dennis E. "A History of the Chortitzer Mennonite Church of Manitoba, 1874–1914." MA thesis, University of Manitoba, 1987.

Tischler, Kurt. "The German Canadians in Saskatchewan with Particular Reference to the Language Problem." MA thesis, University of Saskatchewan, 1977.

Van Dyke, Edward W. "Blumenort: Study of Persistence in a Sect." PhD dissertation, University of Alberta, 1972.

Will, Martina E. "The Old Colony Mennonite Colonization of Chihauhau and the Obregón Administration's Vision for the Nation." MA thesis, University of California, San Diego, 1993.

Index

Page references in *italic* indicate a map or photo.